FRIEDRICH ENGELS

Also by Terrell Carver

A MARX DICTIONARY
ENGELS
KARL MARX: Texts on Method
MARX AND ENGELS: The Intellectual Relationship
MARX'S SOCIAL THEORY

Friedrich Engels

His Life and Thought

Terrell Carver
Lecturer in Politics
University of Bristol

St. Martin's Press   New York

First published in the United States of America in 1990

Printed in Great Britain

ISBN 0–312–04501–8

Library of Congress Cataloging-in-Publication Data
Carver, Terrell.
Friedrich Engels: his life and thought/Terrell Carver.
p.   cm.
Includes bibliographical references.
ISBN 0–312–04501–8
1. Engels, Friedrich, 1820–1895.   2. Dialectical materialism.
I. Title.
B3224.E6C37   1990
335.4'092—dc20
[B]   89–77153
                                                                    CIP

B
3224
.E6
C37
1990

For my friends in America

Contents

List of Plates

List of Abbreviations

Note: Volume numbers appear in arabic before abbreviations, and page numbers after, e.g. *Collected Works*, vol. 25, p. 37, appears as 25 CW 37.

In textual matters I have cited *Collected Works* for preference, and chosen other editions only where absolutely necessary.

AM   Terence Ball and James Farr (eds) *After Marx* (New York and Cambridge: Cambridge University Press, 1984).

COND   F. Engels, *The Condition of the Working Class in England*, trans. and ed. W.O. Henderson and W.H. Chalenor (Oxford: Basil Blackwell, 1958).

CW   Marx and Engels, *Collected Works* (London: Lawrence & Wishart, 1975– (series incomplete)).

D   *Friedrich Engels: Dokumente seines Lebens*, ed. Manfred Kliem (Frankfurt a.M.: Röderberg-Verlag, 1977).

DKM   The Daughters of Karl Marx, *Family Correspondence 1866–1898*, trans. Faith Evans (Harmondsworth: Penguin Books, 1984).

EF   Terrell Carver, 'Engels's Feminism', *History of Political Thought*, vol. 6, no. 3 (1985) pp. 479–89.

FE   Heinrich Gemkow *et al.*, *Friedrich Engels: A Biography* (Dresden: Verlag Zeit im Bild, 1972).

H   W.O. Henderson, *The Life of Friedrich Engels*, 2 vols (London: Frank Cass, 1976).

IR   David McLellan (ed.), *Karl Marx: Interviews and Recollections* (London: Macmillan, 1981).

K   Yvonne Kapp, *Eleanor Marx*, 2 vols (London: Lawrence & Wishart, 1972 and 1976).

KM   David McLellan, *Karl Marx: His Life and Thought* (London: Macmillan, 1973).

L   George Lichtheim, *Marxism: An Historical and Critical Study*, 2nd edn (London: Routledge, 1964).

M   Steven Marcus, *Engels, Manchester and the Working Class* (New York: Random House, 1974).

MBM   David McLellan, *Marx Before Marxism*, 2nd edn (London: Macmillan, 1980).

MEGA[1]   Karl Marx and Friedrich Engels, *Gesamtausgabe*, ed. D.

Ryazanov *et al.* (Frankfurt and Berlin: Marx-Engels-Archiv Verlagsgesellschaft, 1927– (series incomplete)).

MEGA²   Karl Marx and Friedrich Engels, *Gesamtausgabe* (Berlin: Dietz Verlag, 1972– (series in progress)).

MEIR   Terrell Carver, *Marx and Engels: The Intellectual Relationship* (Brighton: Wheatsheaf Books, 1983).

MEOUT   Terrell Carver, 'Marx – and Engels's "Outlines of a Critique of Political Economy"', *History of Political Thought*, vol. 4, no. 2 (1983) pp. 357–65.

MEW   Marx and Engels, *Werke* (Berlin: Dietz Verlag, 1956–68 (series complete)).

MP   Alan Gilbert, *Marx's Politics* (Oxford: Martin Robertson, 1981).

MST   Terrell Carver, *Marx's Social Theory* (Oxford: Oxford University Press, 1982).

R   Fritz J. Raddatz, *Karl Marx*, trans. Richard Barry (London: Weidenfeld & Nicolson, 1978).

SW   Karl Marx and Frederick Engels, *Selected Works* (in two volumes) (Moscow: Foreign Languages Publishing House, 1962).

SWOV   Karl Marx and Frederick Engels, *Selected Works* (in one volume) (New York: International Publishers, 1968, repr. 1984).

YHKM   David McLellan, *The Young Hegelians and Karl Marx* (London: Macmillan, 1969).

Acknowledgement

The author and publishers are grateful to Lawrence & Wishart Ltd for permission to reproduce quotations from Marx and Engels, *Collected Works*.

Germany about 1848

Source: David McLellan, *Karl Marx: His Life and Thought* (London: Macmillan, 1973), p. xiv.

Introduction: Which Engels?

In this biography of Friedrich Engels (1820–95) the reader will not find a compendium of every known fact about him. Those who already know something about Engels will doubtless find some favourite incident or anecdote missing from my account. But I hope that my choice of questions to put to the historical record, and my attempts to find answers, will stimulate interest in Engels the man, his career and the issues that concerned him.

The guiding questions for the work as a whole are as follows:

What is the intellectual and political legacy of Friedrich Engels?
What does an investigation of his life disclose to us about his works, his character, his associates and his times?
How does this knowledge affect our view of Karl Marx (1818–83), the history and current state of Marxism, and contemporary politics?

The guiding questions for each chapter are made explicit as this work progresses. In some cases the reader will note that I offer several possible answers to the questions I have posed, because I have found the record inconclusive. It seems to me honest and informative to explore a number of explanations rather than merely to opt for one at random, or worse, to back up a pre-existing view.

I have considered Engels's relationship with Marx in works listed in the Guide to Further Reading in the present volume, and I have come to conclusions about their relationship which the interested reader can examine. In this biography the focus is on Engels himself, not Engels the junior partner to Marx, the supposed role on which most attention has been focused. Engels put immense emphasis on that view of their relationship, particularly in retrospect, since he outlived Marx by some twelve years. The reader will find that I treat those autobiographical comments with the same scepticism that applies elsewhere in examining sources.

I have set the agenda for the present volume as I think best for exploring and understanding Engels's life and thought as they can be reconstructed from surviving materials. I have not allowed the interpretive tradition established by Engels himself and by various memoirists to dictate the agenda. Also, I have not been swayed by the sheer quantity of materials in constructing my own scheme and narrative, but have instead focused selectively on what was formative for Engels and what has remained influential in politics. I hope that readers will not prejudge my agenda as wrong simply because it is not traditional. In fact I hope that they will see my work in a favourable light precisely for that reason.

Engels is much taken for granted, and very little studied. Even when his writings are scrutinized, the object is very often the curious one of attempting to show that Marx agreed with certain portions of them. The use Engels himself made of Marx's insights is seldom examined, because Engels's thought is almost never taken as an object of study in its own right. His life is similarly subordinated to those points at which he becomes important to the various views intellectual historians have taken about Marx. The present work is entitled *Friedrich Engels: His Life and Thought*, and the subtitle means what it says.

Chapters 1–4 of this biography present a detailed analysis of Engels's early development up to his twenty-fifth year. By then a personal, political and intellectual context was established, and his further important relationships and activities took place within it. Chapter 5 explores the way that Engels's life developed from the age of 24 up to his last years in terms of family, friends and associates. Chapters 6 and 7 cover his work as politician and theorist over the same period, 'nesting' his career within this biographical context. Finally I present my conclusions and assess what Engels achieved. Works by Engels that I have cited are listed in the index, as are the main events of his life.

University of Bristol   TERRELL CARVER

1

Intellectual Awakening

Many of the political issues current in Engels's life and times are similar to those that occupy us now, though there are also substantial differences that must be taken into account. A discussion of nineteenth-century politics as if it did not raise questions of current interest would make a biography of Engels seem pointless, while an assumption that all his battles are recurring in an unchanged world is obviously false to the historical record. The historical and social context for his activities must be established, so that we can see where his concerns resemble ours, and where our situations differ. History has not buried Engels – far from it – but how and why he lives today is a more controversial subject than might appear at first glance.

Engels's early years have been much underrated, not least by Engels himself. His childhood and schooldays provide essential clues to the character that will preoccupy us throughout the work, but we need to examine the young Engels as an agent and personality in his own right, without assuming that the experiences of the youth determined all that he later undertook. The central questions that will concern us in this and the following chapter are:

Why did the young Engels begin to drift away from his family's expectations?
How did he come to perceive his world as one that needed changing in a revolutionary way?
What did he accomplish intellectually in his earliest works?

I EARLY YEARS

Friedrich Engels was the eldest child born to a mill-owning family in the Rhineland town of Barmen, the modern Wuppertal, which lies just east of Düsseldorf in the industrial region of the Ruhr. The river Wupper, a right-bank tributary of the Rhine, had been a centre for yarn-bleaching since the Middle Ages, but in the late eighteenth century it became an important part of the German industrial revolution. Cotton-spinning was established there in water-driven mills, and weaving undertaken by handloom-workers in their cottages. Friedrich's great-grandfather Johann Caspar Engels (1715-87) was a successful entrepreneur, moving from trade to manufacture by founding a firm that made lace and ribbon. The Engels family business passed through successive generations to Friedrich's father (1796–1860), also called Friedrich.

The subject of our biography was born at 9 pm on 28 November 1820, an event which was proudly notified to readers of the local press on the 29th. Three days later on 1 December Engels's father wrote to his wife's cousin Karl Snethlage (1792–1871), a clergyman, of her difficult labour. He described his own feelings of misery at the sight, his devotion to his wife and the joy he felt at the delivery of his healthy first-born and namesake. 'Love', he said, 'prevented me from leaving the scene of her suffering even for a moment, in case there was any alleviation I could help to procure'. In his letter Friedrich senior prayed to God for wisdom to bring the baby up well and in fear of Him, but mingled piety with touching detail: 'Elise has just taken the little boy in her arms and is talking to him; he nearly always sleeps quietly, which is a good thing'.

It is hard to judge whether this fatherly participation at birth was usual at the time, but these deep feelings are certainly all of a piece with what we know of Friedrich senior's involvement, then and later, with his wife and children and their domestic circumstances. About the new baby he wrote, 'His little dwelling-place is beside me, with its sweetly slumbering inhabitant, and it fills me with an utterly new, great joy whenever I look at it' (2 CW 577–9).

Over the generations the Engels family was remarkable for its consistent pursuit of virtue as defined by the successful and respectable classes of the valley. Great-grandfather Johann Caspar introduced machinery into his lace-making concern and provided housing for those recruited to labour in the ranks of the industrial revolution. Two sons expanded and diversified the business, and they pursued the philanthropic activities expected of the fortunate in the Christian community. One of those sons was Engels's grandfather Caspar Engels (1753–1821), who had founded a school and undertaken the charitable distribution of food in 1816 during a famine. His son Friedrich senior, along with two brothers, Caspar

(1792–1863) and August (1797–1874) Engels, had inherited the business, which provided comfortably for them and their children during the 1820s and much later into the century (1 H 2–3).

Along with the entrepreneurial spirit of the Engels clan went a devout, fundamentalist Christianity, which was particularly strong in the region. Pietism, a sect very influential in Barmen, was derived from seventeenth-century puritanism and therefore opposed to the established Catholic and Lutheran churches. Pietist doctrine was democratic in rejecting priestly hierarchy, and individualist in demonstrating a concern with the Christian's personal relationship with God. It was also notably gloomy in emphasizing God's judgement of sinners.

Pietists expected only a few of God's elect to achieve redemption, and members of the sect were strict in observing the Sabbath, condemning levity and idleness. Their practice was supportive of the intellect when they substituted Biblical exegesis for church tradition and ritual, but they were anti-intellectual in placing God's word, as construed by preachers and believers, above rational thought and criticism. Pietists concerned themselves with God's will and the king's bidding, and they rejected any view of public and private morals that left judgement solely to individuals and their reason. Scripture and the collective judgement of the community were their recognized authorities.

While pietists expected toleration from the state and from other Christian churches, they exerted within their own closed community a severely intolerant regime. They attempted to ensure that education, social activities, opinions and morals, very broadly defined, were subject to the supervision of the church. On 18 January 1821 Friedrich was baptized in the reformed Evangelical Church, with his paternal grandfather Caspar Engels and maternal grandmother Franciska Christina van Haar *née* Snethlage (b. 1758) standing as godparents. At 18 he reflected that he had been brought up in extreme orthodoxy and piety drummed in at church, at Sunday school and at home (2 CW 466, 580).

Friedrich's grandfather and godparent was a founder of the United Protestant Church in Barmen, and a municipal councillor under both the Napoleonic regime of the early years of the nineteenth century and its Prussian successor. In the restoration period after 1815, pietism underwent a revival. This was not surprising, as Prussian conservatism was gaining ground over more liberal French notions of rights for 'man' and the citizen.

Those rights were part of a revolutionary, rationalist approach to politics, the hallmark of the Enlightenment. This liberalism was strongly and successfully resisted by pietists, whose worldly authoritarianism and other-worldly mysticism suited established interests in Barmen. They preferred their severely restricted and authoritarian outlook to any democratic, or even republican talk of rights. Until Friedrich's generation the Engels clan cultivated their business and social interests within the confines of their community, social class and church, never lifting their intellectual horizons very much beyond the old dukedom of Berg where they originated.

Friedrich's mother, Elisabeth Francisca Mauritzia Engels *née* van Haar (1797–1873) was of Dutch extraction, and a schoolmaster's daughter. She did not subscribe entirely to the strictly pietist view of things, despite the fact that she undoubtedly heard it every week from the local pulpit. Elise Engels was well-read, musical like her husband Friedrich senior, and absorbed in establishing a home where literature and the theatre were valued, at least in private. Perhaps Elise Engels's interests lifted young Friedrich's horizons just enough, at first, for her eldest son's energies to find their objects further from home. Here we have a clue to his development that begins to explain a remarkable deviation from a well-established and carefully protected family pattern.

For Friedrich home was a securely comfortable but self-contained world of industrial management, commercial skill, civic eminence and public benefaction. He had seven surviving younger siblings, three brothers – Hermann (1822–1905), Emil (1828–84) and Rudolf (1831–1903) – and four sisters – Marie (1824–1901), Anna (1825–53), Hedwig (1830–1904) and Elise (1834–1912). None of them ventured very far for very long from the family and its interests, and none was ever very prominent in the ranks of socialists and revolutionaries. Friedrich's family, while departing slightly from the strictest Barmen norms for thought and behaviour, was never publicly at odds with the community and its leaders. Nor, apart from the dissident opinions of the eldest son, did it ever seem to be internally at odds over fundamental issues, keeping instead to the formalities, at least, of religion and loyalty to the king.

Friedrich's family comedy *Die Verkleidung* (*Dressing-up*), composed for fun when he was 18 and living away from home, portrayed his mother at the centre of a noisy household, beset with small sons and daughters doing French and mathematics, entertaining their neighbourhood friends and persuading her to join them in dressing up in funny clothes to astonish Friedrich senior. Amongst the incidents in the playlet were missed trips to the lavatory and a good deal of childish anarchy, so the family, in the adolescent Engels's mind at least, was a warm-hearted and happy mêlée (2 CW 438–42).

Engels's early life and primary education were anything but disturbing, and he enjoyed the advantages of a large, modern house – built in the year of his birth – and its substantial grounds. The local school, which he attended until he was 14, provided the kind of elementary training that a pietist congregation would support. This included enough literacy for Bible-reading, but nothing further lest young minds should wander too far from the practical activities and wholehearted conformity that the community valued so highly.

The gymnasium or grammar school in the neighbouring town of Elberfeld, where Friedrich was sent as a boarder in the acting director's own house, was rather different. While nominally pietist the school allowed, no doubt inadvertently, some liberal masters in history, literature and languages. They raised their pupils' sights beyond fundamentalist Christianity towards the human experience for its own sake, as embodied in classical literature, science and art. This was a view that departed from the pietist gloss on worldly studies, which was that humanity was sinful in the eyes of God and human works insignificant by comparison with His.

In a letter of 27 August 1835 to Friedrich's mother, who was away tending her declining father, Friedrich senior reported on a communication from the acting director Dr Johann Hantschke (1796–1856). This letter, Friedrich's father wryly observed, was handed by the schoolboy to the household maids very late on a Wednesday evening, though he had had it since the preceding Sunday at least. It renewed the offer of a boarder's place for the coming year, something the elder Engels was keen to accept for his 'peculiar and versatile' lad, who was then 14. Young Friedrich, despite his pleasing qualities, had developed in his father's eyes a disturbing thoughtlessness and lack of character, about which the elder Engels was very concerned. Friedrich senior commented that a secluded life at school would lead the youth to a degree of independence, perhaps from vulgar influences, which would be the best thing for him. 'When it is a question of our child's welfare', he wrote to his wife, 'we should not consider money'. While lamenting that severe chastisements and fear of punishment had little effect in teaching unconditional obedience, Engels's father seemed to take what was perhaps a line of least resistance on some matters. He commented on his son's carelessness in leaving a 'greasy' volume of lending library romances in his desk. Though Friedrich senior did not actually condemn out of hand the youth's interest in thirteenth-century knights, he was fearful for the disposition of his 'otherwise excellent boy' (2 CW 581–2).

Friedrich attended the Elberfeld gymnasium for three years, leaving on 15 September 1837, just two months before his seventeenth birthday, with a good report, but a year short of the normal diploma course for university entrance. While the document has the character of a reference for the pupil, and perhaps for the school as well, it does suggest that the top or prima form interested the adolescent Engels more than the lower school, and that he had a facility for languages. This was mainly for translating Latin, Greek and French into German, rather than anything more philological, though he did compose a poem in classical Greek, 'Eteoklous kai Poluneikous monomachia' ('The Single Combat of Eteocles and Polynices'). On his school-leaving day he gave it as a star recitation. That set him apart from the other pupils as a gifted student of languages, a life-long talent which he developed to a remarkable degree.

The school report also mentions an interest in German national literature and classics. This attests to a degree of accuracy in the perceptions of Dr Hantschke, since Engels displayed a nationalist and literary flair in the years that immediately followed. Friedrich's notebooks on ancient history, 'Von Erschaffung der Welt bis auf den peloponnesischen Krieg' ('From the Beginning of the World to the Peloponnesian War') and his 'Präparation und Bemerkung zu Homers Ilias' ('Revision Notes on Homer's Iliad') demonstrate his keen interest in classicism. Classical studies had been cultivated in Germany since the mid-eighteenth century under the influence of Johann Winckelmann (1717–68), the archaeologist and art historian, and Gotthold Lessing (1729–81), the dramatist and critic. No doubt the enthusiasm of the history master Dr Johann Clausen (1806–77) was also reflected in these notebooks, as Engels later singled him out for praise when he recalled his schooldays. The notebooks on ancient history record two important intellectual developments that drew the young Engels away from the pietist community in Barmen and ultimately from Christian practice and belief.

The first of these developments is the secular, comparative perspective on world history that Engels adopted. Although the title-page of his notebook recorded the supposed Biblical date for the creation of the world, India, China and near-eastern civilizations were mentioned at the outset of his work. And the second is the overwhelming weight he gave to Greek civilization, as opposed to a more traditionally Christian account centred on the Bible. The Israelites were discussed parenthetically between the Phoenicians and the Egyptians, and only briefly mentioned. No doubt other classes at school in religion and Bible study redressed this 'godless' approach somewhat, but the clear thrust of Friedrich's historical education was towards an Enlightenment view of human history.

Human beings were said by the youthful Engels to have sprung from central Asia and to have spread themselves outwards, forming three racial groups – Mongolians, Caucasians and Negroes. The creation of man and woman by God as recounted in Genesis was not even mentioned. In accord with the accepted science of the time Friedrich's characterization of non-Caucasians was unflatteringly racist, and his youthful correspondence after leaving school also displayed a conventional anti-Semitism in which Jews, mentioned in passing, were presented in a supposedly humorous way as grotesques.

On academic subjects the acting director's account was perfunctory, merely remarking on some demonstrable knowledge of religious doctrine, history, geography, mathematics, physics and empirical psychology. In the overtly personal reference for a pupil to whom he was particularly close, Dr Hantschke recommended him for the career in the Engels family business which the young man had found himself induced to choose as his profession in life instead of the further studies that had been his earlier intention (2 CW 584–5; IV/1 MEGA^2 439–532, and IV/1-A 952). Perhaps there is some hint of sadness in the acting director's comments that Friedrich did not go on to university to develop his talents in more academic ways. In fact the enterprising Engels later combined his compulsory military service with attendance at Berlin University as a non-matriculated student, so Dr Hantschke deserves some further credit for prescience.

It is not difficult to see the hand of Friedrich's father in the decision that the boy should forego formal entry to university and join the family firm straight from school. The elder Engels had just gone into partnership that year with the brothers Gottfried and Peter Ermen in order to expand his business activities, first in Manchester and then back in Germany at Barmen and nearby Engelskirchen. The firm of Ermen and Engels manufactured sewing thread, and it seems likely that Friedrich senior wanted a strong showing in the new partnership, since he had left his own two brothers behind in the original business (1 H 4–5). Friedrich was pulled into the dynastic pattern and trained, on the job, for business management in the increasingly mechanized production and international marketing of textiles.

This turn of events need not have impeded Engels's literary talent, which was already developing. A few poems survive from his school days, reflecting his luck in having a maternal grandfather, Bernhard van Haar (1760–1837), headmaster of a gymnasium or academic high school, to tell him tales of Greece and Troy. In a New Year's greeting for 1834 Friedrich sent best wishes in verse to his dear Grandfather, who 'told me many a beautiful story/Of Cercyon and Theseus, and Argus the hundred-eyed monster,/The Minotaur, Ariadne, and Aegeus drowned in the ocean,/The Golden Fleece, the Argonauts and Jason defiant,/ Mighty Hercules, Danaus, and Cadmus the hero' (2 CW 553). At 16 Friedrich had a conventional catalogue of boyhood heroes – William Tell, Siegfried, Faust, Achilles. In another poetic work, 'Mir dämmert in der Ferne' ('The Evening Sky Grows Dimmer'), he made them constellations. He also composed a religious poem or hymn-text 'Herr Jesu Christe, Gottes Sohn' ('Lord Jesus Christ, God's only Son'), in preparation for his confirmation, an event that took place on 12 March 1837. The verses tell of death and redemption, a meditation possibly inspired by grief at the recent death on 20 February of his literary grandfather.

Like Elise Engels, her family and some other members of the clan, Friedrich need not have sacrificed all the arts to trade. He could have cultivated them domestically, while staying within the bounds of conventional manners and decorum. What came between him and this bourgeois idyll?

'Eine Seeräubergeschichte' ('A Pirate Tale') dates from the 16-year-old Friedrich's last year at school and reveals a contemporary political focus for his boyhood preoccupations. The manuscript includes illustrations in ink and watercolour; Engels had a lifelong talent for sketches and caricature. Romantic heroism, brave and noble deeds, cutlass and sabre, high sentiment and heroic self-sacrifice are the familiar ingredients of schoolboy romance. But in his unfinished tale of personal and political vengeance, Friedrich portrayed a struggle of brave Hellenic corsairs against Turkish oppression on the eve of the Greek rebellion of 1821–5. In his account the favoured weapon of the infidel Turk was literally a hammer beating down the noble Greek whose cause was dignified with lines from the Iliad (2 CW 557–71; see I/3 MEGA² for Engels's drawings, reproduced between pp. 16 and 17).

Engels's identification with the Greek rebellion of the 1820s was less conventional and more overtly political than his schoolboy visions of classical and medieval heroes locked in combat. However fancifully he conceived of the Greek struggle for independence, those events were in any case nearer his own time than his other preoccupations, and the popular nationalism of the movement was close, by repute if not always in fact, to libertarian protest movements of the recent past. After the Congress of Vienna in 1815 conservative monarchies were restored throughout Europe, the ideals of the French revolution were denigrated and liberal agitation was forcibly suppressed, especially the *Bursenschaften*, fraternal organizations of protesting students. For the young Engels contemporary rebels were heroes of classical stature.

In identifying romantic heroism with actual political struggle Engels made a move that many of his well-read, well-off contemporaries never managed. Many young romantics existed in a realm of dreamy feeling and literary posturing, but others, including Engels, took romanticism to be the foundation for a movement to sweep away feudalism, intolerance and religious obscurantism. Once engaged in politics the revolutionary romantics of Engels's time were by no means consistent in their political doctrines. Their ideas were a mishmash that included national liberation from foreign oppressors, civil liberation from authoritarian rulers, and personal liberation from superstition and censorship. The Greek rebellion in particular encompassed Byronic ideals of personal intervention and self-sacrifice that were easily linked with the philhellenic classical revival that Friedrich had absorbed at school.

Amongst solid citizens who valued security and stability – such as the Engels clan – the critical character of romantic politics was bound to cause disquiet. Revolutionary romantics called for an assault on vested interests, and they opposed authoritarian states dedicated to preserving the traditional powers of the nobility, clergy and landowners. But this romantic fervour did not determine for Engels any very clear pattern of future political development, since, for some of his contemporaries, democratic sentiments turned in later years to the conservatism of a disillusioned élite, liberatory nationalism turned into racism, and republican ideals into militarism. Engels's adolescent enthusiasms could easily have ended in a few harmless gestures of rebellion, a dusty scrapbook of youthful scribblings and a return to the traditional values of the *ancien régime* – no doubt the outcome his family expected and favoured.

While the 16-year-old Engels did not commit himself in his 'Tale' to a lifetime of democratic political activism, the work nonetheless marks an interesting transitional point between schoolboy fantasy and mature engagement. That engagement was with a fervently revolutionary politics which did not suit the Engels family parlour, and 'A Pirate Tale' shows young Friedrich looking well beyond Barmen. He was led through literary and historical studies to interpret contemporary political events in a way that was not merely controversial at home but, when pursued, was subversive of the values that made that sort of home life possible at all. Rebellion against rulers, armed struggle against the odds and heroic resistance to oppression were not the activities that built textile mills and made profits for the Engels family business.

The schoolboy Engels seems to have started out as a writer some time between 1834 and 1836 by publishing some poems in the literary supplement to the local Barmen paper (copies of which are not preserved), and by contributing in June 1837 *Die brasilianische Braut*, a German version of a novella *The Brazilian Bride*. This was taken from an unknown French translation of the English original, which was attributed by the editors of the Barmen paper to Miss Norton, actually Mrs Caroline Norton *née* Sheridan (1808–77), a grand-daughter of the famous playwright. This translation was signed 'F.E. . . . .', a half-veiled anonymity in which the full points matched the remaining letters of the Engels family name, without utterly hiding the 16-year-old translator's identity from his school-friends.

Author and story are of some significance in the launching of Engels's career. Mrs Caroline Norton was a popular and well-paid Byronic poetess, magazine editor and romantic writer. She began her literary career at the age of 21 with the long and highly successful poem 'The Sorrows of Rosalie', the income from which she used to defray the expenses of her first confinement. She was forced to do this because her husband, George Norton, whom she married in 1827 when she was 19, was chronically unsuccessful in his practice as a barrister and thus dependent on his wife's income from her publications and on preferment through her political contacts with the Whigs, although the Norton family were staunch Tories. Mrs Norton's political and personal friends included Lord Melbourne (1779–1848), who was briefly Prime Minister in 1834 and then again for the period 1835–1841. The Norton marriage was in constant and well-publicized distress during the early 1830s, and in mid-1836 her husband brought an action against Lord Melbourne for seduction. This was unsuccessful, but Norton also denied Caroline access to her children, which was then his legal right. Caroline protested in public, commencing in 1837 a campaign for reform of the law on child custody in order to give women legal redress. Possibly Engels had read accounts of these events, and possibly he had read or heard about Mrs Norton's anonymous poem of the previous year, 'A Voice from the Factories'. Her work, dedicated to the reformer Lord Ashley (later seventh Earl Shaftesbury) and accompanied by a prose introduction, detailed the sufferings of children employed in manufacture. As a mother she called in no uncertain terms for legislation to restrict child labour.

It is unlikely that the young Engels found such a figure for his first published efforts in prose wholly by chance, and his work suggests that his flair for publicizing liberal causes, albeit anonymously, began to show itself around the age of 16. Mrs Norton's fiction was highly personal and political, as one of her favourite themes was the tragic heroine deserted by a cruel lover, trapped in a loveless marriage or victimized by tyrannous males, with no recourse to earthly justice. *The Brazilian Bride*, however, was no overt cry for female emancipation, though it might be read as a radical instruction to men to respect the marital tie and to refrain from sexual deception. It seems to reflect a kind of wish-fulfilment on the part of the author, because the male protagonist is honourable and virtuous despite various trials engineered by his father and his true love. In the end the lady grants him her hand, and they find happiness together in marriage, the reverse of Mrs Norton's tribulations.

Precisely how the young Engels interpreted the story and what he made of Mrs Norton's situation are not recorded, though his own 'Pirate Tale' bears a certain stylistic resemblance to her romantic fiction. Exotic locations, contrived plots, highly charged sentiment and resistance to oppression feature in both. His work in the genre looks back to his boyhood fantasies in a make-believe world and ahead to a lifetime involvement in radical politics (2 CW 554, 555–6; I/3 MEGA² 631–44, and I/3-A 725, 1271–3).

II AWAY FROM HOME

In the autumn of 1837 Friedrich's commercial career was launched in the family firm. He worked for Ermen and Engels in Barmen until the summer of 1838 when, at the age of 17, he was sent to his father's export agent Heinrich Leupold (d. 1865), Consul in Bremen for the Kingdom of Saxony. This was further from home than Friedrich had been before, and the environment was in almost every way very different from the Wupper Valley. The two-and-a-half years that he spent working for the Consul were intellectually and politically formative, indeed exciting, since he began regular publication of his work as a writer.

Bremen was a large seaport which traded extensively with the Americas, exporting German manufactures and emigrants and importing raw materials and luxury goods for trans-shipment. The German Confederation of thirty-four states and four free cities had been established in 1815, and Bremen was a city in the latter category. It was somewhat more liberal than the Prussian and Hanoverian kingdoms and certainly more independent in outlook than any of their towns.

Though Engels was sent to lodge with Pastor Georg Treviranus (1788–1868), a pietist clergyman known to his father, the household regime was not overly strict. Friedrich the lodger was given his own door key, and he had little trouble absorbing the cosmopolitan atmosphere of a trading town. His comments on the Bremen scene for his little sister Marie covered intriguing details of peasant costume at Bremen market, and also urban low-life in the alleys. For his schoolfriend correspondents, the brothers Friedrich (1822–95) and Wilhelm (1820–95) Graeber, he wrote about the latest books and pamphlets on politics.

Engels's political reading included a topical work by Jacob Grimm (1785–1863), the famous philologist and anthologist of folktales, who was one of seven professors dismissed from Göttingen University. On accession to the throne of Hanover in 1837 Ernst August (1777–1851) had abrogated the comparatively liberal constitution of 1833, and then dismissed the academics who protested, a common-enough action amongst anti-liberal monarchs of the restoration period. The Göttingen seven became a *cause célèbre*, and Grimm was forced to emigrate. In 1838 an anonymous pamphlet *Jacob Grimm über seine Entlassung* (*Jacob Grimm on his Dismissal*) in defence of constitutionalism and the sacked professors was published in Switzerland at Basle, and then smuggled into Germany. Engels recommended this work in a letter of 1 September 1838 to two of his Barmen contemporaries, the Graeber brothers, and he praised the rare power of the writing.

More of these quite liberal ideas, as Engels described them, were to be found in seven pamphlets he had read in just one bookshop, which was evidently very liberal in its policy towards browsers. Some of those pamphlets were concerned with the Cologne affair of 1837, in which the King of Prussia, Friedrich Wilhelm III (1770–1840), had had the Archbishop of Cologne arrested for high treason. The archbishop had opposed the religious policy of the Prussian state with respect to the children of mixed Protestant–Catholic marriages, a 'discord' not resolved until after the accession of Friedrich Wilhelm IV (1795–1861) in 1840, when the Catholic position was adopted and religious freedom curtailed.

Pamphleteering was evidently a new experience for the young Engels. He commented that the scurrilous and satirical literature available in Bremen could never have been printed back home in the Rhineland, and he began decorating his letters to schoolfriends with caricatures, done in black and red ink. He seems to have devoted considerable company time to his personal correspondence, for which he used company stationery, and to beer-drinking in the office with his fellow clerks and even the management. Reading, however, was supposed to be forbidden. His major duties were copying letters, keeping records and getting the post out (2 CW 386–92, 396). Engels's letters to his sister Marie gave a vivid and overwhelmingly light-hearted picture of his 'grown-up' life as a junior office-worker:

> We now have a complete stock of beer in the office; under the table, behind the stove, behind the cupboard, everywhere are beer bottles, and when the Old Man [Consul Leupold] is thirsty

he borrows one and has it filled up again for us later. That is now done quite openly, the glasses stand on the table all day and a bottle nearby. In the right-hand corner are the empty bottles, in the left the full ones, next to them my cigars. It is really true, Marie, the young people are getting worse and worse every day, as Dr. Hantschke says (2 CW 499–500).

Evidently this letter produced a predictable, Barmen-type response, for Engels replied, in a predictable, big-brotherly way, 'You must not think, my dearest little goose, that now you are at a boarding-school [in Mannheim] you can at once try to be wise'. He remarked that he could get piles of books from Pastor Treviranus, if he wanted such instruction. So 'the beer stays in our office until it has been drunk, and since your arguing against it our beer trade has only improved ... That's what comes of saucy little boarding-school misses interfering in the affairs of their gentlemen brothers' (2 CW 501). For after-lunch naps, he reported, two hammocks had been rigged up in the packing-house loft, and he drew a caricature of himself swinging in one, smoking a cigar. He also admitted that the home-made fastenings made the hammocks prone to collapse (2 CW 503–5). Here is Engels's account of one afternoon, 18 September 1840:

There was no more work to do, and the Old Man was out, and Wilhelm Leupold [the Consul's son] did not show up often either. So I lit a cigar, first wrote the above [letter] to you, then took [Nicolaus] Lenau's *Faust* [Stuttgart and Tübingen, 1836] from my desk and read some of it. Afterwards I drank a bottle of beer and at half past seven went to [Richard] Roth's [(1821–58), a business friend]; we went off to the Club, I read [Friedrich von] Raumer's *Geschichte der Hohenstaufen* [*History of the Noble Hohenstaufen*, Leipzig, 1823–5] and then ate beefsteak and cucumber salad. At half past ten I went home and read [Friedrich] Diez's *Grammatik der romanischen Sprachen* [*Grammar of the Romance Languages*, Bonn, 1836–8] until I felt sleepy (2 CW 508).

To his favourite sister Engels recounted a plan to horrify the family back home with rebellious gestures:

I now have an enormous moustache and shall presently add to it a Henry IV and goatee beard. Mother will wonder when suddenly such a long, black-bearded fellow comes across the lawn.

Even Bremen itself was not immune from these attacks on bourgeois respectability:

Last Sunday we had a moustache evening [at the town-hall cellars]. For I had sent out a circular to all moustache-capable young men that it was finally time to horrify all philistines, and that that could not be done better than by wearing moustaches. Everyone with the courage to defy philistinism and wear a moustache should therefore sign. I had soon collected a dozen moustaches, and then the 25th of October [1840], when our moustaches would be a month old, was fixed as the day for a common moustache jubilee. But I had a shrewd idea what would happen, bought a little moustache wax and took it with me; it was then found that one [fellow] had a truly very fine but unfortunately quite white moustache, while another had been instructed by his principal to hack the criminal thing off. Enough, that evening we had to have at least a few, and those who had none had to paint themselves one (2 CW 511–12).

The moustache was removed on 18 February 1841 and promptly regrown, as it had been a successful way to *épater les bourgeois*:

In the Academy of Singing I was the only one with a moustache. . . . The ladies, incidentally, liked it very much, and so did the Old Man. Only last night at the concert six young dandies stood around me, all in tail-coats and kid-gloves, and I stood among them in an ordinary coat and without gloves. The fellows made remarks all evening about me and my bristling upper lip. The best of it is that three months ago nobody knew me here and now all the world does, just because of the moustache! Oh, the philistines! (2 CW 525).

Outside work Friedrich read voraciously and studied languages, claiming by the end of his stay in the seaport to be acquainted with twenty-five. This passage, from a letter to Wilhelm Graeber, captures the way in which office work was squeezed in amongst intellectual pursuits and bibulous socializing:

Today (April 30 [1839]), because of the magnificent weather, I sat in the garden from 7 in the morning to half past 8, smoked and read the *Lusiade* [the national poem of Portugal by Luiz Vaz de Camoes (1524–80)] until I had to go to the office. There's no better way of reading than in a garden on a clear spring morning, with a pipe in your mouth, and the rays of the sun on your back. This afternoon I'll continue this pursuit with the Old German Tristan, and his sweet reflections on love. Tonight I'm going to the *Ratskeller* [tavern under the town hall] where our Herr Pastor [Treviranus] is treating us to the Rhine wine which he has been given – in duty bound – by the new Burgomaster. In such stupendous weather I always get an immense longing for the Rhine and its vineyards, but what can I do about it? Write a couple of verses at most (2 CW 445–6, 470).

In Bremen Engels took a further step away from the wishes and interests of his family by writing again for publication. These works could not be mistaken for schoolboy experiments and exercises that had somehow found their way into print, and so they foreshadowed a serious adult avocation at the very least. 'Die Beduinen' ('The Bedouin'), a poem of ten stanzas, appeared anonymously in the *Bremisches Conversatsionsblatt* for 16 September 1838. This is his first original published work to survive, and it contained, according to the 17-year-old author, two main ideas. The first was a line of theatrical criticism, in which the Germanic sincerities of the romantic dramatist Friedrich von Schiller (1759–1805) were contrasted with the flamboyance and exoticism of the playwright Ferdinand von Kotzebue (1761–1819). Engels sympathized with the rebellious Schiller, rather than the socially conservative Kotzebue, who had been assassinated by a student radical in 1819. Intertwined with this argument drawn from revolutionary romanticism was a second one, an aversion to commerce. In that respect Engels's outlook resembled the viewpoint of Ferdinand Freiligrath (1810–76), the Barmen poet known to Friedrich and his schoolmasters. Engels's romantic vision was ultimately derived from popularisations of the 'noble savage' portrayed by Jean-Jacques Rousseau (1712–78). The Bedouins of his poem, who had once been warriors proud and free, were now debased in his eyes because they had been made to jump for coins. But even in their present sorry condition he contrasted them favourably with his audience of foppish Europeans corrupted by commercialism.

Friedrich's reactions to the poem and to the processes of editing and publication were more formative for him and informative for us than the published work itself. His editor had altered the poem, without telling him, and had omitted the concluding lines, in which the tribes of Morocco were praised at the expense of 'civilized' peoples. The editor had destroyed his work, so Engels complained in a letter of 17–18 September 1838 to the Graeber brothers, and in conclusion he wished that he had never written the poem. Its faults were now much clearer with the text in print than they had been in manuscript.

Engels had been reading the advice to young poets given by Johann Wolfgang von Goethe (1749–1832) and had found himself as youthful bard clearly and pejoratively described. Still, the young poet thought that his efforts would neither raise nor lower German literature, and he resolved to continue because others – 'just as big if not bigger asses than I am' – were being published (2 CW 392–8; I/3 MEGA^2 18* and I/3-A 726). Further efforts included 'Florida', a poem which did not appear in his lifetime but is preserved in a letter of 20 January 1839 to Friedrich Graeber. That work is in three parts, each with a different narrator – the Spirit of the Earth, The Seminole and The White Man. The poem links together the politics of contemporary European commercial powers, the philosophy of revolutionary romanticism and the sentiments of an idealized Christianity.

The Spirit of the Earth tells of the seizure by Europeans of a wooded and flowery land inhabited by 'faithful tribesmen of the brown-skinned nation', no doubt a reference to the first Seminole war (1817–18). That conflict broke out when the Indians were punished for harbouring runaway slaves who had escaped from the nearby plantations of the American south. The Seminoles were evicted from their lands by US troops and confined to a reservation in a wilder part of Florida, which was then seized from the Spanish in 1819. European concepts of property and commercial society were portrayed by Engels's earth spirit as alien, unnatural and oppressive.

The Seminole narrator declares war, which he likens unto natural phenomena such as forest fires and hurricanes, and he promises to revenge the wild creatures hunted by whites, since the white men will now become human quarry for the red men's arrows. His remarks also refer to 'cowardly blacks' imported by whites as slaves, a fate for which the strong and courageous red men are said to be unsuited.

The White Man, in Engels's drama, turns out to be a ship-wrecked German youth, crossed in love, punished for seven years for political agitation and then exiled. Presumably this hero was a veteran of the youth movements in Germany which had challenged the reinstated conservative monarchies in the early restoration period. 'Kings themselves have all/Trembled before our League. In trepidation,/Princes have seen how German youth can stand/As one', wrote Engels. This tragic character, hoping to gain freedom in the new world, is executed by red-skinned 'freedom fighters' and so expiates his brothers' sins against innocent, uncorrupted primitives.

Engels seems to have composed 'Florida' as a religious poem for his schoolfriends, some of whom were intended for the ministry. They met in a group for discussions of religious questions and more general topics of intellectual interest. At the time of writing the second Seminole war (1835–42) was raging, as US policy was then to evict the Indians from the reservation on which they had previously been confined, so that new white settlers could benefit. Engels had access at his club in Bremen to a wide range of international newspapers, including American ones. In a letter of 19 February 1839 to 'Fritz' Graeber, Engels complained about the stereotypical character of current religious poetry and suggested that 'Florida' was an attempt, for his friends if not for a wider audience, to set it on to a new path, one of critical reflection on contemporary politics (2 CW 407–17, 470).

Friedrich's letters to family and friends of late 1838 and early 1839 also expressed an interest in hymn tunes, chorales that he had harmonized himself and secular music, including a much enjoyed performance of *The Magic Flute* and a bad performance of *Hamlet*. His reading programme included German folktales, and he asked his little sister Marie to 'keep nagging Mother a little every two or three days to send me the Goethe for Christmas Day [1838]', reflecting his nationalist sentiments and romantic preoccupations. His musical tastes were of a similar character. German composers such as Bach, Handel, Haydn, Gluck, Mozart and especially Beethoven were praised at the expense of Italians, such as Bellini and Donizetti, and also Frenchmen, such as Scribe and Adam, whom he considered frivolous. The 'Eroica' Symphony was a favourite, no doubt because of its deliberate association by Beethoven with the revolutionary struggle in Germany and Austria against the tyranny of feudal rulers. The composer first dedicated the composition to Napoleon (1769–1821), but then withdrew the accolade when the revolutionary general crowned himself emperor and became in Beethoven's eyes a tyrant. For Engels the most talented contemporary composers in the German romantic school were the young Schumann (then in his twenties) and his youthful associates on the *Neue Zeitschrift für Musik*.

During 1840–1 the 20-year-old Engels wrote an operatic libretto, *Cola di Rienzi*, which was discovered only in 1974. Though he was in Bremen, he undertook the work for his Wuppertal schoolfriends, and there the unpublished and presumably unsung work survived amongst the papers of a local poet. Bulwer Lytton's novel *Rienzi* was first published in 1835 and shortly thereafter circulated in a German translation. There had also been a German play on the subject produced in 1837 which Engels might have known from reviews. Coincidentally Richard Wagner (1813–83) set to work on his own libretto and score in 1837, and his *Rienzi* had a successful première in Dresden in 1842 when he was 29.

In Engels's hands the story of the fourteenth-century Roman politician and general was a highly political celebration of popular revolt against a tyrant. This was revolutionary romanticism at fever pitch, and Engels's account is much more democratic than other contemporary versions of the story. The people's vengeance on their former leader turned dictator was wrought in Engels's tale by the character Camilla, a sword-wielding reincarnation of 'Liberty', the French revolutionary emblem of the 1830s, bare-breasted and leading an assault on the barricades (2 CW 150), 159, 396–407, 530, 537–68; I/3-A MEGA² 863–4).

III RADICALISM

Engels was soon in contact with a literary movement known as 'Young Germany', led by the writer and newspaper editor Karl Gutzkow (1811–78). In September 1835 Gutzkow had been accused by the conservative reviewer Wolfgang Menzel (1798–1873) of propounding blasphemy and immorality in his literary works, amongst them the notorious novel *Wally, die Zweiflerin* (*Wally, the*

Doubter), published in Mannheim earlier in the year. It dealt with the question of women's emancipation, amongst other radical preoccupations. His works and those of his associates in the movement were banned in December 1835 by the Federal Diet of the German Confederation. In January 1836 Gutzkow was sentenced to a month's imprisonment for disrespect to the Christian faith and for depicting immoral situations.

Engels's first reaction to the group was hostile. 'The Berlin party of Young Germany are a fine lot indeed!', he wrote to Friedrich Graeber on 20 January 1839. But he had some faint praise for Gutzkow himself as amongst the most reasonable, although Engels chided him for disavowing his views on female emancipation, which were timid enough in any case. At this point Engels was a literary nationalist, enthusiastic over *Volksbücher*, little chap-books containing popular versions of Germanic folktales and legends, and he praised the romantic poets Karl Beck (1817–79), Ferdinand Freiligrath and Julius Mosen (1803–67). Gutzkow's paper, the Hamburg *Telegraph für Deutschland*, was lampooned by Engels the budding satirist in January: 'You call yourself a quick writer, so who can doubt quick-written stuff is what your pages are filled with?' But in a letter of 19 February 1839 he praised it to Friedrich Graeber, and by March he was a contributor, albeit anonymously at first and then regularly under a pseudonym (2 CW 411–17).

In a letter of 8–9 April 1839 Engels wrote again to Friedrich Graeber, commenting that in contemporary German literature there was arising a new generation, which turned to its account the lives and literatures of all peoples, with Gutzkow as its leader. Here his German nationalism merged with a more cosmopolitan perspective, revolutionary liberalism. The July revolution of 1830 in France, he wrote, was the most splendid expression of the people's will since 1789, because it ended the Legitimist Bourbon monarchy by driving Charles X (1757–1836) from the throne and replacing him by popular acclaim with the Orléanist Louis Philippe (1773–1850). The 'citizen king' of the French had granted a constitutional charter which fell far short of popular sovereignty. Nonetheless it represented a liberal victory, compared with the 'divine-right' monarchism of the post-Napoleonic reaction in France and elsewhere in central Europe.

That reaction had followed on from the preceding revolutionary wars. Engels's perspective on the French wars of liberation at the turn of the century identified him clearly as a revolutionary constitutionalist. He sympathized with the largely unsuccessful struggles within the German states and principalities to wrest liberal constitutions from absolute rulers and to secure the freedoms of expression and conscience in civil rights. Those rights had been established in law by the invading French, but were soon revoked by the post-restoration Carlsbad decrees of 1819. Two liberal agitators – the poet Heinrich Heine (1797–1856) and the critic and writer Ludwig Börne (1786–1837) – were already fully-formed characters before the July revolution, he wrote, but only now after 1830 were they acquiring importance as major influences on contemporary intellectual life. Their standard had passed to Gutzkow and Young Germany, in whom the 'ideas of the time' were coming to consciousness. In particular he mentioned 'participation by the people in the administration of the state, that is, constitutional matters . . . emancipation of the Jews, abolition of all religious compulsion and hereditary aristocracy'. 'Who can have anything against that?', he inquired, rhetorically and disingenuously. Freiligrath, he predicted, would yet turn to Young Germany, and he also associated another idol, the poet Beck, with their views.

Politics, as practised amongst the *literati*, absorbed Engels's creative energies. 'I must become a Young German', he wrote, 'or rather, I am one already, body and soul, I cannot sleep at night, all because of the ideas of the century.' He confided that when he was at the post office and saw the Prussian coat of arms, he was seized with the spirit of freedom, and every time he read a newspaper he hunted in it for advances of freedom. But not all aspects of Young Germany met with his approval. He associated some of their slogans and phrases – 'world-weariness, world-historic, the anguish of the Jews, etc.' – with a dreamy, outdated, purely literary romanticism far removed from current issues of real substance (2 CW 420–3).

Engels continued to inform his schoolfriends about Young Germany, and to send them his poetic efforts – until hostility and lack of response 'disqualified' them from receiving any more. In his 'polyglottic' letter of 28–30 April 1839 to Wilhelm Graeber he complained (in Italian and Greek) that he could not accept as either authentic or competent the judgement and sentence passed by the five other students in the discussion group. And he wrote (in Latin) that it would do no harm to liberty if his mind inclined towards Young Germany, for this was not a group of writers, like the romantic, demogogic and other schools, and it was not a closed society. 'Demogogues' in Engels's terms were student demonstrators on behalf of constitutionalism and free intellectual inquiry. After the Wartburg festival of 18 October 1817, which became a vehicle for their efforts, they were repressed by the authorities and given their derogatory name. Friedrich identified the goals of Young Germany once again as the 'ideas of the century – the emancipation of the Jews and of the slaves, general constitutionalism and other good ideas'. Those ideas, he felt, should become part of the flesh and blood of the German people. 'Why should I hold aloof?' he asked with a flourish (2 CW 442–3 n.).

In a letter to Wilhelm Graeber, written over the period 24 May to 15 June 1839, Engels summarized the Young German view on politics and literature as he perceived it. Commenting on the first two volumes of Börne's *Gesammelte Schriften* (*Collected Works*, Hamburg 1829–31 and Paris 1833–4), he referred to the critic as the great fighter for freedom and justice. Börne was concerned in his first two volumes of reviews with aesthetics, and Engels praised him for penetrating to the innermost threads of the action in the plays on which he commented. But Engels's most extravagant comments were reserved for the succeeding generation, particularly Beck – 'a poetic talent without equal since Schiller'. Between the two Engels found a remarkable affinity – the same ardent spirit of freedom, unrestrained fantasy, youthful exuberance, the same mistakes. He interpreted Schiller's *Die Räuber* (*The Robbers*), first produced in 1782 in Mannheim, as an earnest warning to his servile age, but remarked that in the last century such striving could not yet have taken a definite form. But in Young Germany, he wrote, there is now some fifty-odd years later a definite, systematic trend (2 CW 448–50).

Engels sent a manuscript poem to Friedrich Graeber that celebrated the recent 'German July Days 1839', the anniversary of the most recent French revolution begun on 27 July 1830. The poet defies Ernst August, King of Hanover, and abuses other arrogant kings and princes in Germany. He threatens them with revolutionary violence from their no-longer-patient subjects: 'Now a storm blows up out of France, and the people rise up in their masses'. On 27 July 1839 Engels had been sailing on the high waves of the river Weser, and it was from the roaring gale that he drew inspiration for his political verses, using this romantic imagery to make a revolution in Germany seem as irresistible as an overwhelming natural force (2 CW 463–4).

In a letter of 30 July 1839 to Wilhelm Graeber, Engels continued this theme, arguing that Schiller was Germany's greatest liberal poet. This was because he had sensed the new era which would dawn after the French revolution of 1789, whereas Goethe had not shown this historical awareness, even after the July revolution of 1830. When the more recent revolution came so near to him that he almost had to believe that something new was coming, he retired into his room and shut the door so as to remain comfortable. But the youthful critic excused him somewhat, explaining that Goethe was 40 when the revolution had occurred and 'a made man'. Engels was then working on a translation (not preserved) of poems by Shelley, the English romantic and revolutionary (2 CW 464–9).

By late 1839 Engels had a succinct and deeply-felt perspective on the revolutionary struggle being waged by liberal constitutionalists all over Germany against reactionary monarchism in Prussia and elsewhere. That struggle had begun in earnest in 1815 when King Friedrich Wilhelm III broke his promise to provide a constitution, and student protest erupted. Engels summarized his liberal revolutionary views in a letter, composed between 9 December 1839 and 5 February 1840, to Friedrich Graeber:

Napoleon was an angel compared with him [Friedrich Wilhelm III – 'our majestic snotnose of Berlin']. . . . There never was a time richer in royal crimes than that of 1816–30; almost every prince then ruling deserved the death penalty. The pious Charles X, the vicious Ferdinand VII [1784–1833] of Spain, Franz [1768–1835] of Austria. . . . Dom Miguel [1802–66], who is a greater scoundrel than all the heroes of the French Revolution taken together, and whom nevertheless Prussia, Russia and Austria gladly recognised when he bathed in the blood of the best Portuguese, and the parricide Alexander [1777–1825] of Russia, as also his worthy brother Nicholas [1796–1855]. . . . I expect anything good only of that prince whose ears are boxed right and left by his people and whose palace windows are smashed by the flying stones of the revolution (2 CW 492–3).

Engels's revolutionary liberalism embraced a theory of free inquiry, backed up by constitutionalism and participatory politics.

This free inquiry, including as a matter of course access to uncensored publication, extended to certain religious issues which were related to the literary criticism and new literary works associated with Young Germany. In a letter of 8–9 April 1839 Friedrich had advised his friend Friedrich 'Fritz' Graeber, who was studying for the ministry, that he could be as orthodox a Christian as he liked, but 'if ever you become a pietist who rails against Young Germany ... then, truly, I'm telling you you'll have me to deal with'. Engels commented that he had never been a pietist, but mentioned that he had been a mystic for a while. He continued, 'I am now an honest, and in comparison with others very liberal, super-naturalist ... even though inclining now more, now less towards rationalism'. About those religious questions he commented, 'All this will have to be settled' (2 CW 422–3).

IV SCEPTICISM

Engels's boyhood acceptance of Christianity was breaking down, first into an uneasy compromise between Christianity and deism, then into pantheism, and ultimately into atheism. In common with many others at the time he found he could no longer adhere to the literal truth of either scripture or dogma, nor rely on the reassurances of pastoral authorities. As early as 17–18 September 1838 he reported to the Graeber brothers that he had been reading the works of the pantheist philosopher Jacob Böhme (1575–1624). This was significant, because unorthodox theological inquiry and philosophical speculation were an important part of the liberal politics that Engels was beginning to pursue (2 CW 395).

In the eyes of the German authorities theological scepticism concerning established Christian doctrine posed a clear threat to the hierarchical organisation and internal cohesion of the community. To question Christianity was to question the right of established rulers to rule, whether they were rulers of church or state. In any case church and state were deliberately interrelated, and for rulers of that time all authority was at stake in what might appear to us today to be a purely – or indeed merely – religious controversy. Since Engels's day a degree of separation between these two structures of authority, the state and the various churches, has become conventional. Moreover we also enjoy an assumption that religious belief, or the lack of it, is an area of private concern for the individual who stands protected against political 'interference' in a free realm of 'conscience'. Engels's reading of Böhme was a telling foray into an area that was then highly political, indeed revolutionary, because in Prussia in the 1830s the religious *thoughts* of any and all unorthodox writers and their readers were by the authorities' definition a subversive political *activity*.

In his letter of 8–9 April 1839 to Friedrich Graeber, Engels proclaimed himself a 'super-naturalist', i.e. one who believes in something God-like at work in the universe and who values Christianity for attempting to grasp such a deity or supreme being intellectually and emotionally. Some of his emotionalism was communicated in his letters, in particular a view that religious experience is pre-eminently a matter of feelings, as well as reason. This was a kind of compromise rationalism associated with the theologian and preacher Friedrich Schleiermacher (1768–1834). But at the same time Engels tended more and more towards the purely rationalist position which attempted, through intellectual argument, to grasp with reason alone whatever could be discerned about spirituality in the universe (2 CW 453–63).

Over the period 23 April–1 May 1839 Engels wrote to Friedrich Graeber that he was very busy at present with philosophy and critical theology. 'When you get to be eighteen years of age and become acquainted with Strauss, the rationalists and the [*Evangelische*] *Kirchen-Zeitung*', he wrote, 'then you must either read everything without thinking or begin to doubt your Wuppertal faith' (2 CW 425–6). *Das Leben Jesu* (*The Life of Jesus*) by David Friedrich Strauss (1808–74) appeared in Tübingen in 1835–6, and caused a tremendous scandal. By 1840 it was in its fourth edition. In a scholarly way Strauss aimed to treat the Gospels as historical documents, moving – so he hoped – their religious content onto a new level. He sifted the Biblical account of Jesus's life for contradictions, and he found little in what was left that attested to authentic fact. He described the Gospels as pseudo-historical myths created within a more primitive culture. Those myths expressed metaphysical truths and religious feelings in ways that were appropriate to the first and second centuries AD, but for his own time a more philosophical meditation on metaphysical themes was in order, because human knowledge had advanced so remarkably, especially in recent years.

Strauss's view was derived from the philosophical school of

Georg Friedrich Wilhelm Hegel (1770–1831), who interpreted history as the realization of the idea of freedom. Hegel presented human activity as an incarnation of 'reason' that arises from a metaphysical 'idea' and manifests itself as 'mind' or 'spirit'. Christianity as a system of ideas and the historical appearance of Jesus were both treated by Hegel within his philosophical works as part of a developmental process through which reason manifests itself in the world. Strauss embraced Hegel's overall scheme, but aimed as an historian to expand the philosopher's work and to demonstrate its truth. In doing so he offended Christian fundamentalists, such as the evangelicals who wrote for the *Kirchen-Zeitung*, a conservative paper published in Berlin and mentioned by Engels in connection with the Graebers, who had gone there to study. Fundamentalists took the literal truth of the Bible to be a central tenet of the Christian faith, but Strauss had outraged virtually all moderate Christians as well, since almost nothing that was orthodox and doctrinal could survive his textual scrutiny, which seemed to destroy any factual basis for belief. Moreover his Hegelian perspective on history seemed to subsume faith into a system of abstract ideas far removed from Christian dogma.

Some kind of highly intellectual and metaphysically rarified reverence for spirituality still flickered in Strauss's work, but almost no one within the Christian community was impressed with his view that faith could subsist if the truthfulness of the Bible were denied and the historical basis of Christian dogma declared unbelievable. 'Faith in what?' was a question for which Strauss had no very credible answer, and his claim that the essence of the Christian faith was somehow independent of his criticism seemed empty. He was fired from his position at Tübingen University, hounded out of Zürich in 1839, and consigned for the rest of his life to obscurity and disappointment.

Engels took Friedrich Graeber to task for his religious fundamentalism in a letter of 23 April–1 May 1839, complaining about quite obvious contradictions in the Bible, e.g. two genealogies for Mary's husband Joseph, the literal truth of miracles, the authenticity of the works ascribed to the Evangelists etc. 'Not to speak of the Old Testament', he commented, but 'nobody tells you this in dear old Barmen':

Where does the Bible demand literal belief in its teachings, in its accounts? Where does a *single* apostle declare that everything he says is directly inspired? This is not surrendering reason in obedience to Christ, as the orthodox people affirm; no, it is a killing of the divine in man to replace it with the dead letter. I am therefore just as good a super-naturalist as I was before, but I have cast off orthodoxy. Thus I cannot now or ever believe that a rationalist who seeks with all his heart to do as much good as possible, should be eternally damned. That is at odds with the Bible itself, for it is written that no one is damned on account of original sin but only because of his own sins. But if a person resists original sin with all his might and does what he can, then his actual sins are only a necessary consequence of original sin and therefore they cannot damn him (2 CW 425–6).

In a letter of 15 June 1839 Engels wrote again to Friedrich Graeber, declaring Strauss's book to be irrefutable and outlining very clearly his Straussian views:

You think too well of me, I hope, to attribute all this to a sacrilegious scepticism or to boastfulness. I know that I am going to get into the greatest unpleasantness through this, but what forces itself on me so convincingly, I cannot drive away, no matter how much I might like to. If I should perhaps have hurt your conviction by my strong language, then I ask your pardon from the bottom of my heart. I only spoke as I think and as things have forced themselves on me. It is with me as with Gutzkow; when I come across someone who arrogantly dismisses positive Christianity, then I defend this teaching, which derives from the deepest needs of human nature, the longing for salvation from sin through God's grace; but when it is a matter of defending the freedom of reason, then I protest against all compulsion. – I hope to live to see a radical transformation in the religious consciousness of the world. . . . Man is born free, he is free!

Engels's rationalized Christianity was common enough in Hegelian circles, and easy to pick up. But it also arose from very deep concerns, particularly with the allegedly inevitable damnation of his heroes the rationalists and sceptics – just the sort of hell-fire that Wuppertal pietists delighted in:

The Bible teaches that rationalists will be eternally damned. Can you imagine that a man who has striven for union with God all his life (Börne, Spinoza, Kant), indeed that someone like Gutzkow, whose highest aim in life is to find the meeting point between positive Christianity and the culture of our time, that after death people like these should be banished from God for ever and ever and suffer God's wrath physically and mentally without end in the most fearful torments?

'Who gives us the right to believe blindly [in] the Bible?' Engels demanded to know. He wrote quite plainly to Friedrich Graeber that he had reached a point where he could only regard as divine a teaching which could stand the test of reason (2 CW 453–6).

V   RATIONALISM

In a letter of 12–27 July 1839, once again to Friedrich Graeber, Engels explained that pietism must make way for speculative theology, which in his version assured him that mankind was of divine origin and that no part of mankind could ever be lost and that after all the countless struggles of this world mankind must return, divested of all that is mortal and sinful, to God's bosom. In the new rational theology, in which mysticism and dogma gave way to scholarship and philosophy, the sinfulness of man lay in the necessarily imperfect realisation of the 'idea', and the 'idea', of course, was to be fully realized by philosophy. God as revealed by religious authorities, if indeed they could do this, would henceforth have to be greater than, but not different from, a god whose existence was demonstrated by reason. 'Otherwise', Engels concluded, 'all philosophy is not only empty but even sinful', and without philosophy, 'there is no education; without education there is no humanity; without humanity, again, there is no religion' (2 CW 457–63).

On 8 October 1839 Engels declared himself in a letter to Wilhelm Graeber to be an enthusiastic Straussian. Calling himself a poor, miserable poet, he wrote that he had crept under the wing of the genius David Friedrich Strauss. Perhaps Strauss saw too much myth here and there, but only in unimportant matters (2 CW 471). Then on 29 October 1839 Engels announced to Friedrich Graeber that he had taken the oath to the flag of David Friedrich Strauss and had become a first-class mythic. Engels wrote in triumph that

Strauss could not be refuted. He had taken away the ground from under orthodox views, so the historical foundation for Christianity was lost beyond recall, and the dogmatic foundation would have to go down with it (2 CW 480). To Wilhelm Graeber the young Engels denied in a letter of 13–20 November 1839 that he would ever return to Christianity. For the sake of the 'idea' he had stripped off what was fantastical in orthodoxy, and he would never submit to that strait jacket again. 'I am on the point of becoming a Hegelian', he announced. Strauss had 'lit up lights on Hegel for me which make the thing quite plausible', and Hegel's 'philosophy of history is anyway written as from my own heart' (2 CW 485–7).

During the next month or so Engels studied Hegel's *Vorlesungen über die Philosophie der Geschichte* (*Philosophy of History*) compiled by his disciples, edited from lecture notes and posthumously published in Berlin in 1837. 'I read out of it dutifully every evening', he reported to Friedrich Graeber in a letter written between 9 December 1839 and 5 February 1840, and he commented that 'the tremendous thoughts grip me terribly'. By then Engels was not very keen to continue the theological debate with the Graebers, because through Strauss he had entered on the straight road to Hegelianism and was absorbing important things from his colossal system (2 CW 489–90). Chief amongst these was modern pantheism, an interpretation of Hegel in which God and reason merged with the developmental unfolding of the world itself. For Engels as a pantheist reason was no longer effective in rationalizing the Christian God or indeed any deity as such. Divinity was literally everywhere within the universe, and within humanity preeminently, since if there was any meaning to divinity it was in reason itself.

The rationalism with which Engels identified himself was by no means confined to religious questions, such as the foundations of Christian faith and the nature of spirituality, nor to very broad political issues, such as the virtues of constitutionalism and the evils of censorship. In his letter of 29 October 1839 to Friedrich Graeber he mentioned an 'excellent book', *Preussen und Preussenthum* (*Prussia and Prussian Rule*) by Jakob Venedy (1805–71), published earlier that year in Mannheim. In Venedy's detailed political critique, so Engels commented, Prussian legislation, state administration, tax distribution, etc., were subjected to strict scrutiny, and the results were convincing. Amongst the author's criticisms of the Prussian régime Engels picked out favours for the monied aristocracy against the poor, endeavours to perpetuate absolutism, suppression of political education, stupefying of the mass of the people, and utilization of religion to do this (2 CW 480). He mentioned the book again in his letter to Wilhelm Graeber of 13–20 November 1839, boasting that he was now a large-scale importer of banned books into Prussia, including five copies of Venedy's work, which were lying ready for dispatch to Barmen (2 CW 484).

Earlier in the year Engels had had a successful trial run in Gutzkow's *Telegraph* at this polemical style of writing and the use of journalism to promote political action. In March 1839 he created a scandal of his own with a scathing *exposé*, the anonymous 'Briefe aus dem Wuppertal' ('Letters from Wuppertal').

2

Beginning of a Career

Engels wrote the 'Letters from Wuppertal' in early 1839 at the time of his first contacts with the literary movement Young Germany. The 'Letters' appeared anonymously in Gutzkow's periodical *Telegraph für Deutschland* during March and April of that year. At approximately 7500 words they mark the first substantial published work undertaken by the 18-year-old author and the first of his original prose writings to appear in print.

Gutzkow, with whom Engels was not personally acquainted, was still a victim of censorship and not formally named at that time as editor of the paper. After moving about for some years he had finally settled with sympathetic printers in Hamburg, where the local censorship was more liberal than elsewhere in Germany, although posting and receipt of the *Telegraph* were still somewhat restricted within the German Confederation and in the Austrian Empire (I/3 MEGA[2] 666–72). Young Germany promoted a worldly view of literature and a high-toned defiance of philistinism and intolerance. The 'Letters' were a Young German's revenge on his home town and a chance for a native son to settle old scores. The articles also displayed certain characteristics that are traceable to Engels's personal experience and judgement, even in late adolescence, rather than to his undeniable facility for adopting a point of view and defending it polemically.

Engels surveyed the intellectual state of the twin communities in the Wupper valley, Elberfeld and Barmen, and brought them to judgement. He was determined to expose obscurantism, intolerance, prejudice, bigotry, hypocrisy and backwardness. The subject most extensively treated in the work was pietism, a favourite target since pietists were deliberately anti-cosmopolitan, anti-Enlightenment and anti-rationalist. But he also surveyed the local schools, newspapers and periodicals and literary life, such as it was. The immediacy and flair of his personal view make the 'Letters' lively reading today. A very few tributes to individuals were mixed in with his prevailing hostility, but it is plain that the young author saw little hope for his home district. The exercise seems one of shaking the dust from his feet, rather than any serious resolution to spread culture from the city to the provinces.

I   FACTORY TOWNS

The opening of the 'Letters' recalls the romantics' interest in landscape and travel-writing: 'the two towns of Elberfeld and Barmen ... stretch along the [Wupper] valley for a distance of nearly three hours' travel ... the not very high mountains, rising sometimes gently, sometime steeply, and heavily wooded, march boldly into green meadows.' But some of the details noted by Engels are surely unusual in the genre and came directly from experience, notably industrial pollution of the river and his brief but exceptionally vivid descriptions of the living conditions of industrial workers: 'The purple waves of the narrow river flow ... between smoky factory buildings and yarn-strewn bleaching-yards. Its bright red colour, however, is due not to some bloody battle ... but simply and solely to the numerous dye-works using Turkey red.'

At the outset Engels's tour of the region displays a geographer's eye, not merely for the physical details of the landscape but also for the inter-related patterns of human use. The reader is taken up-river from the junction of the Wupper with the Rhine, and so first to Elberfeld, a community of modest dwellings, cramped buildings and accumulated detritus and pollution that gradually diminishes as the journey moves upstream towards the hills. But once over the bridge into Barmen good taste and variety take over. There are modern houses, gardens and a kind of spacious, decentralized development that contrasts with the older, gloomy streets of Elberfeld.

In his articles Engels distributed numerous critical judgements on bastardized architecture, public meanness and indifference to civilized amenity. The museum in Elberfeld, he reported, was burdened by debt and eventually sold off as a casino, and the new town hall was awkwardly situated and only half finished. In this community, so Engels seemed to say, the leading citizens lack taste and civic pride:

Almost outside the town is the Catholic church; it stands there as if it has been expelled from the sacred walls [of Elberfeld – 'the Zion of the obscurantists']. It is in Byzantine style, built very badly by a very inexperienced architect from a very good plan; the old Catholic church has been demolished to make room for the left wing, not yet built, of the Town Hall; only the tower remains and serves the general good after a fashion, namely, as a prison. Immediately afterwards one comes to a large building, its roof supported by columns, but these columns are of a most remarkable kind; they are Egyptian at the bottom, Doric in the middle, and Ionic at the top; moreover, for very sound [financial] reasons, they dispense with all superfluous accessories, such as a plinth and capitals. . . . Incidentally, the building is so clumsily proportioned that at night it looks like a camel.

The author's comments on the ordinary inhabitants display what seems at first to be a romantic vision of simple folk: 'There is no trace here of the wholesome, vigorous life of the people that exists almost everywhere in Germany.' But what really concerned him is revealed to us when we are guided into the factories of the region, where 'people breathe in more coal fumes and dust than oxygen – and in the majority of cases beginning already at the age of six'. That state of affairs, according to Engels, drove people to excessive drinking, and he described the underclass or *Karrenbinder* as 'totally demoralised people, with no fixed abode or definite employment, who crawl out of their refuges, haystacks, stables, etc., at dawn'. Amongst leather workers, he claimed, three years in local tanneries suffices to ruin them physically and mentally, so three out of five died from consumption, and their miseries were compounded by drinking spirits. He described syphilis and lung disease as widespread and damned the terrible poverty that kept half the children of Elberfeld away from school and in the factories instead.

Engels may very well have read descriptive and critical accounts of factory work in English newspapers or in other papers available in Bremen, and his admittedly rough statistics and sweeping generalizations are perhaps best described as impressions mingled with hearsay rather than documented and well-defended facts. But at the same time the picture he painted is very plausible as well as vivid, and there is certainly no reason to dismiss it as fictional or overdrawn. Working conditions in similar factories have been researched since his time, and his view of the factories in his home district is not out of line with what has been historically established.

In Engels's view the factory owners of the region were a particularly nasty species, since he argued that early deaths would not have assumed such horrifying proportions if the factories were not operated in such a reckless way. Moreover he portrayed the workers as divided into two hostile groups, the victims of either religious mysticism or drunkenness, circumstances that destroyed the development of a popular spirit. In any case members of both groups were equally consumptive. His picture of the Wuppertal towns displays very clearly his view of social class, and his sympathy was obviously with the victims of industrialization. About the better-off members of the community he was almost wholly scathing, as he found the most self-righteous to be the most hypocritical:

> But the wealthy manufacturers have a flexible conscience, and causing the death of one child more or one less does not doom a pietist's soul to hell, especially if he goes to church twice every Sunday. For it is a fact that the pietists among the factory owners treat their workers worst of all; they use every possible means to reduce the workers' wages on the pretext of depriving them of the opportunity to get drunk, yet at the election of preachers they are always the first to bribe their people.

Having surveyed the economic geography of the Wuppertal towns from personal experience, Engels moved on to 'mysticism', his catch-all term for a variety of religious views and cults of a broadly pietist character. The relationship between industry and religion was raised in an intriguing way in the 'Letters', because he seemed to suspect that they support each other, but he did not discuss that relationship at any length. He did not consider whether pietism in its local, extreme form was particularly suited to an economy undergoing industrialization, or whether industrialization was pushed on by a pre-existing religious mentality that was favourable to the exploitation of people and resources for profit. Nor did he offer any specific suggestions in his work concerning how the situation might be improved, though he did make vague references to a popular spirit or to modern education that might counter the pietist influence.

Industrial poverty and class-interest made their appearance in

Engels's first expository work, but they were somewhat peripheral to the political perspective that he found available in the writings of Young Germany. Young Germany was not a movement that focused on the plight of factory workers, nor one that attempted to rouse the lower orders of society unduly, since at their most radical these literary romantics were committed to a struggle for rights to participate in politics and to publish political works that were of most interest and use, at the time, to the educated. Young Germans had a revolution in mind, but it was an intellectual one. In their world the principal conflict was not between workers and owners over economic interests, but between the enlightened in society, such as themselves, and the prejudiced, especially narrow-minded Christians.

Engels scorned the Reformed congregations in Elberfeld, into which he had himself been confirmed, and he derided them as the real centre of all pietism and mysticism. The middle-class community, in his opinion, supported a curious kind of Calvinism propagated by extremely bigoted preachers who were savagely intolerant and held regular trials of heretics – persons accused of reading novels, or being rationalists. Rationalists, on the pietist view, were bringing the Bible and the Christian faith into disrepute by subjecting them to historical and factual criticism.

Dr Friedrich Wilhelm Krummacher (1796–1868) was singled out as a target in Engels's attack on pietism, no doubt since he was formerly a liberal 'demagogue' who had carried a banner at the Wartburg festival, but had since that time recanted. His former demagogy broke through once in a while, Engels reported, when he spoke of the contradiction between earthly riches and the humility of Christ, or between the arrogance of earthly rulers and the pride of God. Krummacher's doctrine of predestination was especially strict, and in Engels's opinion, nothing could be refuted once the basis was accepted, namely, the inability of man on his own to desire what is good, let alone do it. This doctrine was in the most direct contradiction to reason and even the Bible, on Engels's reading, and it gave Krummacher a perfect excuse to preach extensively on hellfire, which Engels deplored. His description of the scene must surely derive from first-hand experience or eyewitness accounts:

Then he [Krummacher] thrashes about in the pulpit, bends over all sides, bangs his fist on the edge, stamps like a cavalry horse, and shouts so that the windows resound and people in the street tremble. Then the congregation begins to sob; first the young girls weep, then the old women join in with a heart-rending soprano and the cacophany is completed by the wailing of the enfeebled drunken pietists ... and through all this uproar Krummacher's powerful voice rings out pronouncing before the whole congregation innumerable sentences of damnation, or describing diabolical scenes.

Pietism, Engels argued, pervaded and corrupted every single aspect of life in the Wuppertal communities, especially the schools. For the church schools he had little hope. But in the state sector, where clerical inspectors were present but of less influence, the corrupting effects of religious obscurantism were particularly regrettable, because the more modern curriculum might otherwise tempt pupils to continue their education elsewhere. Even in the Elberfeld gymnasium or grammar school, which he had attended himself, sectarian influence was rife. The guiding principle of school inspectors was to choose 'a mediocre Reformist [teacher] rather than an *efficient* Lutheran, or worse still, a Catholic'. Dr Hantschke, who wrote Engels's largely complimentary school-leaving report, was apparently a victim of this policy, and Engels claimed that he would have been made permanent headmaster if he had not been a Lutheran and if the school inspectorate had been less miserly. The only figure who attracted much praise in the whole of the 'Letters' was Dr Clausen, who was said to be outstanding in history and literature, and the only teacher who could arouse a feeling for poetry among the pupils. His ex-pupil saw him as a hero fighting against the philistines of Wuppertal, the merchants of the older generation who had not a trace of education. Engels concluded with venom that anyone who could play whist and billiards, who could talk a little about politics and pay a pretty compliment was regarded as an educated man in Barmen and Elberfeld. His verdict on the life of a Wuppertal businessman was entirely damning. Though he was himself a merchant, in some more or less tenuous sense, almost all his life, he never went back to Barmen to live as an industrialist amongst his family and his native community:

> The life these people lead is terrible, yet they are so satisfied with it; in the daytime they immerse themselves in their accounts

with a passion and interest that is hard to believe; in the evening at an appointed hour they turn up at social gatherings where they play cards, talk politics and smoke, and then leave for home at the stroke of nine. So they live day in day out, with never a change, and woe to him who interferes with their routine; he can be sure of most ungracious treatment in all the best houses. – Fathers zealously bring up their sons along these lines, sons who show every promise of following in their fathers' footsteps.

No one in the valley knew anything at all about the literary significance of Young Germany, Engels concluded with horror, and it was regarded as a secret alliance, something like the demagogues (2 CW 7–25).

Young Friedrich was evidently not the son of a Wuppertal businessman dutifully following in his father's footsteps. He had rejected his father's world and marked himself out for something quite different and daring – albeit covertly. In his letter of 23 April–1 May 1839 to Friedrich Graeber he exclaimed: 'Ha, ha ha! Do you know who wrote the article in the *Telegraph*? The author is the writer of these lines, but I advise you not to say anything about it. I could get into a hell of a lot of trouble' (2 CW 426). Another schoolfriend, Wilhelm Blank (1821–92), whose elder brother later married Friedrich's favourite sister Marie, was involved in the affair of the anonymous articles. Blank reported in a letter of 24–28 May to Wilhelm Graeber that all copies which had found their way to Elberfeld had been snapped up at once, and that there was a tremendous local guessing-game to determine the author's identity – 'some say Freiligrath, others Clausen . . .' – suggestions that no doubt flattered the novice writer. To Friedrich Graeber, Engels declared himself pleased with his work, since he had not said anything in the article that he could not prove. 'By the way', he continued, 'the article seems to have caused a sensation', and he put his coterie of five schoolfriends under an obligation on their word of honour not to tell anyone that he was the author (2 CW 426–7; I/3-A MEGA^2 740). Remarkably the secret did not leak out in the Wuppertal towns.

On 12 April 1839 Dr Martin Runkel, the editor of the local paper, the *Elberfelder Zeitung*, published his own attack on the anonymous author, much to Engels's disgust. In a letter of 28–30 April 1839 Engels wrote to Wilhelm Graeber, 'I want to let him be given a hint that he should point out to me just one single falsehood, which he cannot, because everything I wrote was based on proven data which I have from eye-witnesses and ear-witnesses.' Blank had supplied him with Runkel's article, and Engels sent it straight off to Gutzkow with a repeated request to keep his name secret. 'God knows what will become of Wuppertal', he concluded to Wilhelm Graeber. But it is evident that he was looking after himself with some care and so sparing his family humiliation (2 CW 446–7).

On 9 May 1839 the *Elberfelder Zeitung* published the anonymous *Herrn Dr Runkel in Elberfeld* (*Open Letter to Dr Runkel*), probably delivered to its offices by Blank. In that work Engels replied anonymously to his critic the local newspaperman. Engels wrote defiantly that 'it does not matter to me that you call me a Young German, for I neither accept the charges you level against Young Literature nor have the honour of belonging to it'. And he objected that the distinguished editor had challenged his facts but not adduced any contrary evidence. In his own defence Engels wrote trenchantly:

> As for ignorance of the conditions, I should have expected this reproach least of all did I not know what a meaningless expression this phrase has become, used everywhere for lack of anything better. I have possibly spent twice as much time as you in Wuppertal, have lived in Elberfeld and Barmen and have had the most favourable opportunity to observe closely the life of all social estates (2 CW 27; I/3-A MEGA² 764).

Blank also sent Engels an account of Pastor Krummacher's next pietist outrage, a sermon of 21 April 1839 on Joshua 10:12–13:

> Then spoke Joshua to the Lord in the day when the Lord gave the Amorites over to the men of Israel; and he said in the sight of Israel,
> 'Sun, stand thou still at Gibeon, and thou Moon in the valley of Aijalon.'
> And the sun stood still, and the moon stayed, until the nation took vengeance on their enemies. Is this not written in the Book of Jashar? The sun stayed in the midst of heaven, and did not hasten to go down for about a whole day.

In his letter to Wilhelm Graeber of 28–30 April 1839 Engels declared this a scandal, remarking that 'Krummacher declared . . .

that the earth stands still and the sun rotates around it, and the fellow dares to trumpet this April 21, 1839.' In May the *Telegraph* published his rationalist critique, anonymously as usual (2 CW 29, 446; I/3-A MEGA² 762).

Later in the year Engels boasted of his journalistic success to his schoolfriends, noting in a letter of 24 May–15 June to Wilhelm Graeber that his 'Letters' had been reviewed in the Nuremberg *Athenäum für Wissenschaft, Kunst und Leben*, where they were described as a true picture of religious life in Elberfeld and Barmen, and moreover praised for an authentic depiction of Krummacher (2 CW 450, 617). But on 8 October he admitted to Wilhelm Graeber that the 'Letters' had been written in haste and had some one-sidednesses and half-truths, so as time passed he began to appraise his work more soberly (2 CW 472).

II 'OSWALD'

Engels's articles had been noticed outside Bremen, Hamburg and Wuppertal, even in Berlin, and the *Telegraph* kept its readers informed of the controversy about the work and the identity of the writer. But Gutzkow revealed only that his correspondent 'S. Oswald', the pseudonymous author of a follow-up article 'Aus Elberfeld' ('From Elberfeld'), published in the *Telegraph* in November 1839, was also responsible for the original work that had caused all the uproar. After 'From Elberfeld' many of Engels's published works were signed 'Friedrich Oswald', 'F. Oswald', 'F.O.' or 'Friedrich O.' The initial 'S', used only once, was probably a printer's error, as the letters 'S' and 'F' were similar in Engels's handwriting. The choice of 'Oswald' for a pseudonym seems to be a mystery. Perhaps Engels was thinking of Oswald von Wolkenstein (1377–1445), a wandering minstrel of noble birth and vastly peripatetic habits, one of the most popular composers of *Minnelieder*. Engels was highly sensitive to the romantic, nationalist revival of folk culture that was taking place in Germany, and he may have been attracted to the medieval poet for political reasons as well, as Oswald took a major part in a revolt of the Tyrolean nobility against their Austrian overlord (I/3-A MEGA² 670–1, 740, 771).

In 'From Elberfeld' Engels, as the romantic critic 'Oswald', reviewed an anonymous collection of poems just published in June 1839. He described the author as a genuine Wuppertal Christian, but intellectually a dead man, because of his childlike beliefs in doctrines now revealed to be contradictory. The short review captures perfectly the moment when Friedrich was balanced uneasily between a powerful scepticism applied to the Christianity expressed in the verses he was considering, and his Schleier-machian view that religion had truly become a matter of the heart. He praised the poetry for its romanticism in some passages which were truly moving in their genuineness of feeling. But he warned his readers not to expect much from any literature that stemmed from Wuppertal. It would not be an unfettered soaring of free spirits, but only a product of pietism. His conclusion also reflected mixed feelings about his birthplace:

> Dear reader, forgive me for presenting you with a book which can be of infinitely little interest to you; you were not born in Wuppertal, perchance you have never stood on its hills and seen the two towns at your feet. But you too have a homeland and perhaps return to it with the same love as I, however ordinary it looks, once you have vented your anger at its perversities (2 CW 30–1).

During 1839 the 18-year-old Engels made his own way through a number of cultural clashes with uncanny speed, testing the con-flicting claims of faith and reason, romanticism and rationalism, intellectual pursuits and political action. Those battles were reflected throughout his correspondence and writings of the period, but nowhere more vividly than in his confrontation with the pietists of the Wuppertal towns.

As Engels's interest in religious questions died down under the influence of Straussian criticism and Hegelian pantheism, so did his interest in the preachers of Elberfeld and Barmen, though it flickered again briefly in another article attacking Krummacher. By 1840 Engels's contacts in journalism stretched beyond the local *Bremisches Conversatsionsblatt* and *Der Bremer Stadtbote*, and Gutz-kow's Hamburg *Telegraph*. For readers of the *Morgenblatt für gebildete Leser*, published in Stuttgart and Tübingen, and then for the *Allgemeine Zeitung* of Augsburg, the freelance correspondent 'Oswald' reported on the Bremen scene in 1840 and 1841. Those reports included an account of the visit in July 1840 by 'the Pope of the Wuppertal Calvinists, the St. Michael of the doctrine of pre-destination', Pastor Krummacher. What was the point, 'Oswald' inquired rhetorically in the *Morgenblatt*, of Krummacher's 'invective against Voltaire (1694–1778) and Rousseau ... except to disguise the very definite, even personal, tendentiousness of the sermons'? 'Oswald' bravely announced his contrasting liberal creed and proposed stirring political tactics, advising his readers that pietists had relied on divisions in the rationalist camp. People in Bremen would have to learn that they must all stand united when it became necessary to fight obscurantism (2 CW 121–2, 126–8; I/3-A MEGA² 1249; the editors of MEGA² note that Gutzkow was probably the author of the article in the *Telegraph* of September 1840 on Krummacher's sermons that is reproduced in English amongst Engels's collected works).

Further articles attacking Wuppertal pietism might have brought Engels's authorship of the 'Letters' and other anti-pietist writings into the open and revealed to the world, and in particular to the twin towns Elberfeld and Barmen, the identity of the notorious 'Oswald'. Indeed by March 1841 'Oswald' had been correctly identified by a Bremen clergyman, who wrote privately to the editor of the *Morgenblatt* demanding a right of reply (I/3-A MEGA² 675). In any case the novelty for Engels of stirring a hornet's nest had probably worn off, and by then he had moved on to larger issues and left the area altogether.

Engels's letter to Friedrich Graeber of 9 December 1839–5 February 1840 was full of plans for novels, poems, reviews, travel writing and political comment within the framework of Young German literary criticism. In 'my last *Telegraph* essay', Engels wrote, 'there are several pieces of very bitter sarcasm about the Bundestag and the Prussian censorship' which the censor omitted to remove. Any 'author who reaches the age of thirty', wrote the 19-year-old veteran, 'or writes three books without cuts by the censor is not worth anything'. 'Scarred warriors are the best', he concluded bravely, '*I* don't commit infanticide on my own thoughts'. But he also admitted that 'whenever I want to write verses in the evening I have always eaten so much that I can't prevent myself from falling asleep' (2 CW 488–92).

The essay for the *Telegraph* that Engels mentioned was part of a series of reviews of *Volksbücher*, chap-books or popular editions of old tales. He evaluated these works along political lines, a method which he favoured over that of earlier romantic critics who had

regarded works in their poetic aspect alone. His tone was highly
didactic, and he judged what was appropriate in books for the
German people without apology:

> If, generally speaking, the qualities which can fairly be demand-
> ed of a popular book are rich poetic content, robust humour,
> moral purity, and, for a German popular book, a strong, trusty
> *German* spirit, qualities which remain the same at all times, we
> are also entitled to demand that it should be in keeping with its
> age, or cease to be a book for the people.

On that score Engels had difficulty recommending a version of
the classic story of Tristan and Isolde, even though there was in it a
close connection with a modern theme, that of the emancipation of
women. But he concluded that in a popular book the question was
out of place, and so the tale might be read as an apology for
adultery. He found it highly questionable whether that issue
should be left in the hands of the people.

On conventional political criteria Engels's evaluations of traditional tales were much more straightforward, since he argued that
popular books should help uneducated people see the truth and
reasonableness of contemporary trends. In that connection he
mentioned the struggle for freedom, the development of constitutionalism, the need to resist the tyranny of the aristocracy, and the
fight against pietism and the remnants of gloomy asceticism (2 CW
32–3, 37–8). He expressed the populist aspect of Young German
politics very clearly, but did so as a Young German, for Young
Germans, in Young German periodicals. At that time popular
politics was by definition a revolutionary idea, and it scarcely
existed in Germany anyway, so Engels can hardly be faulted for his
insularity and intellectualism.

Then in an article 'Retrograde Zeichen der Zeit' ('Retrograde
Signs of the Times'), published again in the *Telegraph*, the correspondent 'Oswald' called in February 1840 for co-operation between science and life, philosophy and modern trends, between
Hegel and Börne. Engels's transition from Young German to
Young Hegelian was underway, and *Telegraph* readers were duly
reminded by 'Oswald' in an article of April 1840 that Hegel had
both conservative and revolutionary aspects, depending on the
way that his notoriously ambiguous writings were interpreted. In
Engels's view the battle over Hegel's philosophy was crucial to the

development of German political consciousness, and he pointed to a developing link between literature and philosophy in the *Hallische Jahrbücher für deutsche Wissenschaft und Kunst*. That periodical had been planned in 1837 by Arnold Ruge (1802–80), sometime philosophy teacher at Halle University and later an independent scholar and writer. It was available from 1838, and its contributors and supporters were generally Hegelians, albeit of different persuasions. It swiftly became the leading journal for Hegel's disciples, amongst whom Engels picked out Strauss and Karl Rosenkranz (1805–79), an idealist philosopher and editor of Immanuel Kant (1724–1804) and Hegel. A year later Engels recommended the *Hallische Jahrbücher* to Friedrich Graeber as the most widely read journal in North Germany (2 CW 50–1, 66, 526).

In a long review, 'Modernes Literaturleben' ('Modern Literary Life'), for the Brunswick paper *Mitternachtzeitung für gebildete Leser*, published between March and May 1840, 'Oswald' turned on Gutzkow and subjected him and Young Germany, also known as Young Literature, to a good deal of criticism, and some faint praise. This was much as he had done in December 1839 in an article for the *Telegraph* on the poet Beck, whom he had formerly admired. His new perspective was that Young Germans had much to learn from the Hegelian school, in its latest, most radical development. The younger generation of Hegelians, in Engels's opinion, were advancing towards a unification of thought which would have the most important influence on the development of literature, and much else. His recommended source for that enlightenment was, naturally, the *Hallische Jahrbücher*.

III   YOUNG HEGELIANS

Engels was aware that the Young Hegelians were not yet a unified school or political tendency. At first they disagreed over theological issues related to the nature of God and the status of Christian dogma. But then they also disagreed politically, holding differing views on the extent to which the historical process on earth – by which reason was thought to manifest itself as freedom – was merely *reflected* in philosophical consciousness or was instead *advanced* by self-conscious acts of the human will. Directly related to this was their disagreement over whether the contemporary Prussian state should be celebrated by Hegelians as the realization of freedom, or criticized as deficient with respect to an idealized free society. They drew conclusions that were variously conservative, reformist and revolutionary. Young Hegelians then had to confront each other, and consider compromising amongst themselves or splitting the ranks. In addition some of them had to face unpleasant consequences when politicians and civil servants took an interest in their ideas and proscribed them.

Young Hegelians and their movement differed from Young Germany in that the Young Hegelians were largely drawn from the universities and found their audiences there, whereas Young Germans belonged to the more commercial and cosmopolitan world of *belles lettres*. But there were also considerable overlaps between the two groups and amongst the various views held from time to time within each one. The opportunities for quarrelling within each camp and between the two were plentiful, and Engels's Young Hegelian critique of Gutzkow was a contribution to those debates.

In June 1840 Gutzkow attacked the *Hallische Jahrbücher*, and Engels referred to this as spiteful abuse. Whilst he was curious how Gutzkow would receive the Hegelian criticism written by his former protégé 'Oswald', no further intellectual reaction from either party on this point is preserved. The relationship between Engels and Gutzkow continued, however, in its characteristically distant fashion, until the end of 1841. Engels's assessment of his first real editor and mentor in the critical essay 'Modern Literary Life' was complex and undoubtedly perceptive. He also revelled in polemic whilst arguing for constructive criticism and unity, and his imagery alone reveals the intensity of his involvement with the radical politics of the time:

> Gutzkow possesses the greatest power of intellect, as is recognised by all German authors – of *belles-lettres*, of course; his judgment is never at a loss, his eye finds its bearings with wonderful facility in the most complex phenomena. Alongside this intellect there is, however, an equally powerful heat of passion which expresses itself as enthusiasm in his productions and puts his imagination in that state of, I would almost say, erection, in which alone spiritual creation is possible . . . I am far from accusing Gutzkow of consciously striving for unrestricted domination in literature, but at times he uses expressions which make it easier for his opponents to charge him with egoism. His

passionate disposition alone drives him to give himself wholly as he is, and so one can discern at once the whole man in his works. – Add to these spiritual characteristics a life continually wounded over the last four years by the censor's scissors and the restrictions imposed on his free literary development by the police, and I may hope to have sketched the main features of Gutzkow's literary personality (2 CW 71–93, 496–7).

The charge of egoism was reciprocated. In a letter of 6 December 1842 to his fellow young German, the writer Alexander Jung (1799–1884), Gutzkow gave his opinion of Engels:

The meagre reward for introducing Oswald into literary life is unfortunately all mine. Some years ago a commercial trainee from Bremen by the name Engels sent me the 'Letters from Wuppertal'. I corrected them, striking out personalities which were glaringly obvious, and printed it. After that he sent me more things which I usually had to revise. Suddenly he forebade these corrections, studied Hegel, discarded the name Oswald and went over to other papers. . . . It's the same with all these new hands. It's thanks to us that they can think and write, and their first act is intellectual patricide (I/2 MEGA[1] xxv).

Certain strands in Engels's writing distinguished him from both the Young German and Young Hegelian schools, and those concerns continued to surface in his published works of 1840. His interest in modern industry, aired in his earlier articles about the Wupper valley, appeared once again in his romantic reflections on landscapes in Germany and Holland. That article was written for the *Telegraph* and published in July and August 1840, and it incorporated an account of a railway journey in England into what is otherwise a set of bucolic word-pictures. Between 22 July and 14 August 1838 he had travelled there by way of Rotterdam with his father, and his depiction of the interplay of modern transport with other aspects of the English landscape is presumed to derive from a notebook that he kept at the time, but is no longer preserved. One of the caricatures that decorated a letter of 15 June 1839 to Friedrich Graeber was a puffing locomotive labelled *Zeitgeist*, spirit of the age. Engels had been taken on the London–Liverpool railway, which he described in dramatic style:

Then comes a tunnel, and for a few minutes the train is in
darkness, emerging into a deep cutting from which one is
suddenly transported again into the midst of smiling, sunny
fields. At another time the railway track is laid on a viaduct
crossing a long valley; far below it lie towns and villages, woods
and meadows. . . . But you have hardly had time to survey the
wonderful scene before you are carried away into a bare cutting
and have time to recreate the magical picture in your imagina-
tion (2 CW 99–100, 453; I/3-A MEGA² 841).

In his articles Engels also looked forward to a new steamship
service across the Atlantic, as the first successful paddleship
crossing had been completed by the Sirius in 1838, and trials of a
screw-driven steamship, the Archimedes, were underway in 1840:
'We will not have to wait long before we can reach New York from
any part of Germany in a fortnight', he wrote for the *Morgenblatt* of
October 1840, anticipating sight-seeing journeys to the United
States and back, the whole trip taking six weeks. 'A couple of
railways, a couple of steamships, and that's that.' In a striking and
unusual way he linked modern industry and transport with the
Hegelian view of history, writing that just as Kant had eliminated
the categories of space and time from the sensory impressions of
the thinking mind, so the material barriers to free movement
through actual space and time were being eroded in practice. For
Engels modern industry was part of the progressive historical
development towards human emancipation that the Young Hegelians were all anticipating (2 CW 128–9).

More striking, and more in tune with the eye for social class and
industrial poverty displayed in the 'Letters from Wuppertal', was
Engels's account of a visit to Bremen's port of Bremerhaven on 5
July 1840. This was written up by the correspondent 'Oswald' for
the *Morgenblatt* later in the month and published in August 1841.
His account of a ship loaded with emigrants for the United States
was harrowing: 'All round the steerage runs a row of berths,
several close together and even one above the other. An oppressive
air reigns here, where men, women and children are packed next
to one another like paving stones in the street, the sick next to the
healthy, all together'. Engels reported that every moment one
stumbled over heaps of clothes, household goods, crying children.
'It is a sad sight', he concluded, and 'what must it be like when a
prolonged storm throws everything into confusion and drives the

waves across the deck, so that the hatch, which alone admits fresh air, cannot be opened!' To his sister Marie he wrote in similar terms on 7–9 July 1840, just after the visit:

> The day before yesterday I was in Bremerhaven. . . . I was on the ships which take emigrants to America. . . . There they all lie, men, women and children, and how horrible this stuffy place is, where there are often 200 people lying, especially during the first days of seasickness, you can well imagine. The air is in any case suffocating. Cabin passengers are better off, however, they have more room and a very elegantly furnished cabin (2 CW 117, 498).

A strike of artisans in Paris in the summer of 1840 caused a tremendous scare in the German press. Engels responded witheringly in the *Allgemeine Zeitung* of Augsburg that the dangers of working-class agitation against employers were much exaggerated, as the Paris *ouvriers* and their organizations were quite distinct from German artisans and their more rudimentary associations. His view of the possibilities for working-class action in the struggle for constitutionalism in Germany was coloured by his general judgement that French politics, in which the Paris workers had played an important role during revolutionary upheavals, was far in advance of any developments in Germany. Amongst German workers demoralization and emigration prevailed, and Hegelian 'freedom' was but slowly manifesting itself in politics (I/3 MEGA^2 208, and I/3-A 889–92).

IV LIBERALISM AND NATIONALISM

By late 1840 Engels had left Young Germans and their literary concerns somewhat behind, but he was by no means as philosophical in ambition and outlook as the Young Hegelians. He had developed his own outlook on the historical development, current state and future prospects of German politics. This was a critical synthesis of the revolutionary liberalism he associated with Young Germany and of the progressive nationalism he associated with the Young Hegelians. He lost no time in getting his views into print, and they provide important clues to his subsequent political career.

In January 1841 the *Telegraph* carried a lengthy review by

'Oswald' of the *memoires* of Ernst Moritz Arndt (1796–1860), published in Leipzig in 1840 and swiftly reprinted. In recalling his part in the struggle during the Napoleonic period to liberate Germany from the French, Arndt was contributing to a complex contemporary debate concerning the extent to which a modern Germany should reflect the democratizing influence of the French Enlightenment or the authoritarian structure inherited from medieval times. The democratic view was taken up by liberals, who were enjoying a relaxation of Prussian censorship granted by Friedrich Wilhelm IV on his accession to the throne in the spring of 1840. But they were open to the conservative charge that they were betraying what was truly German by importing foreign ideas, such as democracy and constitutionalism. On the other hand conservatives wished to see traditional structures preserved, old boundaries restored and German culture protected and glorified. But they in turn were pilloried by liberals for their nationalism and authoritarianism. Romantics found themselves at home in both camps, and their ideas became associated with political forces that were increasingly hostile to each other. Engels was in the difficult position of wanting to reconcile Enlightenment liberalism, including its cosmopolitan internationalism, with German nationalism, excluding its reactionary monarchism.

Between Engels and Arndt there was a generation gap. The younger generation, according to Engels, held Arndt in high esteem but were not satisfied by his ideal of German life. Younger Germans wanted 'more freedom to act, fuller, more exuberant vitality, ardent, impetuous throbbing in the veins of world history which carry Germany's life-blood', than Arndt seemed to advocate. Engels took Arndt to be typical of some Germans, who had had admirable aspirations in ridding Germany of oppression and foreign rule in 1813, but had suffered in the reaction that followed. During that period of repression authoritarian rulers had persecuted those writers, such as Arndt, who were closely associated with a political movement that had been much too popular, too redolent of mass politics, for their conservative tastes. Arndt, amongst others, was proscribed as a university teacher after 1815 and only reinstated in mid-1840. To Engels's evident displeasure Arndt saw this as an act of justice, and had thus misinterpreted the important lessons of his life. He had been betrayed by his own 'mysterious, almost servile, kiss-the-rod manner' in his view of

authority, and had thereby strayed into the blind alley of German-
ization.

For Engels the greatest result of the liberation of Germany from
Napoleonic rule was not simply the freedom that came with the
overthrow of foreign oppression, which he suggested was bound
to self-destruction in any case, but the deed itself, which he
portrayed as a kind of popular uprising:

> That we became conscious of the loss of our national sanctuaries,
> that we armed ourselves without waiting for the most gracious
> permission of the sovereigns, that we actually *compelled* those in
> power to take their place at our head, in short, that for a moment
> we acted as the source of state power, as a sovereign nation, that
> was the greatest gain of those years.

Engels deplored the political disunity which had undermined
this burst of popular nationalism. The result was that the Germans
had reverted to their fragmented political structures and traditional
political quarrelling. 'The moving power [of the German people]
went to sleep again', he wrote, and the Germans subsequently
woke up 'to find themselves back in the old relationship of Your
Most Gracious Majesty and Your Most Humble Servant'.

Engels subjected conservative German nationalists such as
Arndt to a Hegelian analysis, according to which their positive
achievements in terms of national liberation were submerged in
negative ones. This was because they proposed to negate a whole
century of political development – the heritage of the Enlightenment and the progressive aspects of Napoleonic rule – and so push
the nation back into the middle ages or some even remoter time.
Engels was a wholehearted defender of European civilization as
developed by the French, and a proponent of the liberal aspects of
the *Code Napoléon*. He specifically mentioned civil freedoms for the
Jews, the institution of trial by jury and the replacement of
medieval codes or 'pandects' with modern civil law. Germanizers
like Arndt were blindly anti-foreign and philosophically naïve, and
their whole world view was without foundation, in Engels's
opinion, 'since it held that the entire world was created for the sake
of the Germans, and the Germans themselves had long since
arrived at the highest stage of evolution'. Moreover Germanizing
consistently led to theological orthodoxy, which Engels deplored.

Engels advocated instead a contrasting trend, the cosmopolitan liberalism of south Germany. For him this was the progressive line of historical development, and it was associated with religious rationalism, a code-word for Strauss's criticism of the Gospels and his subsumption of Christianity into a Hegelian view of history. In the Hegelian view reason progressively manifests itself in religious consciousness, political life, the arts and (for Engels) industry, thereby advancing human freedom in the broadest possible sense. In Engels's opinion the liberal movement worked for the negation of national differences and the formation of a great, free, united humanity.

In that way Engels developed an admittedly uneasy synthesis of cosmopolitanism and nationalism. The reconciliation was typically Hegelian in that present contradictions, such as the one between liberal internationalists and conservative nationalists, were said to be reconcilable within a higher form of development. This was to be realized in future, and it would include all of humanity.

For his synthesis of Enlightenment liberalism and Germanic philosophy Engels once again identified Börne and Hegel as two important progenitors, 'two men who almost ignored each other in their lifetime and whose complementary relationship was not to be recognised until after their death'. In his view they had been working towards the development of the German, or as he preferred to think of it, the modern spirit. Engels's attempted reconciliation of nationalism and internationalism seems visionary and probably contradictory today, but in his terms a modern 'spirit' of rationality could develop internationally alongside different national and cultural peculiarities. Whilst this is a view that does not emphasize continually conflicting interests, and so appears somewhat naïve, it is not logically inconsistent. As a model of human co-operation it has something to recommend it, namely cultural pluralism and toleration of national differences. Still, his development of this position has a decidedly brash quality, because at a certain point he accepted and possibly even recommended the use of war to settle international political disagreements:

> For I am of the opinion, perhaps in contrast to many whose standpoint I share in other respects, that the reconquest [from the French] of the German-speaking [Alsace on the] left bank of the Rhine is a matter of national honour, and the Germanization of a disloyal Holland and of Belgium is a political necessity for

us. Shall we let the German nationality be completely suppressed in these countries, while the Slavs are rising ever more
powerfully in the east?

Rather airily Engels looked forward to a war between Germany
and France to settle the question, but the worthy victor, in his
view, was the nation with an inner unity and political freedom.
The liberal internationalism of Engels's thought reappeared in his
succeeding argument that 'we are not worthy of the Alsatians so
long as we cannot give them what they now have: a free public life
in a great state'. 'Until then', he wrote, 'let us work for a clear,
mutual understanding among the European nations', recalling
Kant's outlook in *Zum ewigen Frieden* (*Perpetual Peace*, Königsberg,
1795).

Engels defended the liberal writer Börne from charges of undue
Francophilia and anti-German cosmopolitanism. He argued that
Börne was in fact a trenchant critic of the cosmopolitanism taken
up by liberals, because he demonstrated their impotence in failing
to move beyond a realm of pious wishes. Moreover Engels also
argued that Börne was in a sense a truer German than extreme
Germanizers, because he exposed their pretentious claims about
German excellence. In effect Engels created a 'secret' or esoteric
Börne, more liberal than the liberals, more German than the
Germanizers. As early as December 1839 Engels had described
Börne for the *Telegraph* as clear-headed, strong and imperturbable,
and he had commented that Börne's greatness was precisely that
he was above the flowery phrases and cliquish catchwords of the
day. Indeed Börne's *Briefe aus Paris* (*Letters from Paris*) for 1831-3
were very possibly a source of inspiration for Engels's own
similarly titled and ironically inverted 'Briefe aus dem Wuppertal'
('Letters from Wuppertal'), since the Wuppertal was as reactionary
and conservative as Paris was revolutionary and liberal.

Contrasted with Börne, in Engels's synthesis, were Hegel and
the Hegelians. Hegel, the man of thought, had constructed a
philosophical system consisting of abstruse ideas and expressed in
a rebarbative style. He was such a solid, orthodox *German* in his
criticisms of excessive rationalism and of cosmopolitan liberalism
that he was bound to seem admirable to conservative Prussian
politicians, even though they could not take the trouble to read his
works. For that reason they did not appreciate that Hegel's critique
of the rationalism and cosmopolitanism that they hated was

actually in aid of a higher teaching, albeit one that first rooted itself in the nationalistic virtues of the state and of the German peoples in particular. Prussian politicians did not suspect that within Hegel's apparent defence of the traditional order there lurked a much more radical conception, namely a vision of reason developing itself still further in history by realizing in political practice the rights and freedoms for which liberal internationalists, such as Börne, had been fighting since the collapse of the French revolution.

When Börne had attacked Hegel for his excessive nationalism the poet was right, said Engels, and when Hegel's teaching had been elevated almost to a Prussian philosophy of the state, this was perhaps to be expected. But only now, Engels wrote, 'do the faint nebulae of speculation [in Hegel's philosophy] resolve themselves into the shining stars of the ideas which are to light the movement of the century'. After Hegel's death the fresh air of life was breathed upon his doctrine by the younger generation of Hegelians when they exposed the 'secret' or esoteric radicalism of the master, whose true wisdom, contrary to appearances, was quite opposed to the interests of die-hard conservatives and blinkered nationalists. Engels particularly mentioned the contributions of Ruge, Eduard Gans (c. 1798–1839) the Berlin Hegelian, and Strauss: 'Strauss will remain epoch-making in the theological field, Gans and Ruge in the political':

> One may accuse Ruge's aesthetic criticism of being prosaic and confined within the schematism of the doctrine; yet credit must go to him for showing the political side of the Hegelian system to be in accord with the spirit of the time and for restoring it in the nation's esteem. Gans had done this only indirectly, by carrying the philosophy of history forward into the present; Ruge openly expressed the liberalism of Hegelianism.

The Young Hegelian method, which Engels had adopted, was to discover a new, surprising reading of some text, e.g. the Gospels or Hegel's own philosophy, by showing that its real meaning was quite opposite to the usual interpretations. Thus Strauss had revealed that an apparently historical narrative in the Gospels was really a myth, and others had found liberalism lurking within Hegel's apparent defence of the Prussian monarchy. In Engels's Young Hegelian view the master was not to have known that his

philosophy 'would venture from the quiet haven of theory onto
the stormy sea of actuality', that it would become a sword striking
directly against existing practice. The task of our age, he wrote, is
to complete the fusion of Hegel and Börne, and Börne would have
little hesitation in signing many an article in the *Hallische Jahrbücher*, were he still alive. Engels looked for a combination of
thought and action, and he rebuked many 'Old' Hegelians for
merely learning Hegel's *Enzyklopädie* (*Encyclopedia of the Philosophical Sciences*, Berlin, 1833) off by heart. He came to two conclusions:
the practical importance of Hegel's work for the present was not to
be judged by the pure theory of his system, and Börne's importance as a man of action was not diminished by his one-sidedness
and extravagances.

V   THEORY AND PRACTICE

In the review 'Ernst Moritz Arndt' Engels's contribution to the
Young Hegelianism with which he now identified was an impassioned advocacy of Börne, the Young German hero, as the man of
political practice. He continued this theme with a critique of the
political views expounded by Arndt, which formed a programme
for Germanizers and monarchists. Engels described this as utter
reaction and sketched out with horror the implied political consequences: 'Patrimonial courts to promote the formation of a high
aristocracy; guilds to reawaken a 'respectable' burgher estate;
encouragement of all so-called historical seeds, which in reality are
old, cut-off stalks.' According to Engels, the organic state proposed
by the reactionaries was supposed to consist of the three traditional estates – nobility, burghers and peasants, and 'everything else
that goes with it'. He denied that there was still a realistic dividing
line between burghers and peasants, and argued that the estates
system was promoted *pro forma* by Germanizers in order to make
the separation of the nobility more plausible. He stated flatly that
'for the nobility to regard itself as an estate, when no calling is
exclusively reserved for it under the law of any state [in Germany],
neither the military nor that of the large landowner, is ridiculous
arrogance'. Moreover he counselled against tolerating the nobility
as something special as long as they demanded no privileges,
arguing that for as long as the nobility represents something
special, it will desire and must have privileges. His demand was,

'No estates, but a great, united nation of citizens with equal rights!', the battle cry of revolutionary liberals across Europe.

Engels's revolutionary liberalism was founded on individual rights, and on that basis he attacked Arndt's defence of restrictions on the holding and sale of agrarian property, such as entails on the landholdings of noble families. Against that medieval view, which was supposed to protect the general interest by forbidding the successive division of land into uneconomic properties, Engels argued a free-market approach: 'By contrast, freedom of the land allows no extremes to arise. . . . If one scale of the balance goes down too far, the content of the other soon becomes concentrated in compensation. And even if landed property were to fly from hand to hand I would rather have the surging ocean with its grand freedom than the narrow inland lake with its quiet surface.'

Engels the Young Hegelian liberal had a clear vision of the conservative monarchism that predominated in the politics of his day, and he had a vigorous elegance in putting his case against their so-called organic state: 'But these gentlemen [e.g. Arndt] do not know that every organism becomes inorganic as soon as it dies; they set the corpses of the past in motion with their galvanic wires and try to fool us that this is not a mechanism but life. They want to promote the self-development of the nation and fasten the ball and chain of absolutism to its ankle so that it will go ahead more quickly.'

Engels noted that conservatives and reactionaries attempted to denigrate liberalism by calling it mere 'theory' or 'ideology' (an Enlightenment term for the study of ideas) and that they accused liberals of utopianism. But monarchists like Arndt had not realized the power of theory, from which liberalism had emerged within and after the French revolution, so they had not grasped that many liberal ideas which were once just theory had in fact come to life. For that reason, Engels argued, reactionaries, not liberals, were the ones immersed in theoretical utopias. In any case the development of all mankind that liberals hoped for ranked higher in his mind than the nationalistic, one-sided development of the German nation that conservatives were advocating.

Despite the stirring words about political practice Engels's view was still an intellectual's version of politics, and it was somewhat sketchy about practical activity. Of necessity there was little scope for legal political activities anywhere between the censored journalism in which he was immersed and the extreme course of outright revolution. But for Engels, who wrote in praise of political action, the mass politics of the French revolution was barely fifty years in the past, and the July revolution of 1830, in which a form of liberal constitutionalism had replaced a reactionary monarchism, had occurred within his lifetime. The desirability of the Napoleonic legal heritage in Germany was in his own day a matter of intense debate, so perhaps he was hoping that a transition to mass political action in Germany was on its way as well. Engels could claim that Börne was the modern hero in his motto 'all is life, all is vigour', that he was the first to show the relationship of Germany and France in its reality and that his understanding of European nations and their destiny was not mere speculation. But in the end, for all his praise of Börne as a prototypical political actor, Engels had to admit that the émigré writer's major achievement was merely *describing* 'the glory of the deed' (2 CW 41–6, 69, 137–50).

Engels's comments on Börne pose a set of issues that he faced for the rest of his life, since throughout his career he put himself as a writer into a political role. To what extent can *writing* for the public be a political *act*? Under what circumstances is it the only, or the most effective, activity in politics? Under what circumstances are other forms of political activity appropriate instead of, or as well as, writing for the press and producing books and pamphlets? These are questions that political actors and writers must face whenever politicians attempt to communicate ideas and drum up support, or whenever thoughtful people try to influence the outside world through politics. It is remarkable that Engels, at the age of 20, could present the situation with such clarity. To a large extent the rest of this biography is the story of his attempts to address these problems, and his various decisions mark important points at which the success or failure of his work can be gauged.

Engels's intellectual development from Young German to Young Hegelian traces a young liberal's revolutionary encounter with the conservative politics of the day. Virtually all the political problems raised in this tale are with us now, in one form or another. Engels involved himself with the struggle for rights – rights to free intellectual inquiry, rights to uncensored publication on political subjects, rights to popular participation in government, rights to challenge governmental action on the basis of constitutional law, rights of conscience to protect the individual from the oppression of religious conformity, rights for peoples and nations to be self-governing and free from foreign control. His comments on working conditions in industry show that he found injustice in a system which allowed employers to subject their workers to visible miseries, whilst enjoying disproportionate advantages as property owners, and this issue is still topical. The institutional relationship of church and state, the philosophical basis of authority and the best ways to adapt old institutions to new situations are political problems in our time as in Engels's, and the debate about the vulnerability of Christian faith and dogma to historical criticism still rages amongst believers.

Interestingly Engels worked a kind of autobiography into a review of the *Memorabilien* (*Memoires*) by Karl Immermann (1796–1840), which had been published in Hamburg in the year of his death. 'Oswald' had previously marked this event with a panegyric in verse. Engels's piece for the *Telegraph* was written in early 1841, when he was 20, and it appeared in April. Like Arndt, Immermann was for Engels another failed radical of the generation of 1813, when the Germans had successfully risen against the Napoleonic regime. Whilst in Engels's view Immermann stood between the Germanizers and the cosmopolitans, he had a most inadequately grounded preference for Prussianism and a cool indifference towards the constitutional aspirations with which the liberal Engels identified. For that reason Engels the Young Hegelian reviewer concluded that Immermann had not understood the unity of modern spiritual life at all.

The boyhood reminiscences of the writer, critic and poet attracted Engels's attention, because Immermann had attempted to describe the old-fashioned family, the one of his childhood, in order to contrast it, on the whole very favourably, with the modern family, where dissatisfaction and disorder had crept in. Engels agreed that the modern family could not fight off a certain sense of discomfort, but he disagreed with Immermann's complaints. Engels argued instead that the modern family merely displayed the symptoms of a still struggling, uncompleted, epoch. Public life had changed, especially in the geographical area considered by Immermann. This was the Rhineland, which Engels knew well and considered to be the most receptive to modern influences. For that reason the discomfort of the transition process came to light most clearly there, and the causes were to be found in the influence of contemporary literature, politics, and science, which had penetrated the family, causing strains. Those strains were disagreeable,

Engels admitted, but the process just had to be endured and anyway the old family badly needed reformation.

Engels's comments on the young and their education were thinly disguised autobiography. He remarked that young people threw themselves into the arms of modern scholarship and literature. In his view Immermann's education had been completed before the modern movement had formed itself intelligibly, and so Immermann could not see the direction in which the 'whirlwind revolution' in intellectual life was moving. In that revolution, according to Engels, 'philosophy, the soul of all science, and knowledge of the ancient world' were changing dramatically under the influence of Hegelian rationalism as applied to history, politics and religion.

Engels explained the weaknesses in Immermann's account of modern family life and education by suggesting that for Immermann the new romanticism, which had influenced Engels so directly, was only a matter of form for the older man. Immermann had been preserved from its dreamier aspects, but that distance from romanticism was also, in Engels's view, the cause of a certain resistance in Immermann to the most exciting social and intellectual developments of the time. In particular Engels suggested that Immermann had not been able to transcend his allegiance to Prussian monarchical government. Engels's opinion was that the youth of his own day would have to decide political contradictions of ever-heightening intensity, and for that task they had a touchstone in the new Hegelian philosophy and in their enthusiasm:

> He who is afraid of the dense wood in which stands the palace of the Idea, he who does not hack through it with the sword and wake the king's sleeping daughter with a kiss, is not worthy of her and her kingdom; he may go and become a country pastor, merchant, assessor, or whatever he likes, take a wife and beget children in all piety and respectability, but the century will not recognise him as its son.

Engels warned against a regression into Old Hegelianism – its dull clouds of speculation and thin, rarified air in the higher regions of abstraction. Instead he suggested that the youth of today had indeed gone through Hegel's school and emerged with boldest confidence, unrestrained ardour and glowing vigour – without 'fighting shy of the labour of thinking'.

Engels's valedictory for himself and his generation revealed clear signs of family strain: 'The old may complain about the young, and it is true that they are most disobedient'. Indeed his own father had formed just that view about his son, and had virtually given up on him. In the fragments of a letter written during October 1842 the elder Engels remarked:

> I have known since childhood his [young Friedrich's] tendency to extremes and was convinced, although he never wrote to me about his views since he was in Bremen, that he would not keep to those ordinarily held . . . we shall continue entirely our former way of living and read the word of God and other Christian books in his presence. I shall not argue with him, for that would only lead to obstinacy and embitterment. His conversion must come from above. I know for certain that he was moved by pious feelings at his confirmation and I am confident that a person who has once felt the force of God's word in his heart cannot for long be satisfied with the vapid new systems.

Friedrich senior proposed to pray for his errant son, but re-marked to his long-time correspondent Snethlage that it was hard to bear having a son in the house who was like a black sheep in the flock. In the parental view Friedrich junior – at 21 – was the victim of a fashionable trend which he might yet outgrow:

> The most depressive [thing] is that the trend which Friedrich has embraced is becoming or seems almost to be generally prevalent. Friedrich himself does not suspect what influence such a fashionable trend has exerted over him, whom I have always found greatly inclined to imitation. . . . And now that all are preaching *progress* and that the old faith and the old mentality are consigned to the rubbish heap, how easily a young and spirited heart can be ensnared! – Oh, this progress and this modern wisdom, where will they lead to! (2 CW 123–5, 161–9, 586–7).

Engels's stay in Bremen from mid-1838 to late March 1841 was arguably the most influential episode of his life, since he estab-lished himself there as a writer of poetry, travel sketches, political and social criticism, reviews, translations and polemic. For those pieces he was even sometimes paid, but as yet only one had

ppeared under his own name – a translation of a Spanish poem
or an album of 1840 commemorating the invention of movable
ype by Gutenberg. His own verdict on Bremen was decidedly
nixed. For readers of the *Morgenblatt* for 18 January 1841 he
ompared it to other Hanseatic cities with respect to literary life,
nd suggested it had unrealized potential. If only two or three
apable men of letters could be attracted there, he opined, it would
e possible to found a journal which could have an important
nfluence on the cultural development of north Germany. But in a
etter of 8 March 1841 to his sister Marie he dismissed the city
ompletely: 'Thank God that I too am leaving this dreary hole
vhere there is nothing to do but fence, eat, drink, sleep and
rudge, *voilà tout*' (2 CW 158–9, 529). By the end of the month he
vas gone.

3

Autodidact in Philosophy

At 20 Engels's future was unclear. His father's point of view, we may imagine, was that young Friedrich had finished his commercial secondment in Bremen and was now ready to pursue another aspect of the textile business, presumably the manufacturing side in Germany or in England. This plan was subject, of course, to his obligation to complete a period of national service or obtain an exemption. The elder Engels may have thought that perhaps a period at home, some travel abroad and possibly a stretch in the army, would clear the youth's head of the unsettling liberal politics, frivolous literary interests and other wild ideas that he had picked up in Bremen.

Doubtless young Friedrich saw things differently, but we do not have the benefit of any correspondence with the Graeber brothers or other close friends outside the family for this period. Instead we are limited to his letters to his sister Marie, still away at school, first in Mannheim and then in Bonn and Ostend. She was not the ideal recipient for his innermost thoughts about furthering the career in political journalism which must have seemed to him, the notorious 'Oswald', an exciting possibility. Whether he gave serious consideration to journalism as an exclusive vocation, or as one ancillary to the family business, we simply do not know. But by this time it seems that he had developed a certain skill in disguising his activities and interests so as to avoid a break with his family and his income, whilst pursuing his activities as a businessman, albeit with minimum effort.

That is the picture Engels presented to his sister, writing on April 1841 that he had been installed at home in the room next to his old one, which had now become a music room. He was reading Italian books in preparation for a forthcoming trip abroad with his father, and on occasion he emerged to practise fencing with his brother Hermann or other local friends. 'Barmen is still the same old place', he commented. 'The best thing about the whole business', he wrote at the beginning of May, 'is that I smoke the

60

whole day long and this is undoubtedly a great and a priceless pleasure. . . . Father has gone to Engelskirchen and I am sitting in his dressing-gown on his stool with his long pipe, puffing out smoke like anything'. Compared with Bremen, Barmen was pretty dull and repressive: 'Well, it's pretty dry in these parts except for an occasional dinner with some May wine or a student drinking bout, or carousal or rainy weather.' 'And what about me?', he continued, 'I might look interesting if, instead of my present young moustache, I still had the one I had in Bremen and my long hair'. After the trip to Milan in the early summer he wrote again to his sister that he had been smoking a great deal and studying hard, 'although there are some in the higher regions [presumably his father] who maintain that I have been doing nothing'. These habits seem much more like those of a university student home for the summer vacation than those of a trainee businessman returned to headquarters, even allowing for a holiday. As usual Friedrich added well-observed news for Marie of the six younger siblings, and he commented that the letter she had written to their father in English was good on the whole, with only a few serious mistakes (2 CW 531–5).

By September national service loomed. It is tempting to see the year-long stint that Engels undertook in the army in Berlin as a convenient escape from the family firm, which he found dreary, and a back-door entry into Berlin University, where Hegel himself had taught from 1818 till his death in 1831. Subsequently his disciples had congregated there to edit his works and preserve the tradition. Engels would not have qualified for university in the normal way, but in the Berlin milieu he would have the stimulating company of Young Hegelian intellectuals, whom he idolized, and he would be able to follow their radical re-interpretation of Hegelianism at first hand. However, in his letter to his sister Marie of 9 September he commented that he was leaving soon for Berlin 'to do my duty as a citizen, i.e. to do what I can to evade conscription if possible and then come back to Barmen' (2 CW 534). The plan to obtain an exemption did not come off, and he became a one-year volunteer with the Prussian artillery. Whether he moved to Berlin by accident or design, we do not know, but the results are clear enough. He pursued his intellectual and political interests as a Young Hegelian radical and moved in stages towards a more intensely developed engagement with philosophy *and* a more active engagement with politics.

The questions that will concern us in this and the following chapter are:

How did Engels cope with the intensifying contradictions between his outlook and that of his family?
To what extent did he push his career as a journalist into a realm of political action that was new to him?
How substantial were his intellectual achievements by the time he began to collaborate full-time with Marx?

I   CORRESPONDENT IN BERLIN

In the autumn of 1841, during the latter part of his stay in Barmen and perhaps in his first weeks in Berlin, Engels composed another travel sketch, 'Lombardische Streifzüge I: Über die Alpen!' ('Wanderings in Lombardy I: Over the Alps!'). This was eventually published in December in issues 48 and 49 of the *Athenäum, Zeitschrift für das gebildete Deutschland* of Berlin, a revived version of the Nuremberg *Athenäum* that had favourably reviewed his 'Letters from Wuppertal'. 'Oswald's' romantic reflections on awesome landscapes, nationalistic musings on the 'Germanness' of German-speaking Switzerland and earnestly respectful recounting of Strauss's ejection from Zürich were all in order in a journal that, from its first weekly issue in January 1841, had rapidly become a leading organ of Young Hegelianism. Included in the earlier issue number 4 for 23 January 1841 were the 'Wilde Lieder' ('Wild Songs') by Karl Marx, his first published works. These were 'The Fiddler' and 'Nocturnal Love', two very slight romantic poems.

In March 1841 Marx had withdrawn from Berlin University, where he had been a student for five years. His leaving certificate registered attendance at lectures on law given by Gans, the distinguished editor of Hegel's philosophies of law and history. Marx had also followed courses in logic, Greek tragedy and Old Testament studies, and his certificates bore comments from his instructors ranging from 'attended' to 'exceptionally diligent'. He left Berlin in April, but many of his friends amongst the Young Hegelians and their literary contacts remained, such as Eduard Meyen (1812–70), who was virtually running the *Athenäum* by the spring of 1841. He was probably Engels's contact on the paper, which was nominally edited by Karl Riedel (1804–78). It folded in

December, a week after the final sections of the first part of Engels's article appeared, and the work was never completed (1 CW 22–4, 703–4; I/1-A MEGA² 1258, and I/3-A 938–40).

Engels had thus entered a world in which Marx was known for his debating skills, intellectual energy, classical erudition and Bohemian lifestyle, all traits which had begun to appear during 1835–6 when he was a student at Bonn University. On one occasion he had been detained for disturbing the peace and public drunkenness. However he was hardly the leading light in the Berlin 'Doctors Club' which included, at various times, working journalists, high school teachers and sometime academics such as Bruno Bauer (1809–82). Bauer had been a pupil of Hegel, and had lectured on the Book of Isaiah – an important source for the Gospel-writers and hence for their Straussian critics, who argued that New Testament myth-makers had passed off Old Testament paraphernalia as historical fact. Marx attended Bauer's Old Testament lectures and the two became friends. Other associates were Bruno's brother Edgar (1820–86), the liberal newspapermen Adolf Rutenberg (1808–69) and Ludwig Buhl (1814–c. 1882), and the writer Karl Köppen (1808–63), who had dedicated a historical work on Frederick the Great to Marx in 1840. For radicals, Friedrich II of Prussia (1712–86) was an Enlightenment figure, a modernizer and unifier, and so a useful stick with which to beat conservative nationalists and defenders of the semi-medieval, disunited German states.

Marx had retreated home to Trier in the spring of 1841 to finish his doctoral dissertation in classical philosophy. This was his *Differenz der demokritischen und epikureischen Naturphilosophie* (*Difference between the Democritean and Epicurean Philosophy of Nature*), a title that recalled Hegel's first book, *Differenz des Fichte'schen und Schelling'schen Systems der Philosophie* (*Difference between the Philosophical Systems of Fichte and Schelling*), published in Jena in 1801. Marx had undertaken the dissertation in order to explore the philosophical relationship between self-consciousness and historical progress, a matter of intense concern to Young Hegelians who were anxiously trying to clarify their own relationship to established Christianity and the Prussian state. Were these institutions sufficiently rational to satisfy the modern self-consciousness? Was it the task of this philosophical self-consciousness merely to 'mediate' historical contradictions in thought, or actively to assist in their 'negation' through practice? Marx, in his highly academic

philosophical study, defended the latter position, rejecting a
mechanical determinism and arguing the virtues of free human
action (1 CW 657–8; MBM 41–71).

By the time Engels arrived on the Berlin scene he had already
published no fewer than thirty-seven articles, reviews and other
literary contributions – and he was not yet 21. His interests and
experiences allied the young newcomer most closely with the
journalists amongst the Young Hegelians, such as Rutenberg,
Meyen, Köppen and Buhl, who had had to supplement their
academic occupations and scholarly productions with literary
criticism, *belles lettres* and anything else that might interest the
editors of the various weeklies, monthlies and occasional journals
to which they sent their work. Marx, who had been preparing
himself for a university lectureship in philosophy rather than for
the career in law that his family desired, was more like the
professional academics in the Young Hegelian movement. Pre-
eminent amongst them was Bruno Bauer, who had left Berlin
University in 1839 for a post at Bonn, an attempt to escape
harassment by suspicious anti-Hegelians.

It must be said, however, that Young Hegelian journalism was
often highly philosophical, as one would expect, since the writers
had generally been in academic life and were still on its fringes. But
it is also important to note that the Young Hegelian concept of
academic life as a university teacher was not one of withdrawal
from the world into a realm of philosophical reflection. Bruno
Bauer, for instance, was continually in trouble for using his
teaching posts to promulgate unorthodox opinions about Christianity and other topics that were considered politically sensitive.
Indeed the very act of raising religious and political issues for
critical review was considered provocative, especially in the universities. Another Young Hegelian, Ludwig Feuerbach (1804–72),
who – like Strauss and Bruno Bauer – had attended the master's
lectures, was ruined as an academic when his heterodox views on
death and immortality were published anonymously as early as
1830. After the accession of Friedrich Wilhelm IV in 1840 Prussian
universities were singled out for particular attention, as it was
there that unorthodoxy might receive an unwelcome endorsement
from the prestigious academic community. Thus there was no
great difference in principle between Young Hegelian academic life
and Young Hegelian journalism, but there were distinct differences between the scholarly background and academic ambition

of the 23-year-old Marx, and the more worldly experiences and journalistic interests of the 21-year-old Engels.

What Marx and Engels had in common, together with others in the circle of Young Hegelian intellectuals, was a politics that was liberal in inspiration and radical by repute. Indeed Engels's call for a politics of 'the deed' and effusive sympathy for direct revolutionary action in France put him well to the left of the Young Hegelian movement. That made him a more obviously political and more demonstratively radical figure than Marx, who had absorbed himself in philosophical problems, the political implications of which were not as yet entirely clear. Through a variety of intellectual and political experiences the two, who were not personally acquainted, moved steadily but independently towards a more radical political theory and a more direct engagement with political action.

Ironically Marx moved into journalism only when his hopes for a university post were dashed. That happened after the dismissal of Bruno Bauer from Bonn in the spring of 1842 and the purge of other Young Hegelians from German universities. The recently enthroned king and his new minister for religious worship, education and health, Johann Eichhorn (1779–1856), were seeking to rid intellectual life of free-thinking rationalists such as the notoriously sceptical Young Hegelians. After six months as a newspaperman Marx became an editor in Cologne in October 1842 almost by accident. Rather surprisingly, then, he became a recipient for Engels's freelance articles. But in Berlin, where Engels had drifted in late 1841 to fulfil the military obligation which Marx had successfully evaded, the established Young Hegelian journalist 'Oswald' set himself the awesome task of understanding the most important philosophical debate of the era.

In mid-1841 Friedrich von Schelling (1775–1854) had been translated, at the Prussian king's own behest, from the University of Munich to the University of Berlin. This was in order to root out the subversive rationalism of Hegelian philosophy and, in particular, the political radicalism of the Young Hegelians, who were said to have dangerous opinions on theology and other political matters. Schelling was a contemporary of Hegel, but Hegel had always outshone his one-time friend and associate. The two had studied together at the Theological Faculty of Tübingen University and had collaborated for a brief period around 1802, but they broke off over a disagreement concerning the proper definition of the 'absolute', the concept from which their idealist philosophizing began.

Like Hegel, Schelling had been inspired by Kant's philosophical idealism as a way of explaining the rational perception of the world in terms of conceptual truths, rather than empirical perceptions, hence the term idealism – meaning 'of ideas'. Schelling dedicated himself to remedying the alleged defects of Kant's philosophy by producing a new, more comprehensive system. He was also influenced by the philosophy of Johann Gottlieb Fichte (1762–1814), whose idealist account of knowledge and action was rooted more directly in the individual human subject than were Kant's transcendental concepts. In 1800 Schelling published his *System der transzendentalen Idealismus* (*System of Transcendental Idealism*) in Tübingen, and his *Philosophische Untersuchungen über das wesener menschlichen Freiheit* (*Of Human Freedom*) in 1809 in Landshut near Munich. These were works that attempted to incorporate a more explicit view of nature into the idealist concept of the 'absolute', which Hegel had taken to be the 'idea'. Schelling also aimed to develop a view of self-consciousness as active in individuals when humans exercised their wills in material ways upon the world.

But in Schelling's later philosophy his thought became more overtly concerned with Christianity and the doctrine of divine revelation, and less preoccupied with the development of reason and the material results of human self-consciousness. Thus he contrasted a 'negative' philosophy, which developed an idea of God purely through reason, with a 'positive' philosophy of revelation. This positive philosophy was supposed to demonstrate the reality of God from a consideration of history, including His appearance in the world as Christ, and also from an abstract consideration of self-consciousness, particularly the capacity for the will to do evil. Schelling's lectures were deliberately provocative, intellectually and politically, to the Hegelian school, which had become the dominant philosophy in Germany. He gave himself the last word on Hegel's work by treating it critically and incorporating it into his own system, which attempted a similarly encyclopaedic coverage of reality. Moreover he tried to undermine the Hegelian rationalist methodology, which proceeded philosophically from the 'idea', a concept presupposing rationality. In Schelling's view, Hegel's methodology had demonstrably led the Hegelian school away from orthodox Christianity towards pantheism, because Hegelians presumed that the creation of the world and its development were best understood as the work of highly abstract conceptual entities such as 'spirit' or 'mind' (*Geist*), which had been derived from the 'idea'. Hegelian rationalism had even led some of them, the Young Hegelians, towards atheism, when they dared to ascribe self-consciousness and reason solely to human beings, to the apparent exclusion of any supra-human agency such as a deity. For such dangerous rationalism Schelling substituted an almost mystical religious understanding that was supposed to transcend reason itself.

Schelling's inaugural lecture took place on 15 November 1841 and was delivered to an audience of several hundred people. Amongst those attending the series, which lasted until 18 March 1842, were the historian Jacob Burckhardt (1818–97), the philosopher Søren Kierkegaard (1813–55), the anarchist Michael Bakunin (1814–76), and the unmatriculated student or *Hospitant* Friedrich Engels – all, so far as we know, unacquainted with each other (M 81). In his accustomed literary venue, Gutzkow's *Telegraph*, the practised commentator 'Friedrich Oswald' set the scene on what seems even now an extraordinary occasion, a battlefield 'for dominion over German public opinion in politics and religion, that is, over Germany itself':

An imposing, colourful audience has assembled to witness the battle. At the front the notables of the University, the leading lights of science, men every one of whom has created a trend of his own; for them the seats nearest to the rostrum have been reserved, and behind them, jumbled together as chance brought them to the hall, representatives of all walks of life, nations, and religious beliefs. In the midst of high-spirited youths there sits here and there a grey-bearded staff officer and next to him perhaps, quite unembarrassed, a volunteer [? Engels] who in any other society would not know what to do for reverence towards such a high-ranking superior [?irony]. Old doctors and ecclesiastics the jubilee of whose matriculation can soon be celebrated feel the long-forgotten student haunting their minds again and are back in college. Judaism and Islam want to see what Christian revelation is all about; German, French, English, Hungarian, Polish, Russian, modern Greek and Turkish, one can hear all spoken together.

In the European intellectual world, the philosophical school of German idealism, with its 'speculative' methods of conceptual analysis, had challenged Enlightenment materialisms, dualistic philosophies of mind and matter, and what remained of scholastic doctrines of substance and divine creation. Idealism was the most exciting contemporary philosophy, despite the considerable obscurities of style and thought for which Kant and Hegel were notorious. As so much political authority was derived from religious and ultimately theological claims, the relationships between philosophy, correct beliefs about God, and the question of rightful obedience to rulers was a matter on which academic views could be crucial, so the intense international interest in a lecture-series given by an ageing philosopher is understandable. So is Engels's attendance, but in his case this general interest was supplemented by an enlarged intellectual ambition. This was to move beyond Strauss's Young Hegelian challenge to Christianity, in order to clarify for himself at the deepest level the true place of humankind in the universe, to establish the character of any irremediable limitations on human will and activity, and to understand the proper political framework for realizing the human potential.

No doubt Engels's liberal politics suggested certain answers to those questions, but defending them against academic criticism was a matter that required an intensive study of philosophy. This began for intellectual and political reasons with Schelling's current challenge to the whole Hegelian school – 'Old' Hegelians and their Young Hegelian critics alike. Engels's article 'Schelling über Hegel' ('Schelling on Hegel') was his first philosophical work, and in a markedly academic style he quoted Schelling at length from notes taken during the lecture of 2 December 1841. This was particularly important, as Schelling had not published his later philosophy, and until his Berlin lectures there had been no proper opportunity for an academic audience to judge the views that had attracted considerable fame from hearsay versions alone.

'Oswald' wrote as a passionate Young Hegelian, defending the tradition as it had developed through Hegel, his disciple and editor Gans, and then the Young Hegelian Feuerbach, who had already attacked the partisans of Schelling's 'positive' philosophy by defending Hegel in a series of anonymous articles of December 1838 for the *Hallische Jahrbücher*. Engels then mentioned Strauss – famous for his Young Hegelian criticism of the Gospels – and Ruge, now editor of the *Deutsche Jahrbücher für Wissenschaft und Kunst*. This was the Young Hegelian *Hallische Jahrbücher* recently revived in Dresden, in the kingdom of Saxony. Ruge did this in

July 1841 in order to escape the Prussian censorship that had stifled the journal in June.

In Engels's opinion Schelling had trifled with the entire development of philosophy that century by ascribing its achievements to himself. Worse than that, he had argued that his idealist philosophy, and indeed any true philosophy, laid no claims whatever to any influence on the external world, because in Schelling's view 'existence' was to be conceived apart from 'the essence and the concept'. By contrast, in Engels's version of Hegelian philosophy, the whole point of philosophical inquiry was bound up with the opposite dictum that 'existence belongs indeed to thought', so reality is necessarily a proper object for critical reasoning.

Engels rejected Schelling's account of a 'power' ruling over 'being', because that 'power', which supposedly persisted in eternal freedom as the 'absolute', was clearly the Christian God in a philosophical disguise. Overall Engels agreed with the unflattering portrait of Schelling already sketched in a pamphlet of August 1841 by Riedel of the *Athenäum*, and ridiculed the white-haired philosopher for challenging the dead Hegel, who was more alive than ever in his pupils. In Engels's view Schelling was claiming the full power and authority of life, even though he had been intellectually dead for thirty years (I/3-A MEGA^2 942–5; 2 CW 181–7).

II PAMPHLETEER

Engels, now a Berlin Young Hegelian, had become a champion for their cause in a way that was topical, intellectually accomplished, and as politically effectual as anything the others had managed to do. His article on the controversy over Schelling's lectures was his last contribution to Gutzkow's *Telegraph*. He then entered the realm of academic pamphleteering with a highly acclaimed though anonymous work *Schelling und die Offenbarung: Kritik des neuesten Reaktionsversuchs gegen die freie Philosophie* (*Schelling and Revelation: Critique of the Latest Attempt of Reaction against the Free Philosophy*), written between January and March 1842, and published in April in Saxon Leipzig. This was his first use of the philosophical term 'critique' – made famous by Kant – to advertise his work, and in the title he also revealed his identification with 'The Free', the new inner circle of Young Hegelians in Berlin. This was the successor to the 'Doctors Club', which had declined somewhat after Bruno

Bauer's departure in 1839 for the supposed safety of Bonn. Bauer was later suspended from Bonn University and then finally dismissed in March 1842, as the King tightened his net on the Young Hegelians. The circle of café philosophers and radicals seems to have reconvened itself just before the reappearance in Berlin that May of Bauer, Germany's most notorious philosophical radical.

Engels was an assiduous attender at Schelling's evening lectures in early 1842, but to his sister Marie he wrote with relief on 5–6 January that since Schelling was not lecturing one night he would have the whole evening to himself and be able to work seriously and without interruption. *Schelling and Revelation* was a pamphlet of about fifty pages published by a press sympathetic to the Young Hegelians. By May the work was so successful that the publisher had to advertise for the return of all copies not yet sold, in order to satisfy the orders placed directly with him. In an article for Ruge's widely read *Deutsche Jahrbücher* that appeared in July, 'F. Oswald' revealed that he was the author of the booklet on Schelling, which had caused consternation in the conservative press, especially in the *Evangelische Kirchen-Zeitung* of Berlin, which Engels had picked on directly. The *Kirchen-Zeitung* feared that Young Hegelians were popularizing dangerous doctrines already condemned by the champion of conservative monarchism, the historian Heinrich Leo (1799–1878). The Young Hegelians were thereby revealing themselves to be modern Jacobins who, in the words of the *Kirchen-Zeitung*, were bent on bringing the terrible devastation of the French revolution of 1789 to Germany, including such horrors as overthrowing all worship of God, demolishing the churches and melting down bells into cannons. By January 1843 the fame of Engels's pamphlet had spread to St Petersburg. Later in his career he played down this episode of enthusiastic Young Hegelianism, because the 'philosophy of self-consciousness' which he professed at the time did not accord well with the 'material' and 'economic' outlook of his mature years, so he never referred to his youthful attack on Schelling. Curiously the pamphlet was not positively ascribed by scholars to Engels for many years because of a false attribution of the work to Bakunin (2 CW 538; I/3-A MEGA[2] 948–51).

Engels presented Schelling as the long-awaited St George of the conservatives and reactionaries, ready at last 'to slay the dreadful dragon of Hegelianism, which breathed the fire of godlessness and the smoke of obscuration!' For his readers Engels presented the history of the Hegelian school and the development of the Young Hegelian reading of the master's published works and post-humorously collected lectures. The Hegelian method – 'the proud courage which follows truth to its most extreme conclusions' – was employed and defended by Engels, citing the Young Hegelian distinction between Hegel's principles, which were throughout independent and free-minded, and his conclusions, which were sometimes cautious, even illiberal. Crucial for the development of the Young Hegelian school was the historical manifestation of its utter contradiction – a fine Hegelian point, that – in the form of Leo and his attack *Die Hegelingen* on the 'Hegelings' or Young Hegelians themselves, which had been published in Halle in 1838. In a letter to Friedrich Graeber of 23 April–1 May 1839 Engels had already satirized the polemical debates between Leo and Karl Michelet (1801–93), editor of Hegel's lectures on the history of philosophy and a leading 'Old' Hegelian:

Leo
Why that foul-mouthed Hegelian
Would get the Bible in disgrace.
He really must be taught his place.

Michelet
Unpolished boor, and liar too,
He won't let Hegel have his due!

   The voice of Engels, in the form of the resurrected mythical hero Siegfried, comments as he passes:

Although they're peaceful, learned men,
I've never seen such fierce defiance;
They fight with all their might and main,
Though schooled in many a noble science (2 CW 189–97, 436–7).

   In Engels's view Leo had done the hated 'Hegelings' a great service by challenging them. They had had to sharpen up their defence of Hegel's principles and use his dialectical method themselves in order to arrive at new conclusions concerning both science and practice that were ultimately contrary to Hegel's own. In that way many of Leo's complaints about Hegelian philosophy, such as radicalism and irreligion, were borne out when the 'secret'

Hegel emerged from Young Hegelian analysis. However, some Young Hegelians – Engels was probably thinking of Ruge and Meyen – were struggling against the stark truths that other more radical Young Hegelians were deriving from the master's teaching.

Boldly and presumptuously Engels portrayed his contemporaries amongst the Young Hegelians as atheists in all but name. He declared that religious mythologies, including Christianity, were phenomena that had not arisen in human consciousness through the action of an external and supernatural agency, but were instead the innermost products of consciousness itself and so were purely human and natural. In expounding this analysis of religion as an earthly phenomenon he singled out the Young Hegelian *Deutsche Jahrbücher* and three very recently published works for praise. One was Strauss's *Die christliche Glaubenslehre in ihrer geschichtlichen Entwicklung und im Kämpfe mit der modernen Wissenschaft* (*Christian Doctrine in its Historical Development and in its Conflict with Modern Science*), published in Tübingen and Stuttgart in 1840–1. In that work Strauss moved on from criticizing the Gospels to a rationalist critique of Christian dogma, presenting a Young Hegelian interpretation of its significance for the development of reason.

Another book mentioned by Engels was Feuerbach's newly issued *Das Wesen des Christenthums* (*Essence of Christianity*), published in Leipzig in April 1841. In that work Feuerbach advanced from Hegel's rationalization of religion in general, and Christianity in particular, towards a thesis that religions of all kinds, including Christianity, were merely projections of human wishes. Moreover he argued that human capacities and powers became 'alienations', i.e. things which are thought to exist apart from humankind and are apparently out of human control. Alienations occurred when human beings projected their capacities and powers on to supernatural beings, making human capacities and powers the supposed attributes of deities. Feuerbach argued that human beings needed to regain those capacities and powers for their own conscious use, because deities were not properly subjects and human beings were not properly their predicates, as was the case at present. Philosophy could help humanity perform a liberating reversal of subject and predicate by making human beings real, powerful subjects, not mere predicates of fictitious divine activity. In Feuerbach's account, theology was to be dissolved into anthropology, a conclusion enthusiastically taken up by Engels: 'The conclusion of modern philosophy [i.e. Hegelianism] . . . of which

Feuerbach first made us conscious in all its sharpness, is that reason cannot possibly exist except as mind, and that mind can only exist in and with nature, and does not lead, so to say, a life apart, in separateness from it.'

Both Strauss and Feuerbach, however, were at this point some-what pious – in a Hegelian way – about human spirituality, identifying it with philosophy, albeit a philosophy that put human reason and human life at the centre of the universe. Engels's third author was an out-and-out atheist who lacked such piety. The work cited was the anonymous *Die Posaune des jüngsten Gerichts über Hegel den Atheisten und Antichristen. Ein Ultimatum (The Last Trump of Judgement Day for Hegel the Atheist and Anti-Christ. An Ultimatum)*, published in Leipzig in October of 1841. This is now known to be the work of Bruno Bauer, though at the time there were rumours that Marx, who was associating with Bauer in Bonn, was a direct collaborator on the short book. Engels's views on its authorship were not explicitly recorded until the summer of 1842, but he certainly knew that it was written by a brilliant and very radical Young Hegelian. He could easily have guessed or known that Bauer was the author, especially since he was a close associate of Bruno's brother Edgar.

In exile in Bonn, Bruno Bauer had developed a Young Hegelian philosophy of self-consciousness, and he had applied his radical philosophy to further Gospel criticism. He had revised Strauss's interpretation somewhat by arguing that the Evangelists were not merely the supposed authors of communally generated myths, as Strauss had claimed. Rather the significance of the Gospels for Bauer lay in their place in the historical progression of philosophic-al self-consciousness towards rationality. He portrayed the Gos-pels as philosophical works, concocted within the Greco-Roman world using early Christian materials. But in Bauer's view philo-sophical consciousness had progressed enormously since then, so the Gospels were now in any case intellectually superseded, and Christianity was therefore irrational. Although Strauss had por-trayed Christianity as historically *passé*, his attitude towards it was still respectful. The conclusions drawn by Bauer from his work on the Gospels and their sources were more extreme than Strauss's, because Bauer's conclusions emphasized the relationship of the Gospels to ancient philosophy, on the one hand, and the current irrationality of Christian belief and practice on the other.

In 1840 Bauer published his findings on the Johannine Gospel,

which he thought somewhat more modern with respect to the
development of philosophical self-consciousness than its three
predecessors in the New Testament. Then in 1841 there appeared
the first of his volumes on Matthew, Mark and Luke – the Synoptic
Gospels, so-called since the 1780s because of their textual similarity
(synoptic means 'seen together'). Engels immediately took extensive notes (IV/1-A MEGA^2 878).

The *Last Trump* was a work of great importance for Engels, and,
so he argued, for the Young Hegelian movement, because in it the
logical conclusion to the writings of Strauss and Feuerbach on
Christianity – namely atheism – was derived directly from Hegel's
own works without intermediaries like Feuerbach or Leo. The fact
that the *Last Trump* appeared, for the purposes of parody, to be
written by an outraged pietist protesting against atheistic Hegelianism must have caught Engels's fancy as well.

The political message that Engels found in the *Last Trump* was
one specifically for Young Hegelians. Because of that work the
'Hegelings' should not conceal from the world that the basic
principles of Christianity, and even of religion itself, had fallen
inexorably to the criticism of reason. Thus in Engels's view there
was no longer any sense in rationalizing Christianity *within* the
Young Hegelian perspective on intellectual history – as Strauss had
earlier attempted to do – nor was there any room for a humanistic
religion or philosophy of religious experience *alongside* Young
Hegelian rationalism – as Feuerbach was suggesting earlier in 1841.
For Engels the *Last Trump* had cut short any half-hearted drifting
between philosophical religiosity and atheistic rationalism by revealing in Hegel a radical argument against religion and therefore a
triumphant victory for self-consciousness as a purely human
phenomenon.

Moreover in Engels's view the clever, atheistic reading of
Hegel's work in the *Last Trump* also vindicated Hegel's philosophical method. The Hegelian dialectic had been vigorously
defended by Engels as early as his letter to Wilhelm Graeber of 24
May–15 June 1839, and it was said at various points in his *Schelling
and Revelation* of early 1842 to be a profound, restless dialectic of
pure thought and a free, powerful science of thinking.

Because of the development of Young Hegelianism Engels the
nationalist also identified a particular role for Germany in the
progressive unfolding of human self-consciousness:

The great upheaval of which the French [Enlightenment] philosophers of the last century were merely the forerunners has
achieved in the realm of thought its completion, its self-creation.
The philosophy of Protestantism since Descartes has come to an
end; a new era has begun and it is the most sacred duty of all
who have followed the self-development of the spirit to transmit
the immense result to the consciousness of the nation and to
raise it to Germany's living principle.

Young Hegelians of this period, particularly Bruno Bauer, took
an apocalyptic view of the Hegelian doctrine that historical development proceeds through successive contradictions, each negation subsuming and transcending an earlier stage. As historical
progress continued into their own time Young Hegelians were
inclined to see a sharpening of contradictions leading to outright
revolutionary struggles. They also began to view their rationalism
as an active principle in politics, from which they expected a final
victory for revolutionary liberalism. Engels summarized the Hegelian logic of development through intensifying contradictions as:
'That powerful dialectic, that inner motive force which constantly
drives the individual thought categories, as if it were the bad
conscience of their imperfection and one-sidedness, to ever new
development and rebirth until they arise from the grave of negation for the last time as absolute idea in imperishable, immaculate
splendour.'

Hence Engels welcomed not only the intellectual attacks on
Young Hegelianism mounted by Leo and Schelling but also the
political exclusions enforced since 1840 by Friedrich Wilhelm IV
and his minister Eichhorn. The two were successors in the same
year to Friedrich Wilhelm III and his minister Karl Altenstein
(1770–1840), who had been better disposed towards the 'Old'
Hegelian school, and even towards wayward Young Hegelians
such as Bauer himself, whom they shunted away from dangerous
exposure in Berlin to the relative obscurity of Bonn. Bravely Engels
commented on the current political situation, indicating the
opposed positions of the Prussian state and 'The Free' Young
Hegelians of Berlin:

Prussia is a Christian-monarchic state and its position in world
history entitles it to have its principles recognized as valid in fact.
One may share them or not, it is enough that they are there, and

Prussia is strong enough to defend them if need be. Moreover, the [Young] Hegelian philosophy has no cause for complaint on that score ... it can only welcome a sharpening of the contradictions, since its final victory is assured.

In his pamphlet Engels concluded that Schelling's teaching had no foundation either in itself or in anything else that has been proved. The conservative philosopher used a method freed from all logical necessity, one that was arbitrary and empty because it relied on revelation, the reality of which was precisely in question. Schelling had attempted to smuggle belief in dogma, sentimental mysticism and gnostic fantasy into the free science of thinking, and his philosophy was ultimately a gnostic-oriental dream. He had not engaged in any real debate with Strauss or Feuerbach, and had produced something that was neither Christianity nor philosophy.

Engels's paean for the triumph of Young Hegelian atheism was not so much pious intellectualism as paganized rationalism. He ended *Schelling and Revelation* in a blaze of imagery that spoke of 'man, the dearest child of nature, a free man after the long battles of youth', standing in the bright day of self-consciousness where everything has been revealed and true life opens up. A thousand-year reign of freedom would follow a last, holy war won by the all-conquering might of the 'idea' that radicals must follow, even unto death. That mighty 'idea' would be the true religion of every genuine philosopher, the basis of the true positive philosophy, which is the philosophy of world history, and the supreme revelation, that of man to man. The 'self-consciousness of mankind', Engels wrote in a dialectical *Götterdämmerung*, 'is that wonderful phoenix who builds for himself a funeral pyre out of all that is most precious in the world and rises rejuvenated from the flames which destroy an old time' (2 CW 191–240, 451; YHKM 48–97).

At 21 Engels had had an international success with his timely critique of Schelling. But the pamphlet was not itself a work of philosophy, nor a particularly talented scholarly commentary. Indeed the detailed recounting of Schelling's views has distinct *longueurs*, though these are not wholly the author's fault, as the philosophy of revelation is generally considered obscure. *Schelling and Revelation* is a declaration of atheism, and so it marks a significant point in the development of Engels's intellect and character.

Engels's next broadside, an imitation of Bruno Bauer's *Last Trump*, was written immediately after *Schelling and Revelation*. It was published in April 1842, and appeared in Berlin as the anonymous *Schelling, der Philosoph in Christo, oder die Verklärung der Weltweisheit zur Gottesweisheit: für gläubige Christen denen der philosophische Sprachgebrauch unbekannt ist* (*Schelling, Philosopher in Christ, or the Transfiguration of Worldly Wisdom into Divine Wisdom: For Believing Christians Who Do Not Know the Language of Philosophy*). Like Bauer, Engels produced a skilful imitation of a pietist tract, but unlike the *Last Trump*, which was primarily directed at Young Hegelians who had not yet seen the dazzling light of atheism in their hero's work, Engels's parody was directed at the much larger community of Christian scholars and believers. They had expected that Schelling would be able to defend Christianity philosophically and put an end to the doubts concerning the proper justification for Christian belief that Hegel's philosophy was continually creating. Engels's parody was somewhat sharper than Bauer's, because Engels aimed to destroy Schelling's philosophy by showing that it was in essence the kind of dogmatic Christianity that many Christian philosophers and historians could no longer wholeheartedly defend. In effect Engels tried to make 'Christian' as violent a term of abuse for rationalists as 'atheist' was for Christians, and in that way to provoke a crisis *outside* Young Hegelianism by attacking Schelling, who was using philosophy to defend Christianity. But Engels also aimed to continue the struggle *inside* Young Hegelianism by advertising once again the conclusions of the *Last Trump*, which argued that there was no rational defence for Hegel against charges of atheism. The *Last Trump* by Bruno Bauer and the two pamphlets by Engels opened a minor industry in publishing ever more complicated satires. In contributing to the trend Engels developed his skills as a writer of instant intellectual history, synthesizer of current philosophical views and notable publicist for Young Hegelian radicalism.

Part of the reason for publishing parodies, of course, was that they were a ruse for escaping censorship. Bauer's pietist attack on a crypto-atheist Hegel was really a disguised defence of Young Hegelian radicals, and Engels's pietist defence of a crypto-Christian Schelling was really a disguised attack on mainstream conservatives. With *Schelling, Philosopher in Christ*, Engels seems to have fooled its pietist publisher and the Prussian censor alike. The first comments in the press were by Young Hegelian sympathisers who had disguised their identities in order to endorse the views put forward by Engels's pietist. In that way they sought to spread Engels's joke that Schelling's long-awaited philosophy was no more fresh and intellectually satisfying than the 'old-time religion' accepted by very naïve Christians. Ruge attacked Schelling in a long series of articles in his *Deutsche Jahrbücher* in June 1842, giving considerable attention to Engels's works and comparing his parody to Aristophanic comedy. But two whole issues of Ruge's paper were so obviously scurrilous that they were banned (I/3-A MEGA^2 965–8).

Engels's pietist proclaimed that Schelling had brought back the good old times when reason surrenders to faith. The pietist warned his readers against the complicated philosophical language of the worldly wise who had wandered from the simplicity of Scripture, as Schelling had apparently done. Nonetheless Schelling had come through philosophy to the true doctrine of the Trinity, for which the pietist author gave much thanks, and he expected Schelling's new philosophy, a rejection of the wicked Hegelianism, to bring a triumph over the ungodly and blasphemous. Even the Virgin Birth, a perennial problem for Christian rationalists, had been re-asserted as dogma by Schelling albeit in a philosophical guise, and this was one of the most gratifying signs of the times.

Engels's pietist found sin everywhere in contemporary life, and Schelling's inspirational lectures in Berlin were compared with the preaching of St Paul at Athens, where the great teacher had been mocked. Amongst the mockers of Schelling were 'the pagans of the modern world ... Young Germans, philosophers, and what else they may call themselves ... politicians and beer-parlour orators'. They were hypocrites who interfered in government instead of leaving unto the king what is the king's, the traditional doctrine of conservative monarchism. Engels of course identified conservative politics with fundamentalist Christianity, and in his parody he sought to bring free-thinking liberals and Young Hegelian radicals closer together by emphasizing their common opposition to Schelling's crypto-Christianity and to the Christian state that it was supposed to support.

Interestingly Engels's pietist identified the Young Hegelians with classical paganism, echoing the imagery of the earlier critique *Schelling and Revelation*. In his parody Engels recalled the Enlightenment Hellenism of his schooldays and declared his admiration for the anti-Christian ideals of 1789:

Then let us set to work with Schelling, and cast reason out of Christianity into paganism, for there it belongs, there it can rise against God ... and [it] present[s] as models for mankind the suicide of a Cato, the unchastity of a Lais and Aspasia, the parricide of a Brutus, the Stoicism and Christian-persecuting rage of a Marcus Aurelius.... These are the natural consequences of setting reason upon the throne of God, like that whore of old in the gory days of the French revolution.

Engels's characterization of Young Hegelianism as a profoundly political movement, not just a philosophical school, was clear enough in his pamphlet, and very sharp for being couched in parody. In his view Germany was dividing into two great parties, and the subversive one was everywhere on the move:

All enemies of God are coming together and attacking the believers with all possible weapons; the indifferent ones ... are uniting with the atheist worldly wise ... for them this world is supreme, this world with its enjoyments of the flesh, with feasting, boozing and whoring. They are the worst pagans who have made themselves hardened and stiff-necked against the Gospel ... it is open, declared hostility, and instead of all the sects and parties we now have only two: Christians and Anti-Christians.... All shame and respect and reverence have vanished out of them [the Anti-Christians] and the abominable mockeries of a Voltaire are child's play compared with the horrible earnestness and the deliberate blasphemy of these seducers. They roam about in Germany and want to sneak in everywhere (2 CW 241–64).

Precisely what the Young Hegelians were going to accomplish by sneaking in everywhere was unclear, largely because of the lack of opportunity for legal political activity in Prussia. In any case the Young Hegelians were primarily writers and academics who were expecting great transformations in society through changes in élite opinion. Engels, however, seems to have assumed a connection between élite opinion and popular revolution on the French model, but he did not specify exactly what the connection was supposed to be.

III   BOMBARDIER

As a volunteer in the army Engels was permitted to move from barracks into private lodgings after a few weeks, and his lack of commitment to military life seems to have been matched by the few military obligations imposed on him during his year's service in the artillery. His first-floor room, elegantly furnished, had three large windows, and he seems to have had ample time to visit university lecture-halls, stop by the local reading-room for news-papers, drink beer with 'The Free' Young Hegelians and appear at various cultural events strikingly attired in his uniform. He gave this account to his sister Marie in a letter of 5 January 1842:

> My uniform, incidentally, is very fine, blue with a black collar adorned with two broad yellow stripes, and black, yellow-striped facings together with red piping round the coat tails. Furthermore, the red shoulder-straps are edged with white. I assure you the effect is most impressive and I'm worthy to be put on show. Because of this the other day I shamefully embarrassed [Friedrich] Rückert [1788–1866], the [romantic] poet [and orientalist], who is here at present. I sat down right in front of him as he was giving a poetry reading and the poor fellow was so dazzled by my shining buttons that he quite lost the thread of what he was saying. . . . I shall soon be promoted to bombardier, which is a sort of non-commissioned officer, and I shall get gold braid to wear on my facings.

On the letter there is a small self-caricature, and Engels wrote, 'Here you see me in uniform with my great-coat draped round my shoulder in a most romantic and picturesque fashion – but strictly against regulations' (2 CW 536–8).

Another notable event of Engels's time was a visit to Berlin by Franz Liszt, then about 30. Engels caricatured him with his 'Kamchatka hair style' – a severe page-boy. In a letter of 14–16 April 1842 to Marie, Engels recounted the scandal surrounding the celebrity's recitals – a fight amongst ladies over a dropped glove, high fees and prodigious drinking, mementoes and pictures contri-buting to the cult. But Engels did not comment on Liszt's pianism, so perhaps he did not actually hear the great man play. The Berlin opera, he noted in another letter, was not very good, but the theatre was rather better. The attractions of the capital were far superior to those of Bremen, the hours devoted to soldiering less than those demanded by his father's agent at work, and best of all, he could lodge on his own. Altogether the year in Berlin was a great success, not least because he found what he wanted intellectually and politically amongst 'The Free' Young Hegelians (2 CW 538, 541).

IV   RHENISH RADICALS

After joining 'The Free', the most radical of the Young Hegelians, Engels began contributing to the most overtly political of their journals, the newly founded *Rheinische Zeitung* of Cologne. The first issue appeared on 1 January 1842, and during the fifteen months in which it was published the paper was a forum for widely differing viewpoints and interests. The alliance that set up the company involved two distinct groups. On the one hand, the financial backers were Rhenish liberals who were concerned to press the Prussian government for measures favourable to the expansion of trade and for constitutional access by commercial and propertied interests to the political process. On the other hand, the writers for the paper were largely Young Hegelians of the radical sort, who were not inclined to co-operate with the Prussian government nor to thank it kindly for any liberal concessions that it cared to grant. The Prussian censorship was worried about their influence from the very beginning.

A central figure amongst the Young Hegelians was Moses or Moritz Hess (1812–75), a Rhinelander and author of *Die Europäische Triarchie* (*The European Triarchy*), published anonymously in Leipzig in 1841. Hess's father owned a sugar refinery in Cologne, but Hess (unlike Engels) broke with his family at 21 and travelled in Holland and France. On his travels he absorbed the sentiments of revolutionary romanticism from reading Rousseau, and he acquainted himself with the newly developing schools of utopian socialist thought. His first book, *Die heilige Geschichte der Menschheit* (*The Sacred History of Mankind*), published in 1837 in Stuttgart, presented the history of humankind as a transition from the unity of the primitive community to the disorder and inequality of modern commercial society. In that society private property and inheritance had produced a potentially revolutionary class-division between rich and poor. Hess looked forward to the resolution of contemporary material deprivation and spiritual malaise in a new social system – communism. In a communist society of the future, private property would give way to community of goods, and harmony would then prevail amongst humankind.

In *The European Triarchy* Hess mounted his own critique of Hegelian philosophy, arguing that German idealism had focused on rationalizing the past without presenting a vision of the future, and that its philosophizing was insufficiently directed towards practical action in politics. The lessons of the French revolution were still pertinent, so he argued, and he looked forward to a synthesis of German philosophy and French political radicalism, especially the inspirational work of socialist and communist theorists. That synthesis would most likely be realized in England, where the contradictions between rich and poor were intensifying and radical politics was moving into the open. Social unrest had been growing steadily there, and the movement for further reform of the electoral system was underway. Moreover there was considerable agitation over wages and conditions of employment in industry. In conclusion Hess argued for a radical triple alliance of progressive forces in Prussia, France and England, and he pinned the fate of humankind on a communist revolution.

After his travels Hess returned to the family business in the Rhineland and attached himself to the Young Hegelians resident in the area, including Bruno Bauer and Marx. Bauer and Marx were then in collaborative discussions on a number of projects, including the publication of Marx's doctoral dissertation, which had been accepted at the University of Jena in April 1841, just before he left Berlin for Trier. In July he moved to Bonn to be with Bauer, and the two were preoccupied with a Young Hegelian critique of religion, especially Christianity. Marx planned to write on Hegel's view of Christian art and his philosophy of law and politics for a sequel to Bauer's *Last Trump*. These projected contributions never appeared in Bauer's second anonymous parody, *Hegels Lehre von der Religion und Kunst von dem Standpuncte des Glaubens beurtheilt* (*Hegel's Teachings on Religion and Art Adjudged from the Standpoint of True Belief*), published in late May or early June 1842 in Leipzig. Nor was Marx's proposed contribution to the Young Hegelian onslaught on Schelling's 'positive philosophy' ever written, so far as we know, though he added a few notes on Schelling's early philosophy to his doctoral manuscript sometime in 1841. Perhaps Marx read Engels's pseudonymous articles on Schelling in the *Telegraph*, the pamphlet critique *Schelling and Revelation* subsequently acknowledged by 'Oswald', and the anonymous parody *Schelling, Philosopher in Christ*, but we do not know for sure (YHKM 137–47; I/1 MEGA^2 88–91 and I/1-A 883-4, 963–4, 1277–9).

During this period in Bonn, Marx associated with Hess and another of the Young Hegelians, Georg Jung (1814–86). Hess and Jung had been discussing the acquisition of a newspaper, and after the Prussian censorship was slightly relaxed in December 1841, they launched the *Rheinische Zeitung*. From early 1842 Marx was pressed by Bruno Bauer to write for the new paper, and Bauer's brother-in-law Rutenberg, formerly of the Berlin 'Doctors Club', was made editor on Marx's recommendation. That happened in February, just after the resignation of the previous incumbent, who was not in sympathy with the Young Hegelianism of the paper's contributors. Marx was then planning to write for Ruge and had done an article for his *Deutsche Jahrbücher*, but his work had fallen foul of the censorship, and so he began to write for the new Rhenish paper in late March. His first published work of journalism (and only his second published work in total) was a topical article on freedom of the press, signed by 'A Rhinelander', which appeared in early May 1842. Marx was anxious to get married after a long engagement, so he transferred his efforts from the *Deutsche Jahrbücher* to the Rhineland paper in the spring of 1842 in order to make a living and establish a career. His anonymous article was very well received in Berlin by Meyen amongst the Young Hegelians and by Ruge in the *Deutsche Jahrbücher*. Ruge's paper was limping along under attack from the censorship, and as early as March 1842 Ruge and Marx had developed plans to publish their banned and questionable articles in Switzerland. The *Anekdota zur neuesten deutschen Philosophie und Publicistik* (*Anecdotes from the latest German Philosophy and Journalism*) appeared in Zürich and Winterthur in February 1843. This two-volume collection was edited by Ruge and published by Julius Fröbel (1805–93), a Swiss radical. It contained anonymous contributions from Marx on the Prussian censorship, preliminary theses on the reform of philosophy by Feuerbach, and writings on politics by Ruge and Bruno Bauer. Hess was also pursuing the same strategy (I/1-A MEGA^2 963–79, 984–5; MBM 72–87).

Though Marx had been involved in founding the *Rheinische Zeitung*, Engels became a contributor first. For the *Rheinische Zeitung* of 12 April 1842 he wrote an anonymous article 'Nord- und süddeutscher Liberalismus' ('North and South German Liberal-ism'), a swiftly-composed commentary on a current debating point – the state of liberalism in Germany. Engels again praised the liberalism of south Germany, where constitutions had been estab-lished for the monarchical régimes in Baden (1818), Württemberg (1819) and Bavaria (1818) in the early post-Napoleonic period. Elsewhere in Germany paternalistic, 'divine-right' monarchism flourished, especially in the Prussian north and in Hanover, where the king had dramatically rejected constitutionalism by throwing out the constitution altogether.

The liberal movement in the south, however, had revived in response to the July revolution of 1830 in France, but south German liberals, in Engels's view, had mistakenly attempted to derive political theory from their own day-to-day practice. Because the liberal practice of the time was very varied, the theory had ended up as something very general, vague and blurred, which was neither German nor French, neither national nor definitely cosmopolitan, but simply abstract and incomplete. Engels's hero Börne, in whom 'theory wrested itself free from practice', was said to be the epitome of north German liberalism, and worth more than all the south Germans put together. According to Engels the north German liberal had a high degree of consistency, a definite-ness in demands, and a consonance of means and purpose, so north German liberalism could launch a resolute, vigorous and successful battle against each and every form of reaction. South German liberals had proceeded from practice to theory and failed, so he concluded, and he advised all Germans to begin the other way around – working from theory to practice. In that way they would get further towards their goal, the achievement of civil liberties (2 CW 265–7).

Engels had already aired those themes earlier in his review 'Ernst Moritz Arndt', and in all his writings on Börne theory and practice were central to his characterization of the revolutionary liberal. The relationship between theory and practice, indeed the necessity for practice to be informed by theory and for theory to go beyond practice, were common themes amongst the Young Hegel-ians – though they by no means agreed on the way they understood those terms or on the relative emphasis due to one or the other. The ideas themselves were commonplace enough for anyone interested in politics, and they are still commonplace today. But because of the influence of Hegelian philosophy on the quasi-religious world of Prussian politics, the political practice of the 1840s necessarily involved participants with a theory that was highly abstract. Engels and his contemporaries had to come to terms with the theory – practice question at a high level of sophistication, asking themselves three very difficult questions. What were the terms of Hegelian theory? What measures in politics did that theory support? What could actually be undertaken?

Engels's next contributions to the *Rheinische Zeitung* focused on just those points. In his two-part 'Tagebuch eines Hospitanten' ('Diary of a Guest Student') published in May 1842 and signed by 'F.O.', Engels first reviewed the lectures on the relationship of philosophy to theology given by Philipp Marheinicke (1780–1846), a former pupil of Hegel and editor of his lectures on the philosophy of religion. Whilst no Young Hegelian himself, Marheinicke was an associate and defender of Bruno Bauer, and a sturdy advocate of Hegel against the calumnies of Schelling. Engels praised Marheinicke for defending the freedom of science but moved on to another 'Old' Hegelian, Leopold von Henning (1791–1866), editor of Hegel's 'Shorter Logic' and also a former pupil.

Von Henning had taken upon himself the task of extending Hegel's philosophy into areas of scientific inquiry that the master had only sketched in outline, such as a theory of the economy, the financial system and the economic policies pursued by the state. This is the first record of Engels's engagement with economic problems in a theoretical context and with the classic works of political economy. By taking up these matters he expanded the Young Hegelian analysis of German politics in a strikingly original way. He argued that after the defeat of Prussia at Jena in 1806 and the consequent Napoleonic occupation, the natural, organic Germany of the medieval past was over, and the future of Prussia lay with theory, science and the development of the intellect. Modern Prussia had come into being through a process of conscious political settlement, beginning in 1813 with the struggle to overthrow the French invaders. That process had followed the inspiration of reason, not the dictates of national character, so unlike its neighbours Prussia could stand as the model state for Europe, and its institutions could represent the complete state consciousness of its century. Engels had previously defended Enlightenment ideals and theory against the medievalism of the Germanizers, but in his 'Diary' he extended his praise of Enlightenment theorizing to include the eclectic comments on political economy professed by a respected Hegelian. Engels quoted von Henning at some length as his views were not otherwise published at the time, and in fact other sources for von Henning's works on political economy do not exist, since he never prepared his lectures for publication:

> Prussia [said von Henning] stands out among all other states by having a financial system based entirely on the modern science of political economy, and having had the hitherto unique courage to apply in practice the theoretical results of Adam Smith and his followers.... Prussia has firmly recognised the principle of free trade and free industry and has abolished all monopolies and prohibitive customs duties. This aspect of our political system, therefore, places us high above states which in another respect, the development of political freedom, are far ahead of us.... But unfortunately there are still old gentlemen whose narrow-mindedness and peevishness make them carp at what is new and accuse it of being an unhistorical, unpractical, forcibly imposed construction evolved from abstract theory; as if ... it were wrong for practice to conform with theory, with science ... as if there could really be practice devoid of all theory.

Engels was well acquainted with the theory of free trade in a general sense, no doubt from his mercantile training, and he had championed the revolutionary liberal Börne as the man who aimed to bring Enlightenment theory into political practice. Von Henning's Hegelian view that economic theory was an aspect of developing rationality in history, and that rationality required its practical realisation in the political realm of economic policy-making, was clearly inspirational. Within eighteen months Engels had tackled the subject again, writing a Young Hegelian critique – one that was unique to himself – of the essential concepts or categories of political economy, and thus taking Hegelian philosophy deeper into the realm of social science (2 CW 268–73; I/3-A MEGA^2 975–6, 986–7).

V 'THE FREE'

From April 1842 Engels had been in correspondence with Ruge of the *Deutsche Jahrbücher*, the mightiest organ of Young Hegelianism.

Engels had most probably just met Ruge that spring in Berlin, and the young author had suggested that he should contribute to Ruge's paper. What he proposed was an article on Christian poetry of the middle ages, Dante in particular, using the perspective opened up by Feuerbach. That was a project tantalizingly close to the one on which Marx was supposed to be working, at exactly the same time, with Ruge and Bruno Bauer. For both Marx and Engels, interest in Christian art probably derived from a wish to re-interpret the whole of the Hegelian system, which gave promin-ence to the philosophies of religion and aesthetics, as well as the philosophies of law and political life. In that way they planned to attack the use conservative Christians were making of philosophy, including Hegel's, to justify and promote their vision of the world, which extended from aesthetics and organised religion to politics and the law. Marx even expanded his proposed study in a Feuerbachian way by altering his title from a consideration of Christian art to a more general consideration of religion and art, with special reference to the art of the Christian era, much as Feuerbach had pushed the Young Hegelians towards considering Christianity to be a special case of religion in general.

Neither Marx nor Engels wrote the promised articles on Christ-ian art, and it is tempting to think that they both dropped their plans for similar reasons, namely a concern with more immediately pressing political subjects, and with furthering their careers as journalists – instead of devoting themselves to time-consuming research projects. In a letter to Ruge of 15 June 1842 Engels reported that he had put 'the Dante thing to one side for the time being'. He also explained, evidently in answer to Ruge's eager editorial questioning, why he had placed his anonymous critique of Schelling in pamphlet form, instead of in the *Deutsche Jahrbücher*. He corrected Ruge for addressing him as 'Doctor', saying that he was not a doctor of philosophy and could not ever become one, and then he enlightened his editor a little about himself: 'I am only a merchant and a Royal Prussian artillerist', he wrote in a rare moment of self-identification. He also owned up to writing the pietist parody *Schelling, Philosopher in Christ*, and then signed himself 'F. Engels (Oswald)', revealing all. This suggests that his identity as Oswald was not very widely known even in Young Hegelian circles, nor his authorship of the pamphlet critique of Schelling and of the pietist parody of his philosophy that had attained such currency. In the review 'Alexander Jung, *Vor-*

lesungen über die moderne Literatur der Deutschen' ('Alexander Jung,
Lectures on Modern German Literature') for Ruge's *Deutsche Jahrbücher*
of July 1842, 'Oswald' identified himself in print as the author of
Schelling and Revelation, but the reading public was not much wiser
for that.

Alexander Jung's *Lectures* were published in 1842 in Danzig and
were spitefully reviewed by Engels, who denounced Jung and his
fellow Young Germans, especially Heine, Theodor Mundt (1808–
61) and Heinrich Laube (1806–84). Engels charged them with
vanity, shallowness, obsession with personalities, ignorance, and
flirtation with Schelling's 'positive philosophy', especially in the
'boring positivism' of Jung's paper the *Königsberger Literatur-Blatt*.
Engels's review, his sole contribution to the *Deutsche Jahrbücher*, is
notable for the clarity with which he expressed the Young Hegelian outlook, and for his sharply worded break with Young
Germany. This was the group with which he had formerly associated himself and whose importance in a certain phase of his
development he still acknowledged: 'anyone whose own mind has
passed through the recent stages of the development of German
thought will at some time have had a special liking for the works of
Mundt, Laube, or Gutzkow.' However, since then there had been
vigorous progress in German intellectual life, so Engels said, and
the emptiness of most of the Young Germans had become horribly
obvious, compared to Young Hegelianism. Engels's Young Hegelian focus on the development of thought, chiefly in philosophy,
and on the critical relationship of the thinker to social reality, was
summed up in one convoluted but definitive sentence: 'In reality,
however, thought in its development alone constitutes the eternal
and positive whereas the factual, the external aspect of what is
taking place, is precisely what is negative, evanescent and vulnerable to criticism.' 'Young Germany has passed away', he concluded, and 'the Young Hegelian school has emerged'. Breathless-
ly he summed up the situation: 'Strauss, Feuerbach, Bauer, and the
[*Deutsche*] *Jahrbücher* now command universal attention, the battle
over principles is at its height, it is a question of life or death
Christianity is at stake, the political movement embraces every
thing.'

The course of Engels's own politicization, in contradistinction to
what he described as the abstract literary interests of Young
Germans, was then indicated in his familiar citation of Börne
whose influence on Young Germany had not – unfortunately fo

he Young Germans – been so great. Börne had been the conscience f German politics during the dark years 1832 to 1840, and after hat his true sons, the new, philosophical liberals amongst the 'oung Hegelians, had emerged. Engels was particularly damning bout Jung's attempt to deal with Feuerbach's *Essence of Christian-y*, because Jung had constructed a soggy argument that the book vas compatible with Schelling's philosophy and therefore with the Christian religion:

> Feuerbach would be quite right, says Jung, if the earth were the whole universe; from the terrestrial point of view his whole work is splendid, convincing, excellent, irrefutable; but from the universal, the global point of view, it is worthless. A fine theory! As if twice two were five on the moon, as if stones were alive and ran about on Venus, and plants could talk on the sun!

Engels publicly anathematized Jung by pronouncing his exclusion rom 'The Free', the Berlin philosophical radicals, and then dismis-ed him as Germany's most spineless, helpless and confused vriter, yet another crypto-Christian (2 CW 284–97, 543; I/3-A 𝐴EGA² 994–7).

'The Free' were well advertised throughout Germany by yet nother anonymous satire, this one undertaken by Engels and Edgar Bauer. On Bruno Bauer's return to Berlin in May 1842, his rother Edgar and Engels began to collaborate on a satirical lefence of the dismissed lecturer in theology. *Die frech bedräute, edoch wunderbar befreite Bibel. Oder: Der Triumph des Glaubens* (*The nsolently Threatened Yet Miraculously Rescued Bible. Or: The Triumph f Faith*) appeared in December 1842 in Neumünster near Zürich, in he relative safety of Switzerland, but it was noticed in numerous German papers. By 1 April 1843 the authors had been identified as Edgar Bauer and 'Oswald'. Their 'Christian Epic in Four Cantos' old of 'The Terrible, Yet True and Salutary History of the Erstwhile Licentiate Bruno Bauer; How the Same, Seduced by the Devil, Fallen from the True Faith, Became Chief Devil, and Was Well and Truly Ousted in the End'. The plot has a certain undergraduate harm: God and the Devil compete for Bruno Bauer's soul in an obvious parody of the Faust tale. Bauer, aided by the shades of Hegel and other atheists and revolutionaries, chooses the Devil, nd the unholy forces join in battle with the heavenly host and oious philosophers, e.g. Leo and Krummacher. When it appears hat the forces of evil are losing, Bauer dismisses the Devil as a myth and leads the atheists himself against God and Satan, now joined in a desperate alliance of non-existent beings. On the verge of an atheistic triumph over all supernatural forces, the 'licentiate' or lecturer Bauer is stopped short by a one-word message concerning his employment at Bonn University – 'redundant'.

The pamphlet is chiefly remarkable now for its character sketches of the Berlin Young Hegelians, going back to the days of the 'Doctors Club'. This group was known first-hand to Edgar Bauer, though not, of course, to Engels. In their satire the Young Hegelians were presented as followers of Ruge's periodicals and adherents to his 'Hellish congregation'. Included in 'that Atheistic mob/. . . much more wild than ever was the Jacobin Club' were:

Karl Köppen:

That's Köppen you can see there with his glasses on.
. . . He has a sword and wears it dangling . . . like a demon's tail.
He's wearing epaulettes and brandishing about
A stick with which to beat the thirst for knowledge out
Of flaming youth.

Eduard Meyen:

An Atheist born, the vilest love him well: Voltaire
Ever since his birth has been his daily reading fare.

'Oswald', i.e. Engels's self-caricature as the first member of Meyen's 'family' in Hell:

Right on the very left, that tall and long-legged stepper
Is Oswald, coat of grey and trousers shade of pepper;
Pepper inside as well, Oswald the Montagnard;
A radical is he, dyed in the wool, and hard.
Day in, day out, he plays upon the guillotine a
Single solitary tune and that's a cavatina,
The same old devil-song; he bellows the refrain:
Formez vos bataillons! Aux armes, citoyens! [lines from the French revolutionary anthem *The Marseillaise*].

Edgar Bauer:

Who raves beside him [Oswald], with the muscles of a brewer?
It's old Bloodlust himself in person, Edgar Bauer.

... Outside, a smart blue coat; inside he's black, lacks polish;
Outside he's dandified; inside he's sansculottish.

Max Stirner, pseudonym for Johann Caspar Schmidt (1806–56),
who joined 'The Free' about the same time as Engels:

See Stirner too, the thoughtful moderation-hater;
Though still on beer, he'll soon be drinking blood like water.
And if the others shout a wild: *à bas les rois!* [Down with kings!]
Stirner is sure to add: *à bas aussi les lois!* [Down with the laws as
well!]

Ludwig Buhl, editor of *Der Patriot*, a short-lived Young Hegelian
paper:

Next, baring his greenish teeth, comes tripping on his way,
His hair unkempt and tousled, prematurely grey,
A soap-and-water-shy and blood-shy *Patriot*,
So smooth and soft inside; outside a sansculotte.

Then *Arnold Ruge*:

Wild Arnold heads them, Czar of All the Atheists,
And high upon his baton's end he twirls and twists
Copies of *Halle Annals*.

After introducing the Berlin crew, Engels and Edgar Bauer went
on to caricature Bruno Bauer and his followers, who were all
associated with the *Rheinische Zeitung*:

Bruno Bauer:

He raves, a lanky villain in a coat of green;
Behind the leering face Hell's offspring can be seen.
He hoists his flag aloft, and in an arc up high
The sparks of his rude Bible criticisms fly.

Marx:

Who runs up next with wild impetuosity?
A swarthy chap of Trier, a marked monstrosity.
He neither hops nor skips, but moves in leaps and bounds,
Raving aloud. As if to seize and then pull down

To Earth the spacious tent of Heaven up on high,
He opens wide his arms and reaches for the sky.
He shakes his wicked fist, raves with a frantic air,
As if ten thousand devils had him by the hair.

Georg Jung:

Next, from Cologne, a Youngster [from *jung* meaning 'young'],
Something of a swell,
Too bad for Heaven, too good to pass the gates of hell.
He's half a sansculotte, and half an aristo,
A suave rich gentleman. . . .

Rutenberg:

Next, one who indeed disgusts,
The dawdling Rtg, quite handy with his fists.
He has an evil habit: constantly he smokes
Hellish tobacco in an ell-long pipe which pokes
Out of his mouth. . . .

Feuerbach:

A one-man host of Atheists fanatical,
A one-man treasure store of craft Satanical,
A one-man fount of wicked blasphemy and shame?
Help us, Saint John [the Evangelist – in Young Hegelian eyes, the
most 'self-conscious' and 'rational' of the Gospel-writers], it's
Feuerbach of dreadful name [literally 'fire-brook']!
He neither raves nor bounds, but hovers in mid-air [?on the
question of atheism],
An awful meteor girt by hellish vapours there.

Feuerbach's analysis of Christianity, in which the supernatural
was brought down to earth, was brilliantly caricatured by Engels
and Edgar Bauer as a Satanic parody of the Christian sacraments of
Communion and Baptism, reduced to a level of disgusting but
thoroughly human vulgarity:

In the one hand he holds outstretched the cup that shines,
And in the other one, the bread loaf that sustains.
He sits up to his navel in a sea-shell basin,

Trying to find a new church service for the brazen.
Guzzling, boozing, bathing, firmly he maintains,
Are all the truth the holy sacrament contains.
A storm of shouts and cheers succeeds the first *hurrah*!
And then he must be taken to a public bar (2 CW 334–7; I/3-A
MEGA² 1018–22).

Significantly the theory–practice question was raised amongst
'The Free' by the caricatures representing the authors themselves:

Oswald and Edgar cannot wait until he's [Ruge's] done.
They both jump on the table, then they shriek as one:
  'Ruge, we've had enough of all this talk from you!
  What we want now is deeds, not words. We want some
  action!'

Ruge, the most successful man of words but the most stand-
offish politically, was made to reply in 'Old' Hegelian terms, rather
than in the Young Hegelian vocabulary of revolutionary liberalism
that Engels associated with Börne and the July days of 1830:

Then with a mocking laugh shouts Arnold in reply:
  'Our actions are just words, and long they so shall be.
  After Abstraction, Practice follows of itself.'

Ruge was the recipient of a highly revealing letter from Engels,
written on 26 July 1842. In it Engels summed up his achievements
to date and indicated his ambitions for the future, as his one-year
term of service in the army was shortly to expire: 'I have decided to
abandon all literary work for a while in order to devote more time
to studying. The reasons for this are fairly plain. I am young and
self-taught in philosophy [*Autodidakt in der Philosophie*]. I have
learnt enough to form my own viewpoint and, when necessary, to
defend it, but not enough to be able to work for it with success and
in the proper way.'
He continued by mentioning again his lack of proper qualifications in philosophy and the need for further independent study to
defend himself against the criticisms that would inevitably arise
once he started writing again – 'under my own name': 'Regarded
subjectively, my literary activities have so far been mere experiments from the outcome of which I was to be able to learn whether

my natural capacities were such as to enable me to work fruitfully and effectively for progress and to participate actively in the movement of the century. I can be satisfied with the results.'

At the end of September 1842 Engels left Berlin and 'The Free' to return home to the business matters which he knew would occupy much of his time (2 CW 545–6; III/1 MEGA² 235). Whilst *en route* to Barmen he stopped at Cologne in order to visit the offices of the paper to which he had, over the previous year, devoted almost the whole of his journalistic efforts – the *Rheinische Zeitung*.

4

Manchester Man

Engels arrived at the office of the *Rheinische Zeitung* and met the communist Hess for the first time about 7–8 October 1842. In correspondence of the following year Hess reported on this meeting with one of the paper's occasional Berlin correspondents: 'we talked over the issues of the day and he [Engels], a revolutionary of the Year I, departed from me a thoroughly zealous communist'. Engels's 'conversion' to communism is traditionally dated to that meeting with Hess, and it is certainly true that socialist or communist ideas – there was no firm distinction at that time – do not appear in his writings up to then. Hess took credit for such a conversion by implying that he brought Engels forward from a primitive view of social transformation, one characteristic of the opening years of the French revolution, to the most up-to-date ideas of communism, such as his own (I/3-A MEGA^2 685).

However, it is unlikely that Engels needed much persuading, as he was an almost perfect reflection in himself of the 'European Triarchy' that Hess was looking for: revolutionary sentiments in his admiration for French politics, critical Young Hegelianism in his appreciation for German philosophy, and a perspective on industrialization and class that he could expect to develop in England in connection with his family's business interests. Over the next two years communist ideas crept into Engels's works, and they certainly influenced his choice of subject-matter, but the development from revolutionary liberal to communist was not a dramatic change in outlook. This was because the communist or socialist outlook was highly varied, and generally visionary, while liberalism was also for many theorists and politicians a doctrine of revolution and not necessarily anti-communist. Theoretical distinctions and battlelines between constitutional liberalism and revolutionary communism were not then sharply drawn, and in any case Hess, Engels and other radicals were inclined to view communism as a stage in European political development that would build on the achievements of liberal theory and practice by pushing them further forward. Communism was then no simple reversal of liberalism, and liberals were potential allies for communists, not enemies. Communism at the time did not mean much more than community of goods, about which theorists of communism developed widely differing utopian schemes. Practical communists sought to find persuadable liberals – revolutionaries of the Year I – to look beyond the political goal of representative and responsible government and to consider in addition the 'social question' raised by the inequality of property in contemporary society.

After meeting Hess, Engels went to Barmen, presumably to prepare for his move to Manchester in order to continue working for the family firm, a logical stage in the development of his business career, and no doubt a good idea from his father's point of view. Surely, his father might have reasoned, there would be no Young Hegelian philosophy in England, and with luck young Friedrich's upsetting religious scepticism and flighty enthusiasm for intellectual life would disappear. It would be difficult to imagine the young man retaining the manner of a Berlin radical in Manchester, as a Manchester man was down to earth, common-sensical and absorbed in industry and commerce. The Prussian Army had obviously failed to do the trick, continued residence in Barmen as a disaffected intellectual was out of the question, and in any case young Friedrich had to earn a living.

I   MEETING MARX

En route in November to London and Manchester, Engels made another stop at Cologne to visit the *Rheinische Zeitung*, and this time he met its new editor. Marx had taken over on 15 October 1842, more or less by default, as he was the only associate willing to manage the troubled paper. The *Rheinische Zeitung* had been under attack in the German press for criticizing the Rhenish provincial and Prussian national governments, and heavy censorship, even closure were real threats. Presciently Marx had written to Ruge on 9 July 1842 about the situation: 'Incidentally, do not imagine that we on the Rhine live in a political Eldorado. The most unswerving persistence is required to push through a newspaper like the *Rheinische Zeitung*' (1 CW 389; I/3-A MEGA^2 680–9).

Up to July 1842 Engels had published nine anonymous or pseudonymous articles in the *Rheinische Zeitung*. Besides 'North-

and South-German Liberalism' and the two-part 'Diary of a Guest Student', he had written on Rhenish music festivals, the tribulations of liberal writers in connection with the censorship, and the censorship laws themselves in a stinging attack published in July. This was very much in the spirit of his revolutionary liberalism, in which Enlightenment ideals were used to criticize the Prussian *ancien régime*, and it was also an argument very similar to the one used by Marx in his first article for the *Rheinische Zeitung*, published in May.

Four anonymous articles from this period that are published in English amongst Engels's works are now assigned by the editors of MEGA^2 to a list of 'Dubiosa', because they cannot be positively ascribed to Engels, though the possibility of his authorship cannot be totally excluded: 'Participation in the Debates of the Baden Chamber of Deputies', 'F.W. Andreä and the *High Nobility of Germany*', 'Berlin Miscellany' and 'Centralisation and Freedom'. After Marx became editor in October Engels's contributions to the *Rheinische Zeitung* amounted to five anonymous pieces, all published in December (I/3-A MEGA^2 658).

The first meeting between Marx and Engels took place on 16 November 1842 and was described as very cool by Engels himself, writing in 1895 to Marx's biographer Franz Mehring. During 1842 Marx's suspicions about his Berlin contributors amongst 'The Free' had been growing steadily. He seems to have become dissatisfied with Bruno Bauer's failure, as he saw it, to move beyond the 'tone of the *Last Trump* and the irksome constraint of the Hegelian exposition'. Writing of his dissatisfaction to Ruge on 20 March 1842, Marx argued that Bauer's academic high-jinks should be replaced by a more thorough exposition. By 9 July he was asking Ruge for further details of 'The Free', since they had been attacked for their wild ideas and their notorious manners in an article in the *Königsberger Zeitung* for 17 June, a report reprinted in the *Rheinische Zeitung* eight days later.

Marx was evidently afraid that he would be saddled with the antics of the Berlin Young Hegelians by his arch-rival in Cologne, Karl Hermes (1800–56) of the *Kölnische Zeitung*. Whilst Marx sympathized with the emancipation that 'The Free' were promoting, he took exception to the way that they were doing it, and to the kind of characters they were: 'It is one thing to declare for emancipation – that is honest; it is another thing to start off by shouting it out as propaganda; that sounds like bragging and irritates the philistine. And then, reflect on who are these "Free", a

man like Meyen, etc.' Marx feared that the Berliners would make
their good cause into something ridiculous and that they would
commit stupidities, unless someone could restrain them. 'Anyone
who has spent as much time among these people as I have', he
concluded in his letter to Ruge, 'will find that this anxiety is not
without foundation'. It was just as well for Engels that *The
Insolently Threatened Yet Miraculously Rescued Bible* was not published until December, a month after his first meeting with the
firm-minded editor of the *Rheinische Zeitung*, so Marx had not yet
had the benefit of Engels and Edgar Bauer's colourful characteriza-
tions of 'The Free'. The works and manners of these rebels were
intended to be the comeuppance of the very middle classes with
whom Marx was seeking an alliance in his paper's campaign for
democratic reforms (1 CW 385, 390; I/3-A MEGA^2 685, and III/1-A
576).

Edgar Bauer had brought 'The Free' and their anti-bourgeois
views into the *Rheinische Zeitung* itself in a long article 'Das
Juste-Milieu' ('Polite Society') begun in June 1842 and continued in
mid-August. Writing on 25 August from Bonn to an associate at the
editorial offices in Cologne, Marx asked for copies of Edgar Bauer's
work and for agreement to print a reply, discussing dispassionate-
ly the issues that he thought the younger Bauer's work had raised.
Marx's view was that general theoretical arguments about the
political system were more suitable for purely scientific organs
than for newspapers. The sweeping radicalism that Edgar Bauer
promoted was merely a recipe for intensified censorship and even
suppression of the press. Moreover it aroused 'the resentment of
many, indeed the majority, of the free-thinking practical people
who have undertaken the laborious task of winning freedom step
by step, within the constitutional framework'. Demonstrating to
the middle classes their own contradictions, in present political
circumstances, would merely divide the opposition to the current
Prussian régime. Moreover squabbles amongst radicals in the press
would become a convenient excuse for the government to close it
down altogether. 'The Free' were becoming known as atheists and
anarchists, rejecting all religion and authority, and bringing more
responsible democrats into disrepute. Marx's aims, by contrast,
were to develop 'correct theory . . . within the concrete conditions
and on the basis of the existing state of things', to forge an effective
political alliance with constitutional liberals, and to keep the
Rheinische Zeitung open by ensuring that its contributors followed a

policy of moderation (1 CW 392; III/1-A MEGA^2 577–8).

It is small wonder Engels was greeted with suspicion by Marx, but noteworthy that Marx did not enforce a total ban on contributions from members of the group to his newspaper. Perhaps Engels did not go into more detail when writing to Mehring about the first meeting with Marx because he wished to pass over his association with 'The Free' as quickly as possible. His first collaboration with Marx, agreed in late 1844, was in fact *Die heilige Familie* (*The Holy Family*), a satirical attack on the remaining Berliners.

It would be interesting to know if Marx had outlined his editorial and political policies to Engels when they first met, and how closely in any case Engels felt himself allied to Edgar Bauer and the uncompromising and extrovert politicking of 'The Free'. Engels's published work of the period, like Marx's, was generally in praise of the liberal tradition, especially in its revolutionary mode, and hortatory for its survival. But Engels was also the author of a parody, *Schelling, Philosopher in Christ*, and co-author of a satire, *The Insolently Threatened Yet Miraculously Rescued Bible*, that were much more radical, since they were overtly atheistic. Those works were bound to offend many liberals, because in them Engels was generally hostile to the mores of the 'polite society' that Edgar Bauer, to Marx's rage, had explicitly attacked.

When Engels wrote to Ruge on 26 July 1842 that he was forsaking literary work for a while in order to devote himself to study, he was perhaps indicating the kind of dissatisfaction that Marx also felt with respect to the business of theorising in the press, though Engels does not seem to have been quite so alive to the serious political consequences of tangling with the censorship or offending middle-class interests. In that respect Marx perhaps rightly saw him as one of 'The Free', but it is also possible that Engels's intent to undertake a serious theorization of contemporary politics also impressed his strong-minded editor, whose very first leading article announced that the contemporary literature of socialism and communism could not be criticized on the basis of superficial flashes of thought, but only after long and profound study (1 CW 220; 2 CW 545).

Marx continued to accept Engels's work, and he may have implicitly or overtly directed its tone and content. As one of the correspondents in England for the *Rheinische Zeitung* Engels covered 'the concrete conditions' and 'the existing state of things' in politics, just as Marx desired, and his treatment displayed a class-perspective that recalled the best of his early journalism – the 'Letters from Wuppertal'. But at their meeting Engels may also have influenced or at least encouraged Marx in ways that followed on from his previously published views on political economy that Marx could hardly have missed. When Marx took over the *Rheinische Zeitung* in October his own articles were taking just this turn towards cool analyses of the 'social question', and during his editorship he defended his own work and similar pieces by other contributors very vigorously. Many years later in a brief autobiographical note he singled out his investigations of poverty in the Rhineland, begun in the autumn of 1842, as his first contact with the economic questions of material interest in society. To his embarrassment, he could not resolve these questions in terms of liberal constitutionalism. With respect to economic theory and practical observation Engels was more familiar with class politics than Marx, though that is not saying much. Engels had only scratched the surface of political economy, though significantly his contact with it had been in the Hegelian context of critical conceptual analysis. His factual study of industrial poverty in the Wuppertal was highly formative, but even as journalism it was rudimentary. But during his two years in Manchester he made startling progress on both a theoretical critique of the modern economy and an empirical account of its effects on the working class.

After going abroad Engels also devoted less attention to religion as an intellectually important issue. As his political perspective widened beyond Germany, so the importance of Young Hegelian waverers on the religious issue declined. Christianity as a particular object for rationalistic attack, and atheism as an absorbing philosophical crusade, both receded somewhat from his works. Of course Christianity and atheism did not disappear altogether from view, especially when Christianity was conjoined politically with socialism. In Engels's view atheism was the logical conclusion of Enlightenment philosophy and revolutionary liberal politics. Socialists and communists would have to accept it, indeed to refuse to do so was to compromise the cause.

By the autumn of 1842 Engels's attention had evidently focused on material interests so that he was not so inclined to attack, in the first instance, the beliefs that people hold within society – something he had been doing since his early polemics against obscurantism. Henceforth he concentrated his efforts on further analysis of the 'social question' and study of the economic circumstances from which class politics arises. Engels's conception of his career changed definitively as he came to live permanently abroad but to devote most of his attention to German-speaking communists and socialists. Amongst those communists and socialists he favoured the ones whose critical energies were directed towards the 'social question' and whose political programmes included a resolution of the inequalities of class-divided industrial societies.

II CLASS CONSCIOUSNESS

Engels had left Berlin at the right moment in September 1842 and had made contact with Marx just in time on 16 November. By 30 November Marx's hostility to 'The Free' boiled over as he wrote to Ruge. Marx devoted his entire letter to complaints about them, noting that a mass of their articles for the *Rheinische Zeitung* were killed by the censor, but that he had thrown out just as many himself. 'Meyen and Co. sent us heaps of scribblings, pregnant with revolutionizing the world and empty of ideas, written in a slovenly style and seasoned with a little atheism and communism (which these gentlemen have never studied).' Marx was annoyed that they considered the *Rheinische Zeitung* to be their house organ, and he would no longer permit their watery torrent of words. He considered their work to be 'worthless creations of "freedom"', and he complained that freedom, as understood in Berlin, consisted in 'vague reasoning, magniloquent phrases and self-satisfied self-adoration'. He proposed instead more specificity, more attention to the actual state of affairs, more expert knowledge, and less trifling with the *label* atheism. Such trifling reminded him of children who assure everyone that they are not afraid of the bogey man. After meeting with Marx earlier in November Engels can hardly have missed the signals that the 'Berlin windbags' were out of favour. As he was serious-minded and no longer in Berlin, he escaped Marx's wrath and so was able to submit sober contributions to the *Rheinische Zeitung* on English politics, all written within a month of his arrival in London on 19 November 1842 (1 CW 393–5; I/3-A MEGA^2 1055).

Engels's articles on England for the *Rheinische Zeitung* were written swiftly without much research, and they were based on very limited personal experience of the English political scene on which he commented. His views were coincident with previous articles in the paper written by Hess and Gustav Mevissen, a founder and shareholder who had himself visited England that summer. Hess had placed the question of revolution in England on the editorial agenda, and Mevissen had provided a class-analysis of the current situation, covering landed interests, manufacturers and middle classes, and property-less workers.

In Engels's time there were obvious, even violent political clashes to be observed in England, especially the mass strikes in the manufacturing districts that had taken place in mid-1842. The activities of the Chartists and the Anti-Corn Law League both led to noisy meetings, demonstrations, marches and desperate political tensions in Parliament itself. The *People's Charter* had been published in 1838, and it contained demands for universal male suffrage at the age of 21, annual parliaments, salaries for MPs, elections by ballot rather than by public vote, equality in electoral districts, and abolition of property qualifications for parliamentary candidates. The original committee, formed to promote the *Charter* as a Parliamentary bill, consisted of MPs and members of the London Working Men's Association. After the failure of these efforts, the National Charter Association was formed in July 1840 in Manchester to organize a mass petition. This eventually attracted 3.3 million signatures, but it was also rejected by Parliament. During the mass strikes of August 1842 an attempt was made to link the struggle for wages to the Chartists' cause, but the strikes were forcibly suppressed, and the two movements – one for better wages and conditions for working people, and the other for a more democratic and representative Parliament – then diverged.

Overlapping those movements to some extent was the Anti-Corn Law League, founded in December 1838 in Manchester, and dedicated to the repeal of the protective tariffs that kept out foreign grain. This policy maintained high prices for domestic corn, because it suited aristocratic landed interests, and conversely it forced manufacturers to pay high wages, because their workers were denied access to cheap foreign foodstuffs. The Anti-Corn Law League wanted a major reform in policy that the ruling Tories, traditionally allied to landed, agricultural interests, would not countenance. One way of achieving this change in economic policy might be to reform Parliament itself in accordance with the *Charter*. The *Charter*, in so far as it promised universal suffrage, might result in a Parliament more favourable to working-class interests and less favourable to agricultural landlords than the current restricted representation allowed.

This coincidence of interests did not remove the very real differences between these three groups that a reform of Parliament would inevitably expose. In 1846 the Corn Laws were repealed, a policy change that was to some extent forced on the Tories to counter the threat of reform. Reform of Parliament was not achieved in the 1840s, and the unsuccessful attempt of 1842 to promote a mass alliance of opposition forces was not repeated (1 H 20–6; I/3-A MEGA^2 1051–85).

For Engels this was liberal politics on a grand scale far surpassing the political activity that was permitted or even attempted in Prussia. Moreover it was tinged with a kind of proto-communism, in that the interests of the working classes were openly and sometimes violently pursued, though community of goods was not an obvious issue in the struggle. The revolution that he and the *Rheinische Zeitung* had in mind was itself a liberal one – the creation, through violent means if necessary, of representative and responsible government. They reasoned that such a government would have to legislate to protect the interests of the broad mass of voters, including workers, rather than the minority of wealthy property-owners.

The consequences of industrialization were on display in England to a far greater degree than in Germany, and this, too, engaged Engels's interest. Hess had argued that the industrial poor represented the political issue of the future, and England (by which German communists meant Britain) had more of them than anywhere else. In what sense the industrial poor might themselves be an important political actor before and after a liberal revolution was left nebulous. But then the liberal model was itself vague about the exact scope of revolutionary, electoral and parliamentary participation that the industrial poor might expect to enjoy in practice, so neither Hess nor Engels must have felt it necessary to define those matters very distinctly. Making the industrial working class a political issue for educated liberals did not explicitly include – but did not necessarily exclude – some conception of industrial workers as an organized force in politics.

Engels's experience as an international trader entered his articles in a striking manner, and in that respect he contributed something of his own to the radical views developed by Hess and others on the *Rheinische Zeitung*. Their perspective had been internationalist in a somewhat mystical way – a Hegelian synthesis of French revolutionary vigour, English industrial might and German philosophy. For what else could Germany, in the eyes of its intellectuals, contribute but something philosophical and synthetic? In Young Hegelian eyes, and perhaps rightly, Germans were international visionaries, as their political and industrial achievements at home were not yet on a European scale to match those of France and Britain.

But the radicals of the *Rheinische Zeitung* were not wholly bound up with visionary philosophizing. For Hess and Marx and others on the paper there was also the practical, domestic struggle to get Germany moving on both the political and economic fronts. This involved an intense battle against reactionaries, Germanizers, landed interests and other defenders of the remnants of feudalism, so that liberal reforms in the political and economic structures of society could be carried out and the old order pushed aside.

Engels produced an analysis of England as a trading nation. No doubt the motivation for doing this was his expectation that it would reinforce Hess's conclusions concerning the revolutionary potential of an industrialized country, and those are precisely the conclusions that he drew for the readers of the *Rheinische Zeitung*. But in doing this he challenged Young Hegelians to look beyond liberalism in the German context and to give content to Hess's sketchy internationalism. If they could see industry abroad, and see industrialization as an international force, they could then see the relevance of a powerful new analytical tool – political economy. Almost at a stroke Engels conjoined philosophical politics with social science.

Engels's argument flowed in a chain of empirical deductions quite unlike other Young Hegelian discourse. In part this was because the economic issues relevant to a trading country had not yet been fully aired in relation to Germany, and it is therefore unsurprising that they did not play a significant role in Young Hegelian literature or in the politics of the day from which the movement arose. Engels's achievement within Young Hegelianism was to draw on his unusual background in international trade, his current posting to a job in English industry and his academic curiosity about economic affairs. His aim was to make significant alterations in his contemporaries' political perceptions.

Very simply Engels argued that a trading nation such as England must constantly increase its industrial output, or face decline. This was because of the progressive industrialization of the foreign countries which formed its export market. Lower costs abroad would bring a flood of cheap imports, resulting in bankruptcy for domestic manufacturers. Domestic industrialists would consequently demand protective tariffs on foreign goods to protect their position in the home market. This would lead to high prices, to which English consumers would object. Moreover foreign industries would seek barriers to English products, so English export industries would fail and workers would face unemployment. Competition and protection at home and abroad thus formed a two-sided process continuing to infinity, in his view, and those forces would produce an inevitable contradiction in practice.

This conceptual analysis, Engels continued, was also confirmed by direct observation of the existing state of affairs. He took the recent wave of strikes to be a result of changes in the terms of international trade, and an augury of the impossibility for peaceful reform or 'legal revolution'. Because industrialization made more and more people dependent for their livelihood, indeed their very existence, on these economic fluctuations, he predicted a mass revolt against the land-owning nobility and the industrial aristocracy. This would be a matter of political necessity. Writing of the trade crisis that occurred in the autumn of 1842, he concluded:

The slightest fluctuation in trade leaves thousands of workers destitute; their modest savings are soon used up and then they are in danger of starving to death. And a crisis of this kind is bound to occur again in a few year's time. . . . True, the workers have organised their own mutual benefit funds, which are augmented by weekly contributions and are intended to support the unemployed; but these only suffice when the factories are working well, for even then there are always enough destitute. When unemployment becomes general, even this source of relief dries up.

Engels's analysis of the political furore surrounding the Corn Laws was straightforward reporting, but it was augmented by an interesting account of the position of the merchants and manufacturers. He compared their situation in England with the position of similar classes in Germany, who were coincidentally the backers of the *Rheinische Zeitung*. In England he found a relatively enlightened version of the industrialists and traders that he knew from his days in Barmen:

> This middle class . . . is, however, a middle class only compared with the wealthy nobility and capitalists; in relation to the workers its position is that of an aristocracy. In a country like England, which lives only by industry and therefore has a multitude of workers, people will be much more conscious of this than, for example, in Germany, where the middle class comprises the craftsmen and peasants, and where such an extensive class of factory workers is unknown.

Engels expected the Whig party of the English middle classes to be forced into just the kind of squeeze that he would like to see developing in Germany. In England this would happen when the working-class became more and more imbued with the radical-democratic principles of Chartism and came to recognize those principles as the expression of its collective consciousness. At that point political power would flow to the working-class who would have an advantage in terms of numbers and determination over the middle classes. The battle against the old order and its political and economic privileges would be bound to intensify, and middle-class liberals would have to choose which side they were on (2 CW 368–82).

Engels's first articles from England reflect the property-conscious perspective of the Rhenish communists, hence a renewed and politically ambitious concern with the 'social question' as it was developing in the world's major industrial power. His methods of analysis display not only the Hegelian search for conceptual contradictions underlying the phenomena of experience but also the rudimentary political economy that he had absorbed in the textile trade and from the lectures of von Henning. His new analytical perspective obviously excited him as he communicated it to Rhenish liberals and Young Hegelian radicals.

But it was unclear in his account precisely what immediate difference this perspective on international political economy would make in the struggle for constitutional rule in Prussia, and for the abolition of political barriers to trade within Germany. The political problems that intrigued Engels, and to which Hess had to some limited extent directed his attention, were best observed in England and in certain other highly industrialized areas. The best methods for assessing the political situation there, including the critical use of political economy, were not ones that Germans found readily comprehensible in any case. The obvious course for Engels was to find his audience and colleagues in industrialized Britain, Belgium and France – but amongst German émigrés, ordinary workers and communist theoreticians alike.

However, reaching Germans and even German-speaking émigrés was becoming more difficult. Ruge's *Deutsche Jahrbücher* was suppressed in January 1843 and Marx's *Rheinische Zeitung* in March. Their friends the poet Georg Herwegh (1817–75) and the editor-publisher Fröbel had been seeking, against the wishes of the Prussian and Saxon governments, to publish further Young Hegelian literature in Switzerland, and they succeeded again with the single volume *Einundzwanzig Bogen aus der Schweiz* (*Twenty-one Folio Sheets from Switzerland*). This collection appeared in Winterthur and Zürich in June 1843 and included Engels's article (signed 'F.O.') 'Friedrich Wilhelm IV, König von Preussen' ('Frederick William IV, King of Prussia'), as well as contributions by Bruno Bauer on religious belief and civil freedom and by Hess on theories of socialism and communism. Unsold copies of the first edition were seized in July, but the volume was republished the following year.

Engels's article was written in mid-October 1842 while he was preparing to leave Germany for England, and it represents his last forthright attack on the Christian state in Prussia. In the article he argued the case for universal, civic and human rights against the theological defence of conservative monarchism offered by the King and his apologists. Claiming that Bruno Bauer's atheistic critique of theology had exposed Christian conservatism as cant and hypocrisy, Engels exhorted public opinion to continue the struggle for representative government and freedom of the press (2 CW 360–7).

Herwegh had been forced to leave Zürich in February, but after the suppression of the *Rheinische Zeitung* in March, Hess had arrived. He and Fröbel then worked in association on Fröbel's paper *Schweizerische Republikaner*. This was published bi-weekly by the same house that had produced *The Insolently Threatened Yet Miraculously Rescued Bible* and the *Twenty-one Folio Sheets from Switzerland*. It is presumed that Hess encouraged his protégé, resident in England and needing an outlet for his radical journalism, to contribute to the Swiss paper, and Engels's four 'Briefe aus London' ('Letters from London') were published between 16 May and 27 June 1843 (I/3-A MEGA² 689–94, 1032–7).

During his stay in England Engels worked as a clerk at Ermen and Engels, cotton-spinners and manufacturers of sewing thread, at their offices in central Manchester, and he presumably visited their mill-works in suburban Pendleton. Because his correspondence, if any, has not survived, his movements are not accurately known, but he seems to have travelled extensively and certainly visited London. Doubtless 'Letters from London' seemed a more appropriate heading for a Swiss newspaper than 'Letters from Manchester', and the use of the capital city correctly indicated his focus on national politics. The articles continued his reports on English party politics begun for the *Rheinische Zeitung*, but they displayed certain new preoccupations, such as English socialism and Irish nationalism. Presumably those topics reflected his personal experience of politics in industrial districts in England, and his extensive reading of the local press.

Engels's articles were full of praise for the popular agitation in support of the *People's Charter* that he had seen at public meetings in Manchester and neighbouring Salford. He contrasted English matter-of-factness and humour very favourably with French socialism, which in his view was beset with scheming and factionalism, and with German philosophical radicalism, which he considered ill-written and self-regarding. For Engels the Chartist movement for the reform of Parliament was in a sense a popular front for much more radical schemes for revolutionizing contemporary society, including the destruction of landed, aristocratic interests which he considered reactionary, and the curtailment of propertied, commercial interests, which he considered exploitative. His highest praise was for the 'founder of the socialist movement' Robert Owen (1771–1858), who wrote badly, in his opinion, but had lucid moments. Owen's views were comprehensive, according to Engels, and he remarked that his writings teemed with outbursts of rage against theologians, lawyers and doctors, all lumped together. Engels marked with a double exclamation Owen's claim that 'marriage, religion and property are the sole causes of all the calamity that has existed since the world began'.

Owenites and their meetings were undoubtedly influential in Manchester, and the heady mixture of groups, interests and ideas within the Chartist movement of the 1840s was vividly pictured by Engels, an eyewitness and partisan. But he did not pay much attention to the leadership of the movement, which stuck to very limited aims and methods in pursuing the national campaign. His characterization of Chartism as English socialism now seems somewhat odd, since the leadership lost confidence in themselves and then the confidence of their supporters. The first mass political movement to include significant working-class participation fell apart long before any very organized form of socialism emerged in England.

Engels, writing for Germans in a Swiss paper, had no English audience amongst Chartists at this point. As political journalism it was thus doubly removed from real struggles, but his analysis was very confident none the less: 'In the socialists, English energy is very clearly evident, but what astonished me more was the good-natured character of these people. I almost called them lads, which, however, is so far removed from weakness that they laugh at the mere Republicans, because a republic would be just as hypocritical, just as theological, just as unjust in its laws, as a monarchy.'

Engels took much the same view of Daniel O'Connell (1775–1847) and his campaign for repeal of the Union between Ireland and Great Britain. 'Give me two hundred thousand Irishmen', Engels promised, 'and I will overthrow the entire British monarchy'. Engels's Irishmen were 'wild, headstrong, fanatical Gaels' bent on justified revenge for five centuries of oppression. O'Connell's concern to protect Irish property-owners, which Engels termed two-faced Whiggery, obviously made him an unsuitable candidate to lead the revolution that Engels had in mind. This was a revolution that would abolish poverty, which he sketched for German readers in a devastating though second-hand account of Irish peasant life.

The oppressed and poor as political actors were coming into focus in Engels's analysis of contemporary English politics. He clearly wanted an alliance of Irishmen and Chartists, converted to socialism, to march on the British establishment and remove it. And he did not want any constitutional backsliding towards monarchy or any other strategems to defend landed and commercial interests at the expense of agricultural and industrial workers. The French constitutional monarchy of King Louis Philippe was specifically mentioned by Engels as an example of the way in which a mass movement had been betrayed.

Yet Engels's notion of mass political participation was inchoate, so he did not handle the role of leaders at all well, seeing them as either traitors or ciphers. The political process by which the interests of the oppressed and poor were to be pursued and then protected in reformed political structures received little attention in his writings. Instead he left us an account of convivial socializing observed at the Communist Hall in Manchester:

> In their form, these meetings partly resemble church gatherings; in the gallery a choir accompanied by an orchestra sings social hymns; these consist of semi-religious or wholly religious melodies with communist words, during which the audience stands. . . . In one corner of the hall is a stall where books and pamphlets are sold and in another a booth with oranges and refreshments, where everyone can obtain what he needs or to which he can withdraw if the speech bores him. From time to time tea-parties are arranged on Sunday evenings at which people of both sexes, of all ages and classes, sit together and partake of the usual supper of tea and sandwiches; on working days dances and concerts are often held in the hall, where people have a very jolly time (3 CW 379–91).

III   ECONOMIC THEORY

The fifth 'Letter from London', like the preceding four, was sent in manuscript to the *Schweizer Republikaner*, but Engels's contact Fröbel was forced to leave the editorial board of the paper in late June 1843. Fröbel redirected the article in November to Marx, who acknowledged receipt of the pages 'all scissored up' by the postal censors. Marx was then living in Paris and collaborating with Ruge. The two were planning to continue the tradition of radical publication abroad for a German audience by editing a review of French socialism and German philosophy, the *Deutsch-französische Jahrbücher*, using Fröbel, who set up a branch in Paris, as publisher. All three – Marx, Ruge and Fröbel – had had their careers in German journalism cut short for political reasons, forcing them to consider various schemes to work abroad. By working in Paris they came increasingly into contact with a political radicalism that was more intensely revolutionary, more communistic and more concerned with the small but growing industrial working class than the politics they were accustomed to in Germany.

By the summer of 1843 Engels was deep in the study of political economy, economic history and class-politics in England. This heady combination of interests for a Young Hegelian communist had been foreshadowed in his articles for the *Rheinische Zeitung* of late 1842 and was then pursued methodically in its brief reincarnation in the *Deutsch-französische Jahrbücher*. The double number, the first and only issue of the journal, was published in February 1844, and it contained an article 'Umrisse zu einer Kritik der National-ökonomie' ('Outlines of a Critique of Political Economy'). This was proudly signed 'Friedrich Engels in Manchester', the first significant work written for a German audience to appear under his own name. The long article drew together his views on the political economy of industrial society, his criticisms of the terms in which the classic works of economic theory were written, and his conclusions concerning the proper and likely course of development in European class-politics.

Although Engels had corresponded with Fröbel and met his associate Herwegh on a visit to Ostend in August, the most likely source for the commission to write for the *Deutsch-französische Jahrbücher* was Hess, who was regularly in contact with Ruge, Marx and Fröbel, and who probably approached Engels by letter in September, asking him to be a fellow contributor. Hess was the Young Hegelian best versed in the 'social question' as it was developing in industrial society, and the keenest to pursue the theories in political economy which purported to excuse, ameliorate or dispense with it. The 'Outlines of a Critique of Political Economy' was written by Engels in the autumn of 1843 and dispatched to Marx and Ruge in Paris in very late December or early January, just before the *Deutsch-französische Jahrbücher* was published. Engels's work on political economy was a highly orchestrated Young Hegelian critique, firmly grounded in analytical premises and methods established in his earlier writings, but making a forceful argument for communism (I/3-A MEGA² 689–93, 699–703, 1109–14, *contra* III/1-A 604).

As a communist Engels questioned the validity of private property. He argued that in economic science, as in the contemporary industrial economy, private property was central, and that it necessarily presupposed competition. For Engels competition was isolating and immoral, a danger to civilized values in the community and in the family. Moreover the competitive practice of modern commercial society obscured the fundamental relationship between consumption goods, the very stuff of human life, and the productivity of human labour, the capacity to produce goods of any sort. By contrast, in a communist society, a society worthy of the human potential as communists portrayed it, competition amongst individuals would give way to a calculation of the common good by the community: 'The community will have to calculate what it can produce with the means at its disposal; and in accordance with the relationship of this productive power to the mass of consumers it will determine how far it has to raise or lower production, how far it has to give way to, or curtail, luxury.' To bolster this case Engels argued, firstly, that theories of competition contained numerous contradictions, and communism was to be their logical resolution. And secondly, he argued that currently developing social conditions made a communist revolution politically possible.

For Engels there was no way of reconciling private interest and public good in competitive practice, as individual interests were always diametrically opposed, and moreover there was no way of making this opposition morally palatable. A theory of human relationships founded on the rightness of competition was in truth the deepest degradation of humankind, a hideous blasphemy against nature and humanity:

> In other words, because private property isolates everyone in his own crude solitariness, and because, nevertheless, everyone has the same interest as his neighbour, one landowner stands antagonistically confronted by another, one capitalist by another, one worker by another. In this discord of identical interests resulting precisely from this identity is consummated the immorality of mankind's condition hitherto; and this consummation is competition.

Moreover under a system of competition and incipient monopoly, labour's share in production, so Engels argued, would always be inferior to the shares of land and capital. Workers had to struggle for their very means of subsistence, whilst landowners and capitalists, who could live for a time on their resources, were somewhat better insulated from competitive pressures. Then, as ownership of resources became concentrated in fewer hands, the strength of capital and land would increase relative to labour, and the rate of concentration would accelerate.

Thus Engels predicted that pressure on employment would

grow as workers were attracted from subsistence agriculture into the market, and indeed he argued that workers were in fact supplied through population growth to meet the industrial demand for labour. Then he deduced that capitalists and landowners, in order to improve their competitive position in the market, would use new technologies to economize on labour, rather than to increase employment and output for the benefit of everyone in society. Economic crises were of necessity unavoidable, and they would inevitably grow worse.

The workings of the competitive market, far from being a marvel of automatic regulation in everyone's best interests, were in Engels's view, a permanently unhealthy state of affairs. The competitive market necessarily led to trade crises as fluctuations evened out, and paradoxically in equilibrium conditions between supply to the market and effective consumer demand the people starved from sheer abundance:

> The law of competition is that demand and supply always strive to complement each other, and therefore never do so.... [A]s long as you continue to produce ... at the mercy of chance ... each successive crisis is ... bound to impoverish a larger body of small capitalists, and to augment in increasing proportion the numbers of the class who live by labour alone, thus considerably enlarging the mass of labour to be employed (the major problem of our economists) and finally causing a social revolution.

Engels maintained that rigorous adherence to this system would mean the end of trade altogether. In recognition of this logical truth, more elaborate systems of political economy had been developed to disguise the true nature of competitive trade and to allow it to continue, despite the seeds of destruction that were growing within it. The mercantile system had staved off the inevitable to some extent by encouraging nations to balance their trade. But further developments in political economy had merely disguised its central contradiction – the identification of wealth with gold and silver, the root of the mutual destruction inherent in the competition for these precious metals. In so far as riches were identified with an excess of exports over imports, trade had supplanted religion as the impetus for crusades and inquisitions, and thousands of human beings had been slaughtered in warfare:

But in fact there was still the old avarice and selfishness and from time to time this erupted in wars, which in that day were all based on trade jealousy. In these wars it also became evident that trade, like robbery, is based on the law of the strong hand. No scruples whatever were felt about exacting by cunning or violence such treaties as were held to be the most advantageous.

As a Young Hegelian, Engels presumed that there is progress in history towards rationality, and that it was the task of the communist critic to make this plain. He proceeded from a view which, so he said, was universal but purely human. In that way he recalled the Young Hegelian critique of Hegel's philosophy – that it rightly aimed to reveal what is rational in historical experience, but was unfortunately expressed in terms that were metaphysical and quasi-religious. To get the best from Hegel's universalism, any suggestion of supernatural or mysterious entities would have to be stripped away, and humanity restored to its necessarily central place. Otherwise the way that rationality develops in history would remain obscure.

For Engels, as for Hegel, developing rationality in history could be viewed both in theory and in practice, as the two necessarily progressed together. More specifically, developing rationality could be viewed both in economic theory and economic practice, a suggestion made by the Hegelian philosopher von Henning. Just as the Young Hegelians had placed Hegel's philosophy into a context of philosophical progress, in imitation of the way that Hegel himself had treated philosophy up to his own time, so Engels appreciatively surveyed the history of political economy up to the latest developments in communist thought. But just as the Young Hegelians had also taken Hegel's philosophy to be an apology for arbitrary monarchism in contemporary politics, so Engels also took political economy to be an apology for a 'system of licensed fraud' in the contemporary economy. And just as the Young Hegelians had connected Hegel's philosophy with the political practice of conservatives, and the rationality of their own critique with Enlightenment politics, so Engels connected contemporary political economy with the economic practice of the commercial classes, and the rationality of his own critique with the political struggle for communism.

Strikingly Engels subjected the revolutions in philosophical, political and economic theory that had taken place in the eighteenth century to a common analysis, arguing that in all three cases the revolutionaries did not get to the real root of the problems which faced them. Instead they produced antitheses or mere reversals of previous doctrines.

Firstly, in Engels's view, eighteenth-century philosophical materialists had rejected Christian supernaturalism, which humiliated human beings, but had then set up nature as an absolute power confronting humankind. Here his analysis reflected the way Young Hegelians were attempting to construct a purely human point of view by interpreting the supernatural as an alienation of human powers, and by attempting to situate human beings in a non-mysterious natural setting.

Secondly, in politics, according to Engels, eighteenth-century revolutionaries had objected to monarchism, but had not examined the basis of the state. Here he alluded to the descent of the French revolution into the Terror and Napoleonic despotism, and the more recent failures of revolutionary liberals in France and Germany to wrest their states from more or less arbitrary monarchs. These were themes which had occupied him a good deal in his early political journalism.

Finally, and more intriguingly, Engels argued that the eighteenth-century revolution in political economy had produced an outlook that denied the very logical premises on which the theory was constructed. It did this by changing its focus of attention from producer to consumer, by disavowing the 'bloody terror' of mercantilism, and by proclaiming trade to be a bond of friendship and union amongst nations and individuals. Sophistry and hypocrisy in economics were the natural result of the humane spirit of the century, so a supposedly reformed economics attempted to pass itself off as philanthropy.

Moreover Engels made explicit use of the Hegelian dialectic, albeit on Young Hegelian terms. Young Hegelians and their Hegelian predecessors had shared a view that rationality develops in history through contradictions, a development – sometimes referred to as dialectical – of successive negations. Negative forces or tendencies in positive phenomena were thereby considered – despite appearances – to be creative, as it was through such negations that history progressed. Engels attached that notion of dialectic to his criticism of political economy, arguing that the more outrageous the cloak of hypocrisy, the more uncompromising the revelation of truth. After the sham philanthropy of the eighteenth century there had arisen the theories of Thomas Robert Malthus (1766–1834), and in Engels's opinion his work was the crudest, most barbarous theory that had ever existed, a system of despair that gave the lie to beautiful phrases about international cooperation and world citizenship. He identified the premise of Malthusian population theory – that fecundity necessarily outstrips productivity – with the factory system, and he described the factory system as modern slavery, yielding nothing to the inhumanity and cruelty of slavery in the ancient world. In a striking burst of lateral thinking he then argued that crime in industrial societies was pressing on the means of punishment – not on property as such – just as population was pressing on the means of employment – not on subsistence as such. When economic competition allowed industry to develop, a demand for labour led to population growth; when industrial competition allowed unemployment to develop, society was in effect creating a demand for criminals:

> The number of arrests, of criminal cases – indeed, the number of murders, burglaries, petty thefts, etc., for a large town or for a district – can be predicted year by year with unfailing precision, as had been done often enough in England. This regularity proves that crime, too, is governed by competition; that society creates a *demand* for crime which is met by a corresponding *supply*.... How just it is to punish criminals under these circumstances, quite apart from any other considerations, I leave to the judgement of my readers (3 CW 418–43).

Thus the hypocrisy previously introduced into economics would be dissolved when its essential immorality was at last revealed in theory and carried to its highest pitch in practice. Theoretical and practical negations – however horrifying – enabled progress to be made, and for Engels communist theory and practice were necessarily built up from the contradictory logic and contradictory reality of contemporary private property.

In that way Engels argued that the Young Hegelian politics of criticism should be appropriated by communists. As in recent years theology had been decomposed by Young Hegelians into the contradictory concepts blind faith and free philosophy – debates on which the young Engels was exceptionally well informed – so the theory of free trade would be resolved conceptually by communist critics into an inveterate monopolism, on the one hand, and n abolition of private property, on the other. Free-traders would ave the logic of their view exposed to all when the laws of private roperty, which they defended, were fully elaborated in practice nd – thanks to communist analysis – in theory as well. Commun- ts, who argued for the abolition of private property, would be ncreasingly well placed in these economic debates, because their pponents' position would be exposed to all as a sham humanity nd a terrible new barbarism. The inconsistencies and ambiguities f modern political economy would thus dissolve as theoretical vork proceeded – free-traders working away on strictly economic ontroversies, and communists arguing vociferously against the nonopolies that private property permits – so the political issues urrounding the 'social question' would be starkly posed.

Hence Engels argued that communists should gladly concede heir debt to free trade, and admit its justification as a stage in numan development. At the same time, in order to make progress n history and to achieve a more rational form of human society, ommunists would have to expose its utter theoretical and practic- l nullity. Adam Smith (1723–90) had made that task easier, ecause he had departed from purely empirical inquiries and had hus put economic studies on a more scientific footing. He had lone that in *The Wealth of Nations* (London, 1776) by making olitical economy more general and more abstract, drawing back rom the detail of specific problems and the purely national point f view. In that way, Engels suggested, political economy itself was ecoming more responsible for the consequences of the theories it urveyed worldwide, and this new science was ascending to a evel of universal human concern. That, too, was a development in ationality that gave credence to the communist cause.

In Engels's view the judgements of communists must become nore severe as they begin to consider economists nearer and nearer their own time, and they must make these judgements in order to pursue their struggle against the power of private prop- erty:

For while Smith and Malthus found only scattered fragments, the modern economists had the whole system complete before them: the consequences had all been drawn; the contradictions came clearly enough to light; yet they did not come to examining the premises, and still accepted the responsibility for the whole system. The nearer the economists come to the present time, the further they depart from honesty. With every advance of time sophistry necessarily increases, so as to prevent economics from lagging behind the times. This is why [David] *Ricardo* [1772–1823], for instance, is more guilty than *Adam Smith*, and [John Ramsay] *McCulloch* [1789–1864] and [James] *Mill* [1773–1836] more guilty than *Ricardo*.

For Engels the rationality that develops in history was a human rationality identified with science, but in his view science did no exclude morals. The force of his argument clearly relies on the superior status that he accorded to honesty and altruism as rationa principles compared with hypocrisy and selfishness. In the work o the political economists he found irreconcilable contradictions ir social theory, and hypocritical attempts to cover them up.

Engels's outline critique of political economy also drew on his early experience at home of business and industry. From the mutual envy and greed of the merchant class – which he knew intimately from his youth – grew political economy, the theory behind the practice. He associated that science with further recol lections of his upbringing. One of these was the detestable selfishness which he had exposed in his 'Letters from Wuppertal' in which he had accused local factory owners of living comfortably whilst their workers suffered in squalor. Another association between political economy and his early days was the way that the science of enrichment necessarily bore on its metaphorical brow, so he said, the mark of the Beast of the Apocalypse. In that way he turned the hellfire beloved of Wuppertal pietists back on to the prosperous community from whence he came. And his picture of the origins of trade, when people naïvely believed that gold and silver were wealth itself, vividly recalled his contempt for the mill-owners of Barmen and the traders of Bremen: 'The nations faced each other like misers, each clasping to himself with both arms his precious money-bag, eyeing his neighbours with envy and distrust. Every conceivable means was employed to lure from the nations with whom one had commerce as much ready cash as possible, and to retain snugly within the customs-boundary all which had happily been gathered in.'

Engels's Young Hegelian communism promised a great trans formation – the reconciliation of humankind with nature and with itself. In his view this could happen only under the social circum stances created by modern industrialization. Modern industrialization was conceived by him as a stage in the historical development

of rationality and therefore a proper subject for conceptual criticism. Its constituent concepts were expressed in the works of
political economists, though often in a somewhat garbled or
disguised fashion, and his critique was intended to reveal the
correct analysis, so that a true picture of the facts would fall into
place.

Engels's exposure to industrial poverty, revolutionary liberalism,
theological radicalism, Young Hegelian criticism, visionary communism, and economic science had produced a clear result. That
result was a cumulative and well-integrated outlook, one that
presupposed the practicability of sweeping social change, focused
sharply on the 'social question', utilized highly philosophical
methods and claimed to be scientific. Though this application of
philosophy to social science and then to politics was sometimes
abstruse, its abstraction and generality made it intellectually very
powerful.

The outlook of the 23-year-old Engels was thus one of considerable intellectual maturity. Ruge commented to Feuerbach in a letter
of 5 February 1844 that Engels was making himself very useful –
despite his Hegelian style – and that his subject-matter was a
veritable deluge of important material for bone-idle Germans. But
later in a letter of October 1844 Engels admitted to his editor Marx
that only a very few people, to his knowledge, had read the article
on political economy, a circumstance he himself described as
natural enough. One person who had read it, however, was Marx,
and as he did so he prepared a conspectus that prefigured, for the
first time, his own life's work – a critical investigation of the
concepts of private property, trade and value (3 CW 375–6; 38 CW 4;
I/3-A MEGA² 1113; see also MEOUT, *passim*).

IV   ANGLO-GERMAN

Engels's political contacts in England began to include émigré
Germans. In August 1843 he first came into contact with the
League of the Just, a loose organization of political agitators
advocating a republic and a reformed economy in Germany.
Because this was a highly subversive programme, and because on
any realistic view a violent revolution would be necessary to
introduce it, the League was perforce a secret organization dogged
by police spies. Its leading members were not themselves intellec-

tuals like Marx, nor journalists like Engels, but artisans who argued what they imagined was a simple case for social justice. Engels was introduced to a group in London that included Karl Schapper (1812–70), Heinrich Bauer (*c*. 1813 – emigrated to Australia 1851) and Joseph Moll (1813–49). Moll and Schapper had been prosecuted for their part in a communist uprising in Paris in May 1839 and had subsequently exiled themselves again, this time to London. Engels developed links with working-class German communism by beginning an association with these and other members of the League.

During 1843–4 whilst in Manchester Engels broadened his contacts in political journalism to include English newspapers, which were then in the thick of the Chartist campaign, industrial strife and liberal agitation against the Corn Laws. He wrote as a German temporarily resident in England, addressing a much larger and politically more sophisticated public than he had enjoyed with the *Rheinische Zeitung*. His articles covered developments in continental socialism, particularly the visionary schemes of the French utopians and the philosophical critiques of the German communists. These contacts with the socialist press in England brought to the fore his fluent English and put him in touch with major figures in mass politics.

Engels's new associates included members of the editorial group of *The New Moral World*, such as John Watts (1818–87) and the editor George Fleming (d. 1878). This paper was the *Gazette of the Rational Society*, founded in 1834 and originally edited by Robert Owen. Owenite socialism was a rationalistic communitarianism that was not specifically working-class in orientation. During the turbulent early 1840s it was uneasily allied with, and yet distanced from, the Parliamentary reforms proposed by the Chartists and the campaign for better wages and working conditions mounted by strikers. For Owenites Parliamentary reforms and the extended franchise were an insufficient response to the ills of commercial society, but violent demonstrations and strikes were irrational in spirit and divided workers from the middle classes. Engels's attempts to bring continental socialism to the embroiled Owenites were soon noticed in *The Northern Star*, edited by George Harney (1817–97). During May and June 1844 he wrote for this widely circulated Leeds paper, which was then attempting to bring together striking workers, Chartist reformers and Owenite socialists.

(*right*) Friedrich Engels at 19.

(*below, left*) Friedrich Engels, senior, father of the above young man.

(*below, right*) Elisabeth Engels, mother of Friedrich Engels.

4. The Engels house, Barmen, where Friedrich Engels was born in 1820.

5. View of Lower Barmen, 1832.

Friedrich Engels, 1845.

7. Engels's 1842 caricature of 'The Free', the Berlin group of Young Hegelians, identified by him as Ruge, Buhl, Nauwerck, Bruno Bauer, Wigand, Edgar Bauer, Stirner, Meyen, stranger, Köppen.

8. Engels's caricature of himself, December 1840. 'I was furious because the cigar would not draw.'

9. Engels's caricature of himself, August 1840. 'My hammock, containing myself smoking a cigar.'

10. Cartoons by Engels, June 1839 (*left to right*): World-weariness; Modern Stress and Strain; (*above*) Discord of Cologne; the Noble Modern Materialism; (*below*) Emancipation of Women; Spirit of the Times; Emancipation of the Flesh.

11.   Friedrich Engels, 1865.

The Chetham Library, Manchester, 1870.

13. (*left*) Friedrich Engels in mid-life.

14. Helene Demuth, servant to the Marx family and later housekeeper to Friedrich Engels.

15. (*right*) Lydia 'Lizzy' Burns, briefly Mrs Friedrich Engels.

16. Louise Kautsky-Freyberger, last housekeeper to Friedrich Engels.

17. Friedrich Engels, 1880.

18. Friedrich Engels, 1890.

19. Friedrich Engels, *c.* 1895 (the year of his death).

For Engels the communist outlook transcended nationalism and national boundaries, but as a political agent he was a German, oriented towards Germans and German political development. In that role he sometimes advised others – generally in their own languages – about the international development of communism, especially communist theory in which Germans had been especially progressive. In particular he advised English readers on 3 February 1844 of the forthcoming *Deutsch-französische Jahrbücher*, edited by Dr Ruge and Dr Marx. Moreover his writing for the English press continued after he returned to the Continent in August 1844, and whilst in Germany during the next year he also used the English press as a source for articles to inform Germans about socialism in England. In this journalism Engels, who once signed himself 'Anglo-German' and used other variations on that theme to sign his articles, was keen to report details of industrial unrest on the continent to readers in England, and to communicate the latest news of working-class agitation in England to continental communists. In his view the distinction between socialists and communists, in Germany anyway, was that socialism meant only the vague, undefined and undefinable imaginations of those who could see that something had to be done about private property, but who could not yet make up their minds – as communists supposedly had – to go the whole length of the community system (I/3-A MEGA² 694–9, 706–8; 3 CW 416; 4 CW 241).

Engels's signed article 'Progress of Social Reform on the Continent' appeared in *The New Moral World* on 4 November 1843, and in it he promised a reconciliation of such minor differences as there were between the socialist movements in England, France and Germany. Those minor differences arose, in his view, from the different origins of the socialist movements in each country. English socialism had developed from practical concerns, which were chiefly with industrialization and the immiseration of workers. French socialism had grown out of political concerns with liberty and rights, which expanded to include economic equality. And German socialism was proceeding from first principles, which led philosophically to communism. English readers were also advised by Engels that there were expanding communist movements in numerous other European countries. These were movements distinct from less radical organizations for social reform, on the one hand, and from out-and-out utopian schemes to start society afresh, on the other.

Engels subjected communist writers and movements to critical scrutiny, drawing his judgements from two axioms. The first was the absolute evil of private property and the necessity for any communist society to abolish it totally. In its place they would erect a rational scheme through which to organise the production and distribution of resources. The second was an absolute endorsement of democracy and the liberty of the individual, extending from the economic realm to political institutions and even to marriage, education and the treatment of the aged. In a phrase communists were radical anti-proprietarians and highly principled atheists.

Engels promised his readers another article spelling out his own communist system, but this was never fulfilled at any length. In a subsequent short article of 13 January 1844 he appeared to favour some of the proposals of Wilhelm Weitling (1808–71), an artisan generally credited with being the first German communist and the leader of the League of the Just in its earliest days. Weitling's first influential writings began to appear in 1838, and his later works included, according to Engels, some noteworthy suggestions – superior to those of the French utopians – on how a communist society could be run:

> The abolition of all government by force and by majority, and the establishment in its stead of a mere administration, organising the different branches of labour, and distributing its produce . . . [the nomination of] all officers of this administration, and in every particular Branch, not by a majority of the community at large, but by those only who have a knowledge of the particular kind of work the future officer has to perform; and, one of the most important features of the plan, that the nominators are to select the fittest person, by means of some kind of prize essays (3 CW 413; 4 CW 213).

In an article written for German readers immediately after his return from England, Engels defended at length some of the many experimental communist communities founded in Europe and America, drawing his material from press reports. Amongst the associations picked out for praise were the Rappites of Pennsylvania, whose rules were quoted by Engels without criticism, and so with some measure of approval:

1. Each member surrenders all his possessions to the community, without gaining any privileges from this. All are equal within the community.
2. The laws and regulations of the society are equally binding on all.
3. Each member works only for the benefit of the whole society and not each for himself alone.
4. Whoever leaves the society has no claim to compensation for his work, but is given back everything he put in; and those who have put nothing in and depart in peace and friendship receive a parting gratuity.
5. In exchange the community undertakes to provide each member and his family with the necessities of life and the necessary care in sickness and old age, and if the parents die or withdraw, leaving their children behind, the community will bring up these children.

Engels argued pragmatically that the systems of communism variously worked out by different communities proved that communism – social existence and activity based on community of goods – was entirely feasible, given the way that modern technology had been harnessed to perform tasks that humans found unpleasant and the way that it had developed human productivity to the point where riches and abundance outstripped what people could consume.

Engels's overall strategy as a German communist was clear. Firstly, he disavowed the religious character of American and French socialism and described the current contributions of French theorists to the cause as necessarily limited. Secondly, he argued that the chances for a communist party amongst the educated classes of society were greater in Germany than elsewhere, because the Germans were a philosophical nation. Their own philosophical tradition, so he announced, had reached its culmination just as the Young Hegelians were resolving their philosophical enquiries in a theory of communism. In his view they would soon be joined by workers, to whom the social question mattered most. Clearly he expected industrial unrest to create working-class agitation for communism and to provide the opportunity for allying working-class strikers and communists to middle-class liberals and socialists. He argued that communism was developing

internationally as a common struggle against a common complaint
– the factory system – and that communism represented a solution
to the 'social question' for middle classes and working classes
alike. And thirdly, Engels praised the English socialists for their
concern with the facts of the present state of society, noting that
Germans had a great deal to learn from their work. Indeed he had
already embarked upon such studies himself, and on his return to
the continent he announced to English readers that he had formed
an association with Hess. The two communists planned a German
periodical (to be published in Elberfeld) that would 'contain facts
only, showing the state of civilised society'. According to Engels
they would argue the necessity of a radical reform and preach this
to the world through 'the eloquence of facts' (3 CW 392–408; 4 CW
213, 214–15, 218, 227, 230, 235, 240).

V   'THE ELOQUENCE OF FACTS'

The autumn of 1843 proved to be a remarkable period in Engels'
life, notably because his work advanced on three fronts at once.
Over the months from late September to late December he wrote
three rather different works. One was the highly original Young
Hegelian 'Outlines of a Critique of Political Economy' for the
Deutsch-französische Jahrbücher, which promoted the communist
case against industrial society to an audience of German intellectuals. For the English popular press he wrote the 'Progress of
Social Reform on the Continent', suggesting that the English were
behind continental socialists in theoretical terms but ahead in their
factual investigations into its effects on industrial workers. And as
a companion to the theoretical work in the *Deutsch-französische
Jahrbücher*, he contributed a review of *Past and Present* by Thomas
Carlyle (1795–1881), just published in April 1843 as a book and then
excerpted in *The New Moral World* between August and November.
This review was the opening instalment of Engels's own research
into the contemporary factory system and the historical development of industrial society. His choice of English conditions as his
object for research and his use of English sources mark this as a
considerable advance on the 'Letters from Wuppertal', which in
any case predated his exposure to socialism, communism and
political economy.

The review of Carlyle, addressed to German intellectuals, was he beginning of a projected series of articles on 'The Condition of ngland'. Carlyle's vivid and deeply-felt indictment of the factory ystem and laissez-faire economics provided Engels with useful naterials to relay to German readers, who could respect Carlyle as n intellectual with interests somewhat akin to their own. Indeed arlyle, a biographer of Schiller and translator of Goethe, was nstrumental in bringing German literature to an English audience, s Engels reminded his readers in the *Deutsch-französische Jahr- ücher*. Moreover Carlyle's crippling deficiency – lack of acquaint- nce with German philosophy – was one which Engels could use ɔ interest and flatter his audience. His criticisms of Carlyle's noralism, medievalism and pantheism, and the political conclu- ions which followed from them, were also useful in warning German intellectuals off similar vices.

Because the *Deutsch-französische Jahrbücher* collapsed after the rst double number, Engels's further work of early 1844 on 'The ondition of England' was held over by Ruge and Marx whilst they egotiated another outlet for themselves and their associates. Two rticles in Engels's series on England – 'The Eighteenth Century' nd 'The English Constitution' – finally appeared in the autumn of 844 in *Vorwärts*, a radical German-language paper edited in Paris. ɔver the summer of 1844 the influence of a communist circle ecame predominant amongst the editorial collective of *Vorwärts* vhich included, amongst others, Marx, Heine, Herwegh and akunin. Engels himself was probably involved with the group vhilst he was on the scene for ten days in late August and early eptember, and some of the figures in the Paris section of the eague of the Just, such as August Ewerbeck (1816–60), were also ssociated with it.

The political strategy behind Engels's critical history of indus- rialization was clear enough – middle-class Germans, artisans and actory workers alike, were to take notice of their future and act on his information. For Engels communist conclusions were acces- ible from philosophy as well as from experience, so his rationalistic pproach to a revolutionary remaking of society was inherently riented towards a broad, popular front. This movement was to ght for democratic reforms of the political system in the first nstance and to move on directly to the 'social question', for which ommunism was the ultimate resolution. Engels expected demo- racy to progress further and faster in England than in France ecause of the thorough-going social revolution wrought by

industry, and he sketched a model of democratic political develop
ment as follows:

> The democratic party originated at the same time as the indust
> rial revolution. . . . As in France, the democrats were exclusively
> men with a philosophical education, but they soon found tha
> the upper and middle classes were opposed to them and only
> the working class lent a ready ear to their principles. Amongst
> the latter class they soon founded a party, which by 1794 was
> already fairly strong and yet still only strong enough to act by fits
> and starts. From 1797 to 1816 it disappeared from view; in the
> turbulent years from 1816 to 1823 it was again very active bu
> then subsided once more into inactivity until the July revolution
> From then on it has maintained its importance alongside the old
> parties and is making steady progress.

Though he supported democratic politics, indeed the whol
process of democratization in England, France, Germany o
wherever, Engels also viewed democracy as distinctly limited in
what it could achieve with respect to the 'social question':

> But democracy by itself is not capable of curing social ills
> Democratic equality is a chimera, the fight of the poor against
> the rich cannot be fought out on a basis of democracy or indeed
> of politics as a whole. This stage too is thus only a transition, th
> last purely political remedy which has still to be tried and from
> which a new element is bound to develop at once, a principl
> transcending everything of a political nature.
>   This principle is the principle of socialism.

The elimination of religious appeals from both kinds of approac
– philosophical arguments for intellectuals and factual argument
for others – was crucial to Engels's outlook. Indeed his intellectu
strength derives to a large extent from his conviction that argu
ments from first principles were more convincing, not less, whe
they proceeded from atheism and applied a dialectical logic t
human experience. But there was a certain political weakness i
his conviction that arguments from fact could persuade ordinar
readers as effectively as the religious enthusiasm so common, an
so astoundingly influential, in the early nineteenth century (3 CW
487, 513; 38 CW 28; I/3-A MEGA^2 703–5).

Work on 'The Condition of England' grew into Engels's first full-length book *Die Lage der arbeitenden Klasse in England* (*The Condition of the Working Class in England*), published in 1845, and arguably his masterpiece. In effect this study combined his plans for a social history of England with his intention to make a thorough investigation of the contemporary factory system, though he saw these as separate projects at the time. He wrote the book from notes and other materials between mid-September 1844 and March 1845 whilst back home in Barmen, and it was published in early June under his own name. Thus *The Condition of the Working Class in England* was written before he began to work extensively with Marx, and indeed the young author may have delayed moving abroad to join his communist contacts until the book was completed. He felt that his talents were best utilized on the book and on other German activities, and commented that the Paris communists were doing well enough on their own. He wrote to Marx on 19 November 1844 about the political character of his project, showing how the work was intended to convey the same message of communism to both his German and his English audiences:

I shall be presenting the English with a fine bill of indictment; I accuse the English bourgeoisie before the entire world of murder, robbery and other crimes on a massive scale, and I am writing an English preface which I shall have printed separately and sent to English party leaders, men of letters and members of Parliament. That'll give those fellows something to remember me by. It need hardly be said that my blows . . . are meant for . . . the German bourgeoisie, to whom I make it plain enough that they are as bad as their English counterparts (38 CW 9–11).

Indeed Engels's attack on the English middle classes was razor-sharp. In his special preface he accused them of authorizing parliamentary inquiries into working conditions in industry but leaving these reports hypocritically 'in ever-lasting slumber among heaps of waste paper on the shelves of the Home Office'. Never had the ruling middle classes authorized a readable book from which ordinary people could get information on the degrading circumstances in which many 'free-born Britons' found themselves. The English middle classes exemplified the wholesale selfishness that he had identified as the root of market rela-

tionships in his 'Outlines of a Critique of Political Economy'. They
manifested this in their nationalistic prejudices and their profit
taking from the labour of others. For Engels this was an 'indirect
trade in human flesh'. Despite protestations of concern and bouts
of ineffectual philanthropy, the English middle classes intended
nothing else but to get rich on the labour of working people, and to
abandon them to starvation as soon as profits dried up.

Engels also advertised his research as an eyewitness account
because he had abandoned 'the port-wine and champaign [*sic*] of
the middle classes', their 'fashionable talk and tiresome etiquette'
in order to observe workers in their everyday lives. This personal
approach was founded on his view that there is a 'great and
universal family of mankind, who know their interest and that of
all the human race to be the same'. This family included everyone
earnestly pursuing human progress and making common cause
with humanity. Though technically a foreigner, Engels argued that
he spoke plain English and was in fact no stranger to working
people anywhere. Thus his work was founded on the Young
Hegelian philosophy of rational progress through historical contradictions. This was then politicized in his theory of the contemporary class struggle, and personalized in a programme of practical
activity – research, publication and direct contact.

In a preface for German readers Engels explained why he
thought a study of the English working classes to be of contemporary political interest. Firstly he suggested that Germans, whether
communists or reformers, were preoccupied with theory and
ill-informed about fact, so a study of conditions in England was at
least a model for similar work in Germany. Secondly he argued
that the root causes of oppression in England were also in
existence in Germany and that in the long run the same result
would ensue. Finally he averred that his factual study was not
merely of political interest – it had a dual political purpose. It
would provide a sound basis for socialist theories and judgements
and it would put an end to sentimental dreams and utopian
fancies. Engels clearly defined himself as a Young Hegelian communist working to merge science with philosophy, theory with
practice, writing with politics, intellectuals with workers, and
future progress with present fact (4 CW 297–305).

The originality of *The Condition of the Working Class in England* lies
in Engels's attempt to realize Hess's European Triarchy through
transformation of liberal politics. Factual material was selectively

quoted, sometimes hurriedly, in support of broad generalizations linking the industrial revolution in England to the political revolution in France – for the benefit of readers in Germany. Perhaps the best way to judge the book today is as a political tract, which is of course the view that the author himself had of it. His political project was extraordinarily ambitious in that it encompassed the principal powers in European politics: 'The industrial revolution is of the same importance for England as the political revolution for France, and the philosophical revolution for Germany; and the difference between England in 1760 and in 1844 is at least as great as that between France under the *ancien régime* and during the revolution of July [1830]' (4 CW 320).

The mightiest result of this industrial transformation, according to Engels, was the English proletariat, from whom he expected world-historical actions in the very near future. He predicted, as he had in his 'Outlines of a Critique of Political Economy', that English industry would expand, that the proletariat would increase in geometrical proportion and that commercial crises would grow more violent. The working classes would eventually embrace the whole nation, with the exception of a few millionaires. But even before economic development reached that late stage, there would come a point at which the proletariat could well perceive how easily existing power might be overthrown, and a revolution would ensue. Only one more commercial crisis, which he predicted for the early 1850s, would be necessary to drive the proletarians to despair, and then the people's vengeance would descend with a wrath 'of which the rage of 1793 gives no true idea'. He was clearly anticipating a re-run of the French revolution on economic, rather than merely political terms, and he commented that the war of the poor against the rich would be the bloodiest ever waged. But he also argued that in proportion as the proletariat absorbed socialism and communism, so the revolution would diminish in savagery. In making this claim he discounted any middle-class tendency to ameliorate the economic circumstances of the working classes, and argued instead that the prospects for peaceful change depended on communists themselves. The 'communistic party', building on intelligent comprehension of the social question amongst the proletariat, would exert its influence in order to conquer the brutal element in the forthcoming social revolution. Communists, according to Engels, saw the present class struggle in the context of humanity as a whole and did not regard world revolution as a way to settle personal scores (4 CW 307–23, 580–3).

Engels promoted this stirring political message with a combination of abstract economic theory and vivid reporting. Much of the book consists of generalizations and analysis drawn from horrors such as this:

> On the occasion of an inquest held Nov. 16th, 1843, by Mr. Carter, coroner for Surrey, on the body of Ann Galway, aged 45 years, the newspapers related the following particulars concerning the deceased: She had lived ... with her husband and a nineteen-year-old son in a little room, in which neither a bedstead nor any other furniture was to be seen. She lay dead beside her son upon a heap of feathers which were scattered over her almost naked body, there being neither sheet nor coverlet. The feathers stuck so fast over the whole body that the physician could not examine the corpse until it was cleansed, and then found it starved and scarred from the bites of vermin. Part of the floor of the room was torn up, and the hole used by the family as a privy.

and this:

> The coal-mine is the scene of a multitude of the most terrifying calamities, and these come directly from the selfishness of the bourgeoisie. The hydrocarbon gas which develops so freely in these mines, forms ... an explosive ... and kills every one within its reach. ... Further, every few days the roof of a working falls in, and buries or mangles the workers employed in it. ... All these accidents ... carry off yearly, according to the *Mining Journal* [of 9 September 1843], some fourteen hundred human beings.

Engels admitted that there were numerous counter-examples to his generalizations, but argued that the truth of the situation was clear-cut, not least because under a competitive system everyone's well-being was at risk. For some the risk was much greater and the consequences even more serious than for others: 'I know very well that ten are somewhat better off, where one is so totally trodden under foot by society; but I assert that thousands of industrious and worthy people ... find themselves in a condition unworthy of human beings; and that every proletarian ... is exposed to a similar fate without any fault of his own and in spite of every possible effort' (4 CW 334–5, 537–8).

Amongst Engels's foremost academic critics are W.O. Henderson and W.H. Chaloner, who argue in an introduction to their own translation of *The Condition of the Working Class in England* that Engels was 'a young man in a bad temper who vented his spleen in a passionate denunciation of the factory system'. They criticize him for 'unrestrained violence' in his language and a 'complete failure to understand any point of view different from his own'. In partial explanation they suggest that he had conceived 'a bitter hatred' of capitalists through his early life and circumstances in Barmen and was therefore suffering from acute frustration with having to live at home over the winter of 1844–5. In my view these conclusions trivialize Engels's early experiences and achievements, and suggest quite wrongly that his work is meaningless abuse. The brief commentary by Alan Gilbert in his book on Marx's politics is far more to the point. Steven Marcus is a much more sympathetic critic, but he also complains of Engels's inability to give the middle classes 'a fair shake', just as Henderson and Chaloner remark that 'as far as Engels was concerned no employer was ever in the right and the factory owner was always the villain of the piece'.

Engels's claim that he could establish communist conclusions through 'the eloquence of facts' obviously needs careful examination. His acceptance of proletarian communism was grounded in a conviction that the essential human enterprise was to make rationality unfold in history, and that this development would take place through the contradictions of class conflict. Such beliefs about humanity and its mission in the world rested on 'undeniable facts, partly of historical development, partly facts inherent in human nature'. For Engels these were just as real as the specific facts recounted in his eyewitness reports on the proletariat. Contrary to Marcus's claim that he set the realities of life over against mere abstract knowledge, the two forms of knowledge were marshalled together in his tract.

Thus Engels believed that workers were in fact the victims of their employers, that communism was in fact the resolution of the class struggle, and that human progress was in fact political action towards this goal. Charges of inaccuracy and wish-fulfilment do not overturn the case for communism that Engels offered, because his view of what constitutes a fact is significantly different from that of his critics. For that reason a successful attack on Engels's conclusions would have to challenge his premises – a Young Hegelian understanding of the human experience – and his method – an analysis of Hegelian contradictions. Engels is highly vulnerable, but so far his critics have not made much impression. The fault in Engels's work is that Young Hegelian premises and Hegelian methodology are presumed to be valid, and very little in the way of argument is offered to persuade the sceptic. As a political philosopher Engels was not doing much better than preaching to the converted.

Engels's critics also attack him for poor political advice. Marcus argues that he contradicts himself by claiming that the middle classes cannot be blamed as individuals for their role in oppressing workers, but that workers ought to be outraged at middle-class indifference to their plight. But for Engels communist political action would necessarily be the work of individuals, both working-class and middle-class. Their motivation would arise from a conviction that the system as a whole was blameworthy. Thus in Engels's view individuals have choices and are responsible for their actions, but praise and blame for individual actions is inadequate as a platform for communist politics. However, it must be admitted that with such a rationalistic and individualistic message Engels found it difficult to attract many new adherents to his cause (M 70 n, 92–3, 115, 137–9, 145, 178, 198–9, 217–18, 232–4, 237–9; COND xxiii–xxiv, xxvii–xxx; 1 H 69–73; MP 50–9).

The Condition of the Working Class in England received mixed reviews in Germany and Russia, and was the subject of academic and political controversy. Uniquely amongst Engels's early works it was reprinted within a few years of publication. Because it was a full-length book, rather than a brief article, it consolidated his reputation, and it has been widely circulated from the 1880s to the present.

5

Personal and Political

In early 1845 Engels was 24 and apparently a young man with the world before him. As it happens, however, the pattern for his life over the next fifty years was largely in place. He could not have been aware of this, and indeed his experiences and career did not follow an inevitable course. But in retrospect it is remarkable how clearly his life and thought were prefigured in the events so far considered.

Engels was now enmeshed in a number of ambiguous activities and relationships. He maintained a relationship with his family that included large elements of economic support and personal strain. His sexual affairs with women were neither completely committed nor wholly casual. He had a lifestyle that combined, albeit uneasily, bourgeois tastes and proletarian sentiments. Although already brilliant and successful in radical circles, he had just attached himself to the little-known Marx. His advocacy of political action figured far more largely in his life than the sort of action that he was advocating.

In this chapter we shall be examining the major personal relationships of Engels's life and exploring the way they inter-relate with his political career. In fact the personal context is the one in which his life as politician and theorist was conducted, so I cover this material chronologically from 1845 up to his last years in the present chapter, in order to 'nest' my account of his political work in chapters 6 and 7 within his life as he actually lived it. Once he left his family in Barmen, Engels's domestic and political world were in a certain sense the same, in that his intimates were chosen precisely because they were politically sympathetic. For that reason they were not part of his public activities 'at work', as business at Ermen and Engels was the political antithesis of the communism pursued 'at home'.

Thus the central questions for this chapter are:

What constraints – financial and emotional – were imposed on

Engels by his continuing relationship with the Engels clan?
What bearing do his relationships with women, notably the
Burns sisters, have on our understanding of his character and
political thought?
What was Engels's relationship with the Marx family, and how
did it affect his life?

I   SON AND BROTHER

Engels's communist convictions, his writing and his political
associations strained his familial ties considerably. Indeed his
whole outlook was an attack on the way family relationships were
traditionally conceived in certain respects. Writing to Marx from
Barmen at the beginning of October 1844 he commented on
Elberfeld communists who had begun to revolutionize their family
lives. According to Engels the communists lectured their elders
whenever they tried to act the aristocrat over the servants or
workmen – 'and that's saying a great deal in patriarchal Elberfeld',
he wrote. From the family's point of view he was merely returning
to hearth and firm after a spell of working abroad, improving his
knowledge of the trade before pursuing further his career in
business, acting the dutiful son and brother, and possibly getting
married. From his own point of view he was forced back home for
economic reasons, but he planned to make the best use of his time
by working on *The Condition of the Working Class in England*. This
meant spreading communism locally and raising what money he
could for the cause, including money from his father for his own
maintenance. It soon became apparent that he would have to
spend more than a few weeks in Germany enduring his family, but
in turn he sought to make himself so unendurable to them that
they would eventually pension him off with an allowance. There is
no sign of any other strategy on Engels's part, and this is in fact
what happened after six months. Father and son did not conceive
of their financial relationship in the same terms, however, as for
Engels senior the threat of non-payment was a central element in
his strategy for Friedrich's moral renewal. By contrast Friedrich
gloated that his father was obliged to keep him 'primed' and
objected strongly to his 'old man's' moral blackmail. The young
Engels simply wanted funds with the minimum of fuss, and this is

the keynote of his personal and economic relationships with the Engels clan (38 CW 3–4, 22).

Unsurprisingly the worst problems for the 24-year-old Engels whilst he was living at home were boredom and his parents. He complained that there was never any opportunity for high spirits and that he was instead stuck with an uneventful existence, replete with godliness and respectability, working on his book in his room and hardly ever going out. Moreover he had allowed himself to be persuaded by his parents to have another go at business, which he referred to as 'huckstering' (*Schacher*). In January 1845 he wrote to Marx that he wanted out by Easter, as an enervating existence in his dyed-in-the-wool Christian–Prussian family was intolerable, and he might end up by importing philistinism into communism in spite of himself. A few heartfelt lines then defined not only his immediate circumstances but also the central contradiction of his life: 'huckstering is too beastly ... most beastly of all is the fact of being, not only a bourgeois, but actually a manufacturer, a bourgeois who actively takes sides against the proletariat. A few days in my old man's factory have sufficed to bring me face to face with this beastliness, which I had rather overlooked.'

Engels had planned to stay in business only as long as it suited him, then to write something offensive to the police and make off across the border into France. But working on his book, recording daily the most horrifying tales about English society, had caused his rage to rise to boiling point. Perhaps he could have maintained the outward appearance of a bourgeois and a 'brutish' huckster, if he had not been writing. But as it was, he felt he could not carry on communist propaganda on a large scale and at the same time engage in industry. But whether existing on an uncertain allowance, as he did during his communist sojourns in the remainder of the 1840s, working for his family in Manchester as he did in the 1850s and 1860s, or living on investments as he did afterwards in retirement in London, he was burdened with circumstances that he found inconsistent, embarrassing and hard to bear (38 CW 19–20).

By March 1845 Friedrich senior had evidently agreed on some compromise form of words whereby he would support his eccentric son's studies, in some vague sense, but not his communist aims – as if the two, on young Friedrich's terms, could be disentangled. It is certainly difficult to imagine exactly what else the elder Engels thought his son might be planning to study when he departed in early April for Brussels in order to join Marx and his communist associates, recently expelled from Paris on suspicion of political subversion.

Engels's last days at home in Barmen were, in his own words, 'a real dog's life'. His sketch of familial relations portrayed a situation that never improved, as both sides preserved the outward civilities and never let the underlying conflicts cause a definitive breakdown. Indeed they rather prided themselves on keeping silent when the issues that really divided them threatened to come up. In correspondence with Marx, Engels objected particularly to his 'old man's' religious fanaticism, to his bigotry and despotism and to his hold over his wife. He found his father stupid, because he lumped communism and liberalism together as revolutionary and then blamed young Friedrich 'for the infamies perpetrated by the English *bourgeoisie* in Parliament'. But Engels also commented that he really loved his mother, who had a rare fund of humanity, though she showed no independence whatever towards his father. She was constantly fretting and making herself ill with headaches through worrying about her eldest son. But the family as a whole was excoriated by Engels for their aggressive piety: 'I can't eat, drink, sleep, let out a fart, without being confronted by this same accursed lamb-of-God expression ... today the whole tribe went toddling off to Communion ... this morning the doleful expressions surpassed themselves.'

A late-night session on communism with Hess resulted in long faces over his late return and hints that he might have been in gaol. When it was discovered that he had been with Hess there was a pause, then intensified Christian dismay and *sighs* – enough to drive one mad, Engels reported to Marx. The worst was that 'these people ... positively *want* to flay and torture themselves with their infernal fantasies' and were immune to 'the most platitudinous principles of justice' (38 CW 25, 29–30).

Earlier on Engels had had more hope for his family, certain members at least. In his article 'Rapid Progress of Communism in Germany' for *The New Moral World*, written in late 1844 shortly after arriving in Barmen, he had advised his English readers that amongst his own family, which he described as very pious and loyal, he could count six or more communists, each of whom had been converted without being influenced by the remainder. His sister Marie was then engaged to Emil Blank, a London merchant and friend of Ewerbeck – of the League of the Just. Emil was thereafter a soft touch for loans when circumstances intervened between Engels and his Barmen remittances. Emil's brother Wilhelm, who had been Engels's schoolfriend, Engels's own brother Hermann, and other old friends such as Richard Roth featured in a list of sympathizers, but it is difficult to see who else Engels had in mind as communist conversions amongst his family. None of these conversions, if indeed they were more than passing sympathies, was a commitment anything like his own. In a letter to Marx of 1856, ten years later, Engels described Emil Blank as naïve, but 'a good chap, communist of principle, bourgeois out of interest', who always used *'we'* when referring to communist matters. But it is unclear whether he was paying Blank a compliment or complaining about his presumptuousness (4 CW 231; 38 CW 5–6; 40 CW 65).

After Engels left the Wuppertal for what became a life of exile – broken only by temporary residence in Germany during the revolutionary months of 1848–9 – his family no longer featured as sympathetic figures in his communist career. After the revolutionary rising of February 1848 against King Louis Philippe and the establishment of the Second Republic in France, insurrections broke out in Germany and Austria, and the communist exiles made their way back to aid the struggle. Engels then collaborated with Marx on his paper the *Neue Rheinische Zeitung* – a self-styled 'organ of democracy' – which he edited from Cologne. In the autumn conservative forces mounted an offensive against revolutionary democrats in the Rhineland, publication of the paper was suspended for two weeks, and Engels fled abroad to Belgium, then France and Switzerland.

Engels's overtly revolutionary activities then brought a rare outburst of plain speaking from within the family group. Letters from his mother followed him on his peregrinations, which had necessarily interrupted the flow of funds, some of which – in Marx's eyes – were destined for the ailing newspaper. 'Now you have really gone too far', Engels's mother wrote in October, 'you have paid more heed to other people, to strangers, and have taken no account of your mother's pleas'. Elisabeth Engels had picked up a Rhineland paper, the *Kölnische Zeitung*, and had found in it a notice of the warrant for her son's arrest. Her letter was deeply maternal – 'I often see you as a little boy still, playing near me. How happy I used to be then and what hopes did I not pin upon you.'

And it was also firmly practical, in the family tradition, suggesting to Engels that since he was now separated from his friends he should reconsider his position, consent once again to be her child and 'walk the same path with us' – by going to America and finding work with a good firm.

From a letter of 5 December it is apparent that Engels's father had threatened to cut him off unless he took up the American option, and his mother said that she agreed with this plan. If he were in fact deprived of funds, she hoped that he would find something else to do in order to make a living, since it was self-evident to her that revolutionary communism was not a viable mode of life. Having rebuked Friedrich for unreasonably expecting prompt remittances whilst he was travelling – some of the time on foot – Elisabeth Engels moved on to his politics: 'I have learned from a fairly reliable source a thing or two about your plans in Cologne, and I must say that when one plans to build barricades one is not so far from murder.' In previous letters to Friedrich she had related her suspicions that the editors of the *Rheinische Zeitung* were taking advantage of his absence to exclude him from the paper. Indeed Engels's father, who had visited Cologne in Friedrich's absence, seems to have offended Marx and no doubt misrepresented the chief editor's intentions concerning the journalistic collective, as it was clearly in his paternal interests to drive a wedge between his son and his communist associates.

At the conclusion of her letter Elisabeth Engels turned to certain essential aspects of her relationship with Friedrich on which there was no need to hold her peace:

> Now that you have got the money from us, I entreat you to buy yourself a warm overcoat so that you will have it when the weather turns colder, as it soon will; also to provide yourself with drawers and a bed jacket so that you will be warmly clad should you catch a cold, as can very easily happen. I only wish I had occasion to send you some warm socks. Your father, however, thinks it would cost more than they are worth and says I ought to keep them and everything else until you are closer to us again (38 CW 178–9, 181, 540–1, 543–5).

By July 1849 the revolutionary campaigns were over in Germany, and Engels began to make his way to England, which was largely untouched by revolutionary democracy and was as safe a place of exile as could be found within reach of Germany. Marx had made his way there a few months previously with his family, and Engels joined him in dire poverty in London. A year later in November 1850, aged 30, he left for Manchester in some desperation to work for the family firm. By January he reported to Marx that the ever-useful Emil Blank had got rid of the proposed American business-partner, and there would be no further family plots. Indeed the elder Engels had to some extent come to a compromise once again with his errant son. After 'trailing around' Manchester for a week with his 'old man', Engels reported to Marx on 6 July 1851 that he had agreed to steady work at the accounting offices of Ermen and Engels – not at the mill – for at least three years at approximately £200 per annum, with no long-term obligations 'either with regard to my writing, or to my staying here in case of a revolution'.

Engels's 'job' was to keep an eye on his father's partners the Ermen brothers, Gottfried and Peter, who were also running a textile business of their own from the same premises. The elder Engels was obviously concerned that his capital might be going to finance another enterprise in which he had no share, and that his own firm might be cross-subsidizing the one belonging to the Ermens through price manipulation. Friedrich's role was pretty obviously that of a spy, and his contacts with the Ermens veered between mutual suspicion and outright rows. His intention was to make himself indispensable to his father – for financial reasons.

However, relations between father and son were inevitably strained, and it did not take much to set one or the other off. The 'stupid and tactless' Friedrich senior indulged himself in defences of conservative politics in Prussia, and the younger Friedrich, in view of his financial dependency, had to keep his ripostes under control, commenting that a dispassionate business relationship was obviously preferable to any kind of emotional humbug. The arrangement was for Engels to represent his father and to draw an expense allowance, rather than to work for the firm directly. Unsurprisingly this did not go smoothly, as Engels wrote to Marx in September 1851 before even the first year was up: 'I suddenly got a letter from my old man in which he tells me that I'm spending far too much money and must make do with £150. Naturally I shan't stand for this ludicrous imposition, all the less so that it is accompanied by the threat that, if necessary, the Ermens will be instructed not to pay me more than that amount.'

With the help of 'my brother [probably Hermann] and mater', Engels continued, 'I shall be able to settle the matter', but for the time being he would have to retrench, especially since he had already gone through £230 in the year to November 1851 (38 CW 253, 265, 302–3, 378–9, 452).

By mid-1852 Friedrich Engels senior was determined on a change in the Manchester firm. From these negotiations Friedrich junior secured a pay rise and confidential use of funds, and he commented to Marx that the best thing was that he had had to sign nothing at all, since his 'old man' did not trust him on the political score, and rightly so. Loyally Engels seemed to show some real concern about his father's interests and feelings: 'I can arrange to be replaced by one of my brothers in such a way that my old man would lose nothing by my departure save, perhaps, a few illusions, and it would be I, not he, who would be making the sacrifice.' But Engels also observed that, when he could, he was charging things to his father's account with the firm, though in reality these 'extras' were sums going to Marx. His creative accounting also included such schemes as renting cheap lodgings until his father was due to arrive and then – when the 'old man' was on the scene – living as his inflated expenses had indicated.

Ermen and Engels was reorganized in 1852–3, when Friedrich senior bought out Peter Ermen and renewed an arrangement with Gottfried. In April 1854 Engels wrote to Marx about his life at the office in terms that made it seem very like the old days at Consul Leupold's in Bremen, when radical journalism and earthy amusements filled the day far more satisfactorily than doing ledgers and reckoning accounts: 'What with the [newspaper articles I am writing on the Crimean] war . . . sundry drinking bouts, etc., etc., I have of late fallen very much behind with my work at the office and . . . have perpetrated a mass of blunders . . . I shall now have to make up for this, for the very good reason that my old man is coming over in 3 months time' (39 CW 109–10, 148, 283, 437).

By 1855 Engels was taking a share in the firm's profits, but was often short of money. Relations between him and his parents, however, were cordial enough for him to accompany them on a tour of Scotland in September 1859. When his father died from typhoid in 1860 Engels visited Barmen for the first time since his revolutionary travels some eleven years earlier, staying from 23 March to 3 April. After his departure his mother caught the infection as well, and he reported his distress to Marx on 11 May, relating his plans to return urgently to Germany. Settling his father's estate in early 1861 began the process by which he was moved into a partnership in the Manchester firm, rather than into the German business. This was now run by his three brothers Hermann, Emil and Rudolf, who were not keen to have him on board. For the sake of his mother – once again avoiding family rows – he accepted the arrangement, but complained that he had been presented with a *fait accompli* by his younger brothers and denied his rights:

> Not for anything in the world would I contribute in the smallest way towards embittering the evening of your life with family disputes over inheritance. . . . It was extremely disagreeable for me . . . when something I looked upon as a *right* to which I was entitled was lightly passed over for all kinds of reasons . . . my assent being, so to speak, demanded as a matter of course. . . . But having done so, I regard it as settled and you can count on me not to bear any of my brothers the slightest grudge about that.

Engels – then 40 – concluded a letter on this subject with filial thanks to his mother for a dressing-gown she had sent, but commented that the red epaulettes were 'a trifle *outré* for the local taste'.

The business arrangements concocted by his brothers set Engels free very largely from any definite obligations to them, no doubt the object of the exercise in reverse from their point of view. But his partnership in Manchester enmeshed him further with the hated Gottfried Ermen, whom he accused of wanting to take advantage of his recently widowed mother and of himself. 'He had imagined that we in Barmen were urgently in need of money (as to which I enlightened him)', Engels wrote to his brother Emil in April 1860. By 1867 Friedrich was attempting to sever relations with the firm and get his capital out, even threatening to set up in business on his own. It is estimated that he got £12500 in settlement from the firm when he retired in 1869, and that Gottfried had driven a hard bargain, as the Engels share had originally been about £10 000 (40 CW 490; 41 CW 120–1, 138–9, 260, 266; 1 H 195–230).

There is no doubt that Engels had had enough of 'huckstering', and he proposed instead to pursue his communist associations full time, now that his income was assured. Why he bore a distasteful life in commerce for so long is a mystery easily solved. He had very clear ideas how much money he and his dependents needed 'in retirement' and how much capital was required to produce it. The negotiations that successively improved his situation in Ermen and Engels were protracted, and he balanced his increasing years against his chances of securing a better settlement. Eventually the right moment arrived, after which he openly rejoiced in a letter to his mother that 1 July 1869 was 'the first day of my freedom' and that he could think of no better use for it than to write at once to her with details of the settlement. From the previous evening onwards he had become another person and had felt ten years younger. Such joy was no doubt shared in purely personal terms, but it is hard to imagine that Elisabeth Engels had ever seen office work in quite the same light as her son, who wrote rapturously of the open air and his escape from the gloomy warehouse at the age of 48 (32 MEW 615–17).

To his mother Engels had been very loyal, meeting her during the 1860s in Ostend, the family's traditional watering place, and in October 1871 he had urged her to come the following year for a month at Ramsgate, then his favourite spot for sea-bathing. Only an event the size of the Paris Commune of that year brought politics overtly into their correspondence. He suggested that she was once again the victim of the Rhineland press, which had previously decried the patriotic rebels against Napoleon, the 'demagogues' of 1817, the liberals of the 1830s, and of course the '48ers – the very roll-call of progressive politics to which he had attached himself in his early youth. Moreover, so he suggested, the local press had not reported the conservative reprisals taken against the communards, which were viciously bloodthirsty. He then offered the definitive summary of his own political career as he saw it, stressing the continuity in his outlook right back to his days as an unofficial student at Berlin University and pointedly emphasizing the independent origin of his politics:

> You know that I have in no way altered the views which I have held for thirty years, and it cannot be any surprise to you that I, as soon as I heard of such events, would not only champion them but would also act on my obligations. You would be ashamed of me if I had not done so. If Marx were not here or had not ever existed, nothing about the situation would have altered. Hence it is very unjust to blame him for this, and I cheerfully

recall that a long time ago Marx's relations maintained that *I* had corrupted him (33 MEW 299–300).

Engels's surviving parent Elisabeth Engels died not long after in 1873, and he spent 28 October to 20 November with his siblings and in-laws in Engelskirchen where the family business was now principally located. Young Friedrich had not fulfilled her hopes, but he had by no means deserted the family and disgraced it. He had managed to compromise his political vocation by pursuing a career in business, thus preserving the appearance of respectability for his relations and the fervour of revolution for his friends. In effect he had redefined 'work' and 'retirement' so as to meet minimal parental expectations, and for that he secured enough return to maintain himself and to finance the communist activities of his associates (33 MEW 608).

In effect Engels was working not merely for himself but for others, most notably the Marx family, for whom he also provided an annual maintenance when he retired. He put up with his ambiguous life as a Manchester industrialist, and his no-less-ambiguous retirement on family capital, to keep his communist associates from death's door, the workhouse or the kind of menial labour that would have broken them physically, emotionally and intellectually. By burdening himself with tedium and guilt he made considerable sacrifices for them, but in terms of sheer pain and suffering his situation bore no comparison to that of the Marxes. Indeed he had pleasures and advantages, not to mention real financial security through his family, that Marx himself envied on behalf of his wife and children – three surviving, three dead of childhood diseases and a still-birth. All the Marxes suffered physically and emotionally from their continual struggles to get money and pay off creditors.

This contrast was not lost on Engels. On 20 January 1857 Marx – then 38 – wrote that he was without any prospects. With growing domestic liabilities, he was in a more desperate situation than five years earlier. Engels replied, promising £5 in early February and the same every month thereafter, plus help in case of hardship. He continued honestly but somewhat tactlessly:

For my Christmas present my old man gave me the money to buy a horse and, as there was a good one going, I bought it last

week. If I'd known about this business of yours I would have
waited a month or two and saved the cost of its keep. But
NEVER MIND, that doesn't have to be paid for straight away.
But I'm exceedingly vexed that I should be keeping a horse here
[for the Cheshire Hunt] while you and your family are down on
your luck in London (40 CW 94, 96–7).

A letter of 15 July in the following year vividly displays the kind
of appeal to Engels that Marx repeatedly made, suggesting 'it
behoves us to put our heads together to see if some way cannot be
found out of the present [financial] situation, for it has become
absolutely untenable'. Marx continued that he was 'COMPLETELY
DISABLED from doing any work' and that his wife was 'the victim
of daily pressures and haunted by the spectre of final and
unavoidable catastrophe', which he described with Dickensian
realism:

Even were I to seek to reduce expenditure to the utmost – e.g.
take the children away from school, move into a wholly working-class lodging, get rid of the maids, live on potatoes – not
even the auction of my household goods would suffice to satisfy
the creditors in the vicinity and ensure an unhampered removal
to some hidey-hole. . . . I for my part wouldn't care a damn about
living in Whitechapel [in the working-class East End of London],
provided I could again at last secure an hour's peace in which to
attend to my work. But in view of my wife's condition just now
such a metamorphosis might entail dangerous consequences,
and it could hardly be suitable for growing girls (40 CW 328, 331).

Reliable estimates show Engels's receipts from the family business rising from approximately £100 p.a. in the very early 1850s to
almost £3000 p.a. by 1869, giving a total in excess of £23 000 over
the twenty-year period. Of that sum at least £3000 or about
one-seventh went to support the Marx family, and he gave or lent
further sums to other émigrés as well. At times the Marxes
consumed up to one-half of Engels's annual income. The pathos of
this arrangement is readily visible from surviving letters, such as
this one of June 1867 from Marx:

My children are obliged to invite some other girls for dancing on
2 July, as they have been unable to invite anyone for the whole of

this year, to respond to invitations, and are therefore about to LOSE CASTE. So, hard-pressed though I am at the moment, I had to agree to it and am counting on you for the wine (claret and Rhenish), i.e. on your supplying me with it in the course of next week (42 CW 385).

On retirement in 1869 Engels aimed to cover Marx's debts and settle about £350 p.a. on him, paid by quarterly allowance, and the arrangement seems to have worked more satisfactorily (D 329–31, 341–7, 409–11).

Engels was valued and loved on both sides of the class struggle – by his friends for his steady support, material and otherwise, for the communist cause; and by his parents, siblings and in-laws for his loyalty and restraint in preserving family relationships. He lived in two worlds, so to speak, friends in one and family in another, but he was the point at which the two overlapped. There he was the object of conflicting financial claims – from the Marx family, to whom he was doggedly devoted; from the Engels clan, who wanted his work-time and inheritance; and from his own tastes for wine, travel, exercise and other amusements. But the passage of money was strictly one-way – from the Engels family to son-and-heir to unofficial dependants. As son and brother he pursued contradiction and lived in ambiguity, and in that he was markedly consistent. He made no clean breaks and no ultimate sacrifices, and saw no great advantage for anyone in doing so. His affections flowed in both directions – to family and to friends – though not at all in equal measure, and not without a streak of egoism, especially in his relationships with women.

II ENGELS IN LOVE

Engels's earliest remarks about women, so far as they are preserved, were made in the context of the struggle for female emancipation as it existed in the 1830s. As perceived by Engels this was part of the struggle for democratic rights in politics and public life. Amongst prominent radicals – almost wholly male, of course – rights for women were associated with sexual liberation. They argued that women should have proper recognition as human subjects and intellects who could exercise choice over their lives with respect to sexual affairs, marriage and divorce. Engels supported these causes, admittedly with what seems today a large amount of residual male chauvinism. One of his letters of 1839, when he was almost 19 and a supporter of Young Germany, caricatured the Emancipation of Women as a cigar-smoking female exposing her backside, and the Emancipation of the Flesh as a male bearing a priapic flagpole from which female undergarments (?) are displayed (2 CW 453).

As a communist Engels identified the revolutionary reform of heterosexual relations with the liberty of the individual, reporting this to English readers in 1843. His early articles in German on political economy and the factory system revealed considerable sensitivity to the plight of children – obviously weak and dependent – and women, who seemed to some extent to fall into that category as well. In his writings communists and working people were generally 'chaps', 'lads' and 'men'. His sensitivity to the 'woman question' and to the particular horrors of factory work for females must be balanced today against his presumption that political actors are male and that women are the weaker sex. Of course in his time political actors were in fact overwhelmingly male, so his references to political actors as generally male are not surprising. Indeed it would have been surprising for him to refer to women as political actors on terms of equality with men, or even to think of advocating this in full, as the notion of equal participation in public life for women had hardly surfaced. It was easy for Engels – as for virtually everyone else – not to see the issue of democratic participation in politics as one of *complete* equality between the sexes, because of the prevailing assumption that female nature was essentially domestic. Housework, child-rearing, caring for family members and so forth were taken to be the proper functions in society for women. Marx's wife Jenny *née* von Westphalen (1814–81) put precisely this view to her husband in 1845, two years after their marriage, whilst he was associating with the communists in Brussels. She was living at home in Trier with her mother, pregnant with their second child and looking after their first, her namesake Jenny (1844–83), who was not yet 2:

> People are petty here [in Germany] . . . but there [in more liberal France and Belgium] heroes are not giants either, nor is the individual one jot better off. For men it may be different, but for a woman, whose destiny it is to have children, to sew, to cook and to mend, I commend miserable Germany. There, it still does one

credit to have a child, the needle and the kitchen spoon still lend one a modicum of grace and, on top of that, and by way of reward for the days spent washing, sewing and child-minding, one has the comfort of knowing in one's heart of hearts that one has done one's duty.

Jenny Marx then defended the 'lowlier duties of life' against the 'advanced' views and 'egoistic' concerns of some of the communists, and mentioned their desire to experience THE HAPPINESS OF MANKIND in their own persons with some degree of irony (38 CW 527–8).

Thus the prevailing view of woman's lowly role – and the counterbalancing dignity of woman's work – was by no means inconsistent with liberal views stressing the liberty of the individual, because male and female individuals were taken to have different natures and therefore different spheres in which liberty was relevant. Engels's *Beschreibung der in neuerer Zeit entstandenen und noch bestehenden kommunistischen Ansiedlungen* ('Description of Recently Founded Communist Colonies still in Existence'), written in Barmen in October 1844, contained an approving account of Owenite communal living arrangements that expressed this outlook succinctly: 'The members live together in a large house, each with a separate bedroom, which is most comfortably furnished; the housekeeping is done for all of them together by some of the women, and this, of course, saves a great deal of expense, time and trouble' (4 CW 226).

The most likely reading in context of this ambiguous passage is that Engels was conceptualizing the members of the community as males, each furnished with a bedroom and a woman, the women then undertaking the domestic labour of the commune collectively. Similar presumptions reappear in *Der Ursprung der Familie, des Privateigentums und des Staates* (*The Origin of the Family, Private Property and the State*), published by Engels some forty years later in 1884, when he took up the historical position of women in detail. He argued that the first premise for the emancipation of women in modern society is their reintroduction into public industry. On his view the reorganization of the domestic sphere as an industrial activity, including communal catering and cleaning services, would have to follow. Even so, he referred explicitly to women's family duties, but did not detail exactly what they were – childbearing and the care of small children are obvious guesses – nor did he consider how the performance of these duties might then undercut equal participation for women in community life. The issue of men's domestic duties did not arise at all, possibly because he really thought that there were none to discuss, or possibly because his own circumstances made this kind of oversight an easy one for him to make.

Engels lived in a world – by no means vanished – where lowly domestic tasks are generally done by housewives, female relations, maid-servants and housekeepers who tidy up. In 1852, for instance, he wrote to his sister Marie Blank in London inquiring about their little sister Elise, then about 18, connecting these four categories of female, one way or another, with his domestic needs:

> What is Elise up to? If she's a good cook, and can darn stockings, she might well come over here [to Manchester] after Christmas and keep house for me. . . . Elise would undoubtedly be able to do the honours of the house quite famously, while all your old stick-in-the-mud bachelor has is an ancient, crotchety, six-foot-tall, skin-and-bone, intimidating, snarling, blear-eyed, doddery, unkempt, ex-kitchen maid of a housekeeper, but never a wife, despite his gallantries at concerts, balls and suchlike (EF 488–9; 39 CW 249).

Even if there is an element of dated jest in some of these remarks, they nonetheless illustrate Engels's consistent assumption that women are essentially domestic creatures, and that men are the natural recipients of their services, waged or otherwise. Moreover he was markedly more respectful throughout his life in his remarks concerning wives and female relations than in his comments on maid-servants and housekeepers – his sister's (?physical) description of her new maids made him 'eager to see them', and the housekeeper (unnamed) in Manchester was referred to as a 'witch'. He did not see 'women' as a comprehensive group in any real sense, but instead saw broad categories of females, who were then the subject of commonplace discourse – solicitous concern for female relations, lustful appreciation for serving-maids, abusive dislike for housekeepers, etc. (38 CW 270, 515).

There were intimate relationships with women in Engels's life. After returning to Barmen in 1844 Engels – then turning 24 – reported to Marx that he had been involved in an unhappy love affair. However, nothing further is known about this 'girl-friend' or just possibly 'fiancée'. But in his letter to his sister of 1852 the phrase 'never a wife' throws into relief yet another major ambiguity in his life. This is because to his brother-in-law Emil Blank and others in communist circles he had already announced 'a wife' – Mary Burns (*c.* 1823–63) (38 CW 37).

Mary was an Irish-born millworker whom Engels met in Manchester, so it is assumed, when he was working there between 1842 and 1844. This is the time when, according to his own account, he was making personal visits to the homes of the proletariat, and Mary was possibly his guide. For Engels she did not occupy one of the categories of female enumerated above. She was a mill-girl, who worked outside the home in modern industry, and so she was not a female relation, maid or housekeeper. Neither was she a wife (or girl-friend or fiancée) as understood at home, because she and Engels were never legally married nor even continuously co-resident. Instead she was an 'honorary Mrs', his sexual partner – so we presume – and political associate, who accompanied him to Brussels in 1845 at the start of his communist career. During his subsequent time in Paris and Cologne – a period that is very well-documented – she almost disappears from view.

In the 1850s and early 60s Mary was maintained by Engels in a domestic establishment in Ardwick in suburban Manchester separate from his lodgings near the centre. Crudely, this made her his mistress, 'kept' in semi-secrecy away from his 'public' life with Ermen and Engels, the Albert Club, the Manchester Athenaeum, the Cheshire Hunt, the Schiller Anstalt and other middle-class obligations and amusements. An 'unsuitable' marriage with a working-class and very possibly illiterate Irish girl would have threatened Engels's position in these institutions, as he could have been drummed out of the purely social ones and penalized financially on the business side. When his circumstances were discovered by his 'philistine' associates, he was not pleased. Had the two been married, the working-class Mary would of course have had no position in 'polite society', and her removal to middle-class circumstances would very probably have deprived her of friends and family in the Irish community (39 CW 443).

Engels's family reacted with horror to these possibilities early on. In December 1848, during an enforced absence from Germany, some of his belongings arrived at home from Cologne whilst his father was away. That was just as well, his mother wrote, because she had discovered various letters which she proposed to withhold from Friedrich senior:

> I consider it unnecessary to tell him everything I know, but if asked I do not knowingly tell anything but the truth. . . . Amongst the letters in your trunk I found one addressed to 'Madame Engels' [Mary Burns?] and one from a lady to yourself, written in French, though from Cologne [probably from Félicité André – see below]. . . . Both these letters I burnt unread. . . . Do not write to me about it, for I am most anxious that your father should hear nothing. . . . Later you might give me an explanation by word of mouth. But I only wish to hear the truth.

Characteristically she continued: 'If you cannot tell me that, it would be better for us not to speak at all on the subject.' A working-class Frau Engels would not have been a welcome addition to the family circle in purely social terms, and in financial terms – the management of current property and the transmission of inheritance – the idea was unthinkable (38 CW 545).

Some of Engels's communist associates were not at all amused that a mill-owner's son was taking advantage, so it seemed, of a factory girl who had nothing to sell but her labour in that most personal of ways. The émigré Stephan Born (pseud. Simon Buttermilch, 1824–98), a German typesetter and one of the Brussels communists, recounted that Marx and his wife had attended a workers' association meeting in late 1847 or early 1848 at which Engels had arrived with a lady, unnamed but presumed to be Mary Burns. She had joined Engels *à deux* (Jenny Marx's reference to the matter) in Brussels sometime in the latter part of 1845, after Engels's trip during the summer to Manchester in company with Marx. In memoirs written long after the event Born recalled that Marx had indicated by glances and smiles that his wife would not meet Engels's companion. Obviously there is some room for doubt here concerning exactly what was going on. Born drew the conclusion that Marx's 'noble lady' (the von Westphalens had aristocratic connections) held strict views about marriage and morals. But there is room for doubt here as well, because Born may have misunderstood her intention – if such it was – of not acknowledging Engels's 'wife' in public, even amongst communists. Born continued his recollections by commenting that Engels should not have brought his 'mistress' to the gathering at all, as it was a tactless reminder to workers that the sons of rich mill-owners were often accused of using working-class women and girls for their own pleasure (38 CW 529; 1 H 104).

The Marxes in particular have come in for criticism from modern writers such as Henderson, McLellan and Raddatz for their supposed snobbery towards Mary and unfeeling slights towards Engels. The Marxes may well have found Engels's relationship with Mary open to misconstruction by others, who could have pointed to communism and atheism as merely a convenient cover for old-fashioned sexual exploitation. 'Free love' was not at all the kind of publicity that the Marxes sought for the communist cause, because it had connotations of an irresponsible use of women by men, and an unwillingness on their part to acknowledge their obligations, especially to offspring. Indeed the Marxes may have regarded the affair as an exploitation of Mary's economic vulnerability that could compromise her life amongst her working-class family and associates, and yet offer her nothing in the way of middle-class comforts, financial security and personal dignity. More simply the Marxes may not have found Mary good company in a family where literary classics in German, French, English, Latin, Greek, Hebrew and further modern languages were standard fare. And there is some suggestion from as early as 1846 that Jenny Marx did not like Mary personally, finding her ambitious, scheming, arrogant and overly critical of trifles, indeed referring to her as 'Lady Macbeth'. Others in the Brussels group do not seem to have cared for her either (38 CW 530–1; KM 178–9; 1 H 104; R 148–9).

Yet the Marx family and the Engels ménage maintained adjoining accommodation in various locations and for a time stayed in the same inn in Brussels, where Engels's friend Georg Weerth (1822–56) – another communist businessman working at times in England – gave the impression that there was nothing untoward in the close association. In a letter to his mother in 1846 he observed: 'The famous Marx is living in the room opposite to mine with his very beautiful and well-educated wife and two bonny children. Fried[rich] Engels, whose book on England you have read, is staying here too. His wife is an English [*sic*] girl from Manchester so we converse half in English and half in German' (FE 116–17).

In the later 1840s Engels was not shy in declaring in correspondence that he was occupying himself with girls, as Mary did not accompany him on his trips to Paris on behalf of the Brussels communists. In particular Engels once boasted of two conquests to Marx. This happened when, as Engels had it, Sibylle Hess – the wife of his former mentor – conceived a passion for him which he did not return. Meanwhile Hess went on a jealous rage – not at all the first – over his wife's infatuation and reportedly accused Engels of rape. Engels portrayed this accusation of rape as absurd, since he had been the one pursued, and in any case Hess – said Engels – was 'perfectly at liberty ... to avenge himself on all my present, past and future mistresses', and then listed two: '1) the Flemish giantess who lives at my former lodgings ... whose name is Mademoiselle Joséphine, and 2) a Frenchwoman, Mademoiselle Félicie [André] who, on Sunday, the 23rd of this month, will be arriving in Brussels by the first train from Cologne on her way to Paris. It would be bad luck if he were to succeed with neither ... I WILL GIVE HIM FAIR PLAY' (38 CW 153). During the early days of the 1848 revolution in Paris Engels and Mme André were living at the same address (38 CW 166).

Certainly Marx seemed to take Engels's relationship with Mary to be rather casual, even in the 1850s. Engels had written on 29 January 1851 that Marx's previous letter had been mislaid by his 'old witch of a landlady' in a pile of books. 'Had I been studying Russian this month instead of physiology', Engels continued, 'this wouldn't have happened'. Marx inquired lubriciously on 3 February, 'Is it on Mary you're studying physiology, or elsewhere?', and Engels's reply of 5 February offered no reproof. Indeed on 13 February Engels described himself to Marx as a 'BACHELOR', and said that he was bored. During the cotton crisis of the early 1860s, caused by the American civil war, Engels reported to Marx that as the firm had no orders he was working only half-time, and living almost all the time with Mary – 'so as to spend as little money as possible'. 'Unfortunately', he continued, 'I can't dispense with my LODGINGS, otherwise I should move in with her altogether'. Accommodation for Mary and her sister Lizzie or Lizzy (otherwise Lydia, 1827–78) was rented in the name of 'Frederick Boardman', and Mary was 'Mrs Boardman'. Lizzie 'kept house' for the 'married couple', acting the unmarried female relation in a household that was neither respectably middle-class nor conventionally proletarian – nor genuinely egalitarian by modern standards. By Engels's standards it may have represented some contemporary approach to communism, as it was a cross-class alliance between workers in industry, albeit very much on his own terms in the domestic arrangements (38 CW 270–81, 290; 41 CW 344, 370, 634 n. 425).

The Burns sisters were Fenian sympathisers and supporters of the movement for Irish independence, and Engels toured Ireland with Mary in 1856. Through his relations with them Engels was possibly in discreet contact with an organization of revolutionaries – or at least revolutionary fighters. He was inclined to see such movements as working-class threats to middle-class exploitation, or at least potential threats that might eventually bring Irish workers to communism. In that way the Ardwick establishment perhaps recalled the communist contacts between intellectuals and workers in Brussels and Cologne, where he worked for a democratic, but violent revolution. During the Manchester years he was largely isolated from the communist politics of German émigrés, because it was centred on London which he could only visit from time to time. Possibly his semi-secret life with Mary appealed to him politically, as his English associations never lived up to the standard of revolutionary radicalism that as a German communist he expected and required (1 K 116).

When Mary died suddenly of heart disease – at about 41 – she was almost overlooked by the Marxes, and for that Engels rebuked his friend Karl quite sharply. But as the Marxes were not generally insensitive, that rebuke may tell us something about the way Engels's relationship appeared to outsiders. Evidently he had failed to make his regard for Mary completely clear to those who in all other matters were his complete intimates. On 7 January 1863 Engels wrote very briefly: 'Mary is dead . . . I simply can't convey what I feel. The poor girl loved me with all her heart.' Marx responded by return on the 8th, 'The news of Mary's death surprised no less than it dismayed me. She was so good-natured, witty and closely attached to you.' He then launched into yet another heart-rending account of his family's financial embarrassments and his attempts to raise money, saying:

It is dreadfully selfish of me to tell you about these *horreurs* at this time. But it's a homeopathic remedy. One calamity is a distraction from the other. And, *au bout du compte*, what else can I do? . . . In my own home I play the silent stoic to counterbalance the outbursts from the other side [i.e. his wife Jenny]. It's becoming virtually impossible to work UNDER SUCH CIRCUMSTANCES. Instead of Mary, ought it not to have been my mother . . . ?

Marx's mother was then ill, and she eventually died at the end of that year, when Marx set off to Trier to determine his legacy. 'You can see what strange notions come into the heads of "civilised men" under the pressure of certain circumstances', he said. He then continued, perhaps with some envy for the comfortable domestic surroundings that Engels reputedly enjoyed: 'What arrangements will you now make about your ESTABLISHMENT? It's terribly hard for you, since with Mary you had a HOME to which you were at liberty to retreat from the human imbroglio, whenever you chose.'

Five days after Marx's urgent pleas, Engels replied on the 13th, referring to Marx's 'frosty view' of his misfortune and saying icily in turn that he had found it impossible to reply any earlier. 'All my friends, including philistine acquaintances, have on this occasion . . . given me proof of greater sympathy and friendship than I could have looked for.' He then outlined various ways for Marx to raise money, none of them promising, and said he might be able to send £25 in February. This was 'if the worst comes to the worst', and Marx had found no further money from his uncle in Holland, with whom he had been pleading.

On the 24th of January Marx replied, after allowing 'some time to elapse', saying that he had been very wrong to write as he had done. He had been 'shattered' when the original letter had arrived, but the events of the day had made him desperate, as the family had been 'in the same plight as the Manchester workers'. Now he thanked Engels for his unpromising remarks about money, as Jenny had finally given in and would go along with a plan for the two elder children, Jenny and Laura (1845–1911) to find work as governesses, for the family servant Helene Demuth (1820–90) to enter service elsewhere, and for himself, his wife and the youngest child Eleanor (1855–98) to enter the City Model Lodging House, where they could leave behind the 'false appearances' and financial turbulence of the last few years. This would mean the end of them as a family, exposure of the elder girls to the abuse of domestic service, exploitation as an unsalaried journalist for Karl, and degradation for his already long-suffering wife. The Marxes lived for ideas and politics, and the plan outlined by Karl was truly last-ditch, as it meant losing contact with virtually all that they as educated people considered worthwhile in life, and gaining nothing save peace from their creditors. Modern commentators such as McLellan and Kapp have presumed to lecture the long-dead

Marxes on thrift, but Engels – to his credit – saw much more acutely the identity-threatening character of their family crisis, and the need for funds to maintain them in minimally comfortable circumstances where they had some chance of being themselves (KM 264; 1 K 22–63).

On the 26th Engels replied, patching things up. Having extracted what he considered to be the appropriate emotional response to Mary's death, he then found a way to save the Marx family from ruin after all:

> Thank you for being so candid. You yourself have now realised what sort of impression your last letter but one had made on me. One can't live with a woman for years on end without being fearfully affected by her death. I felt as though with her I was burying the last vestige of my youth ... That letter, I tell you, obsessed me for a whole week; I couldn't get it out of my head. NEVER MIND. Your last letter made up for it and I'm glad that, in losing Mary, I didn't also lose my oldest and best friend.

In 'an exceedingly daring move' Engels swiftly obtained a bill of credit for £100 due on 28 February and endorsed it over to Marx. Freiligrath, the former Barmen poet, communist associate on the *Neue Rheinische Zeitung* and now clerk to a Swiss bank in London, would be glad, so Engels said, to discount the bill for cash. But there would be nothing further for the Marxes till 30 June, 'save for trifling amounts'.

Engels's treatment of his dependents – the Burnses and the Marxes – was indeed self-sacrificing and generous. But there is an air of egocentricity and condescension in his account of his relationship with Mary, since he rather implied that her life was wrapped up in loving him. Indeed hardly anything is known about her and their relationship other than his own brief testimony in the letters that survive. Even there he never said anything of substance or interest to his correspondents, so it is not surprising that they made little response save a few formal inquiries. Only in the case of her death was this pattern broken, and then Engels construed it exclusively as an event in his own emotional life, not something that affected anyone else, even her sister Lizzie who had discovered the body. Mary's own voice is unheard in the historical record, unlike that of Jenny Marx, for instance, whose lively correspondence is well represented in modern collections – though she hardly ever mentioned Mary, either. And there are no photographs or other likenesses of Mary Burns, as there were at the time for virtually everyone else in these circles, even the servant Helene (M 98–101; KM 331–2; R 148).

'Mrs Lizzy' fared somewhat better, and she at least was photographed. Possibly the image that survives is the one that Engels described in 1868 as awful but the least bad of five. The 'Mrs' was again honorific, though it went with 'Burns', not with 'Engels'. She resided, as before, at his 'private address', not his 'official dwelling' – as Marx put it. Marx carefully sent his family's greetings to Engels and his own to 'Mrs. Lizzy' in a letter of 5 August 1865, and on 9 August he reported that he had been severely cross-examined by his girls about this 'Mrs. Burns'. He solicitously sought Engels to persuade her into membership of the International Working Men's Association, then just starting up in early 1865, as 'LADIES ARE ADMITTED', and he hoped that she would follow her namesake the poet in thinking 'a man's a man for all that' (42 CW 67, 91, 177, 181, 193; 32 MEW 182; 34 MEW between 336–7).

'Mrs Lizzy' emerges from the Marx–Engels correspondence – indirectly of course – as a considerable character. Like Mary she did not meet his family. In the summer of 1867 Engels planned to take her with him to the continent, mentioning sights in Denmark and north Germany, but proposing to send her home by way of Grimsby before he journeyed himself 'to the Rhine' – where the Engels clan resided. Marx promised Engels in the same year that he would buy Lizzie a 'London dress' with the proceeds from an English translation of *Capital*, but the plan fell through and she never received the gift. The suggestion seems a curious one in view of the family's chronic poverty, but Marx was possibly trying to make up for the past. In 1868 Lizzie went to visit her relations, who were farm labourers in Lincolnshire, and Engels reported excitedly that she described word-for-word the gang-labour system that Marx had portrayed in his book *Capital* (42 CW 389, 394; 32 MEW 200).

As Marx's daughters were growing into young women, and as his family's circumstances improved somewhat when Engels's income began to rise, social relations between the two households increased, particularly when Eleanor visited Manchester and acquired fervent Fenian sympathies. These were nourished on trips to Ireland with Engels and 'Mrs. Burns'. A letter from Eleanor to her sister Jenny gives a 14-year-old's view of the Engels household in July 1869:

> On Saturday it was so warm that we, that is Auntie [Lizzie] and myself and Sarah [Parker – the maid], lay down on the floor the whole day drinking beer, claret, etc. ... In the evening when Uncle [Engels] came home he found Auntie, me, and [Mary] Ellen [Burns – born *c.* 1860, Lizzie's niece], who was telling us Irish tales, all lying our full length on the floor, with no stays, no boots, and one petticoat and a cotton dress on, and that was all.

'Uncle' and 'Aunt', Eleanor reported, were new forms of address she had acquired from Mary Ellen, because 'Mrs. Burns, more to tease me than anything else, persisted in calling me "Miss Marx"', so Eleanor had retaliated by forcing the household to address her by her pet name 'Tussy', and she had adopted the Engels' household names in return. For entertainment they were off the next day to view a royal visit to Manchester and sing 'The Prince of Wales in Belle Vue jail/For robbing a man of a pint of ale' (DKM 51–2).

Lizzie was considered a suitable companion for the Marx girls, and they occasionally spent time at the seaside together. Much of the correspondence that survives is about the lung complaints and other ill-health for which the sea air was considered beneficial, no doubt rightly in view of the notoriously polluted air in London. On Engels's retirement from business in June 1869 he gave up his 'official dwelling' and lived full time with Lizzie in Manchester, but by early 1870 he was planning to move to London, saying that she had had words with her relations and did not wish to stay (32 MEW 453).

Engels could hardly have wanted to remain in Manchester, so this development was obviously convenient, and a new domestic establishment – Engels, Mrs Lizzie, Mary Ellen and their maid Sarah – was set up in September in the salubrious Regent's Park Road. Marx's wife Jenny had located the spacious house for them, commenting that 'all round in the side-streets there are shops of various kinds, so that your wife can look after everything herself'. The two – Jenny Marx and Lizzie Burns – struck up a friendship as they were now within easy reach and had, if nothing else, their ailments in common. They treated their ills together at resorts such as Shanklin and Ramsgate, and Engels fortified them on their 'cures' with glasses of port (32 MEW 714; 33 MEW 281; 34 MEW 26; 1 K 183–4).

By the 1870s Lizzie was 'Mrs. E' in Engels's correspondence with Marx's daughter Jenny, but to his foreign correspondents she was 'Miss Burns' of the Regent's Park Road, so that his name would not be linked with anything politically suspect. In the autumn of 1875 Engels and Lizzie journeyed through Germany to place Mary Ellen (known as 'Pumps') in a finishing establishment in Heidelberg – again bypassing the Engels clan. To his German correspondents Lizzie was 'my wife', though not in a letter to his brother Rudolf, in which Engels reported on his trip in a rather mysterious first person plural (33 MEW 320, 417, 633; 34 MEW 164, 166).

Engels was always very genuinely solicitous about Lizzie's health, taking her to Brighton in 1877, and Marx made frequent inquiries, as she was continually ailing. 'Pumps' was recalled early from Heidelberg to help with the household, as there had been all manner of trouble with maids, and Engels's own efforts to make beds and light kitchen fires were laughable, so he said. By 30 July 1878 he pronounced Lizzie's condition very serious and feared the worst. She died on 12 September 1878, and Engels wrote at once to his brother Rudolf in Barmen of the death of 'his wife', saying that he had legally married Lizzie the previous evening. This is presumed to have been her deathbed wish, and the couple were married by special licence. The marriage was performed by the local vicar, though Lizzie was buried in a Roman Catholic cemetery. Whether her aim was to be right with the world or right with God is unclear, but from Engels's point of view there could be little scandal or bad feeling in Barmen about the match. The new Frau Engels – already the late Frau Engels – would have no claim on the family socially and no chance of inheriting Friedrich's estate. It is difficult to escape the supposition that Lizzie might have preferred marriage at an earlier date, and was refused it by Engels who wished to keep his family affairs in order (34 MEW 252, 255, 336, 342; 1 K 184–92).

A few days later Marx recounted to his wife certain events at the Engels residence – retailed to him by Eleanor. This concerned the discovery of a small bundle of letters amongst Lizzie's things, and Marx commented that the scene was reminiscent of Balzac and the sentimental novelist Paul de Kock. Engels is supposed to have ordered the letters burnt, saying melodramatically 'I need not see her letters. I know she was unable to deceive me'. Mrs Lydia Renshaw, a relation of 'Pumps', was in attendance, and said later to Eleanor, 'Of course, as he had to write her letters, and to read to her the letters she received, he might feel quite sure that these letters contained no secrets for him – but, they might do so, for her.' Marx and his wife seem to have had a private view that Engels was rather pompous and lacking in self-awareness, and there is perhaps some truth in this (34 MEW 344).

In love Engels does not seem to have gone searching for his intellectual equal. Rather he seems to have sought political and domestic compatibility, both 'private' pursuits by comparison with the 'public' life he led as son and heir in the family business. Throughout his life he was strongly associated with the Barmen clan, through affection as well as necessity, and significantly he did not marry in the usual way and start his own family independently, as that would have cut him off altogether. His retirement allowed him to live openly with Lizzie Burns, as he had not been able to do with Mary. This was because he did not have business contacts to keep up, and because he had a politically sympathetic social life available in London, so he did not need diversions with the 'philistines' of Manchester. But there was little that was overtly unconventional in his arrangements in Manchester or London, as they corresponded closely to the way cross-class liaisons were handled in the mid-nineteenth-century – the second household in the suburbs, the housekeeper who was not quite a wife. Later in life he said that he preferred Irish girls far above any blue-stocking with social pretensions. Whilst no doubt a true comment on his tastes, the remark is consistent with his general attitude towards women. Engels's intellectual mates were not women but men, and foremost among them was Marx (38 MEW 298).

Though Marx and Engels had an overwhelming amount in common politically and intellectually, the contrast between them in terms of personal life and career is very striking. Marx was strongly attached to one woman, and she seems to have been his only love. Jenny died in late 1881 and Marx followed within eighteen months, so there was no prolonged period of widowerhood. Whilst she was not his intellectual equal (who was?), they were on terms of intellectual intimacy with respect to his career and work, and he in turn was on far more intimate terms with her concerns in family life than he sometimes wished. The two were devoted parents to their children. They have sometimes been accused of over-protection, though this protectiveness must be balanced against the exploitation and abuse that they feared would be their daughters' fate if they were left to fend for themselves, unprotected by economically reliable husbands. Economic insecurity kept the family tightly together, and they struggled to remain united rather than to try their luck separately. Karl and Jenny kept up with their various relations to a certain extent, and financial calculations played a role in their actions. But compared with Engels, their parents and other relatives played a smaller role in their lives. Their relations had less money than Engels's, but their children and their inability to make ends meet gave them an even stronger motivation to pursue whatever family resources were available. Karl was notably distanced from his parents and siblings, almost from the age of 18, when he became engaged to Jenny and left the Rhineland for Berlin University. The intellectual and political concerns that he began to develop there consumed him for the rest of his life, and his role as son, brother and brother-in-law – though not non-existent – was minimal.

Engels on the other hand was notably unencumbered with domestic ties of his own, and more consistently involved with his parents and relations. Though the industrialists of the Engels clan possessed far more resources than the Marxes and von Westphalens of Trier – who were of the professional classes – Friedrich could well have struck out on his own in business or possibly supported himself as a journalist and writer, despite the obvious advantages of sticking with the Barmen clan. He could still have provided for his communist dependants, though not as generously. He stayed with the family firm reluctantly in order to support the Marxes and the Burnses for personal and political reasons, but he showed little sustained interest in making himself truly independent of his parents and siblings by throwing himself into full-time domesticity and full-time communism as fervently as Marx.

From mid-1845 onwards Engels made Marx the intellectual focus of his life, and he had to struggle somewhat to keep up with his friend. There was a considerable emotional investment in the relationship from Engels's point of view, as can be judged from the surviving correspondence. His other emotional involvements – with the Burns sisters or otherwise – were not so voluminously recorded, so the precise balance of his attentions and the varied qualities of his affections cannot now be determined. Marx was far more ruthless than Engels in his devotion to the things that mattered to him, narrowing them down and pursuing them almost irrespective of the consequences. What Engels lacked in single-mindedness he made up in loyalty, tolerance, open-heartedness and a certain tendency to find workable compromises that suited his interests.

III   WIDOWER AND TESTATOR

When Mrs Lizzie died, Engels was nearly 58, and he seems to have settled into a celibate widowerhood. He was assiduous in looking after the Marxes in their last years, and in assisting the surviving Marx girls Laura and Eleanor – Jenny the eldest daughter had predeceased her father in early 1883. 'Pumps' was now the chief domestic of the Engels household, and from all accounts she was thoroughly disliked for her flightiness and bad humours. But it was also acknowledged by observers such as Mrs Marx that her life had been a hard one. Her working-class family in Manchester would not support her, and she was left to find a 'situation', such as the one with Engels and her Aunt Lizzie – or a husband. She found one in Percy Rosher, an accountant, though he was perhaps not over-eager at the prospect of matrimony. Engels had a hand in arranging the marriage settlement. 'Pumps' was pregnant when she married in 1881, and Engels saw to it that Rosher's father set young Percy up in business. Engels's advocacy of marriage reflected sound economic and social principles, in that 'Pumps' – and her awaited offspring – had everything to gain from legal ties and practically nothing to lose, and marriage was an obvious way to force parental acknowledgement of Percy's need for support. This was rather the opposite of Engels's own involvements, as his family was evidently willing to keep him on, provided he did not marry unsuitably. Rosher eventually failed in business, and Pumps's family was faithfully helped along by Engels, who often put them up in his house. On Marx's death in March 1883 a replacement for the difficult 'Pumps' became available: the servant Helene, known in family circles as 'Lenchen' or – in various spellings – 'Nim' or 'Nimmy' (1 H 564–5, 724–30; 1 K 185–91; 2 K 213).

Lenchen was the daughter of a Rhineland village baker, and at an early age she had become the young Jenny von Westphalen's maid at home. As such she had joined the Marx family in their Brussels days in the mid-1840s in order to help look after the infants. From all accounts she was good-humoured and literate, and in later years she helped the married daughters Jenny and Laura with their babies. But by 1883 the Longuet children – Jenny's – were settled with their widower father Charles (1839–1903) in France, and the three children of Laura and Paul Lafargue (1842–1911) had all died in childhood by the early 1870s. Lenchen ruled over the Engels household until her death at 70 in November 1890. Engels wrote to his old friend Friedrich Sorge (1828–1906), an émigré '48er living in New Jersey, giving this tribute: 'My good, dear, faithful Lenchen died yesterday afternoon. . . . We have lived for seven happy years together here in this house. We were the last two of the pre-1848 old guard. . . . If Marx for many years, and myself in the last seven, found peace for our labours, it was basically her work. . . . I will sadly miss her wonderfully tactful advice on party affairs.' Engels spoke at her funeral, and she was buried with the Marx family. In her will she left everything – amounting to £95 – to her son Frederick Lewis Demuth (1851–1929), born Henry Frederick according to his birth certificate, which gave no father (KM 138; 1 K 278–97; 2 K 429–40; 37 MEW 498).

Frederick Demuth has recently become an important character in Engels's life, though he was certainly no such thing at the time. Freddy, nearly 40 when his mother died, was evidently well known to the Marx girls as Lenchen's son. Jenny wrote to Laura in 1882 about a debt to Freddy and her inability to help 'Nim' make a journey to Germany. Shortly after Freddy's mother died, Eleanor wrote to Laura, mentioning past wrongs and a sense of guilt: 'Freddy has behaved admirably in all respects and Engels's irritation against him is as unfair as it is comprehensible. We should none of us like to meet our pasts, I guess, in flesh and blood. I know I always meet Freddy with a sense of guilt and wrong done. The life of that man! To hear him tell of it all is a misery and shame to me.'

In the next few years Eleanor, Laura and their brother-in-law Charles Longuet helped Freddy out financially, and in 1892 Eleanor wrote to Laura: 'It may be that I am very "sentimental" – but I can't help feeling that Freddy has had great injustice all through his life. Is it not wonderful when you come to look things squarely in the face, how rarely we seem to practise all the fine things we preach – to others?'

Engels did not mention Freddy in his will of 29 July 1893, in which there were numerous bequests, even to 'Pumps' – though her share was cut down from £3000 to £2230 in a codicil of 26 July 1895, as she had perhaps had her eye too obviously on Engels's estate. Eleanor and Laura were asked by Engels in a letter to hold one-third (some £3000) of their combined share in trust for Jenny Longuet's French children, who could not be named for legal reasons. The two women, in conjunction with their brother-in-law Charles, managed to channel some of the funds from Engels's estate to Freddy.

In late 1897 and early 1898 – just before she apparently committed suicide – Eleanor was in a terrible state about money, her relationship with the philandering socialist Edward Aveling (1851–98) and his deteriorating health. She wrote a series of moving letters, confiding in Freddy as Lenchen's son: 'I don't think you and I have been very wicked people – and yet, dear Freddy, it does seem as if we get all the punishment.' 'I say to you what I would not say to anyone now', she continued, 'I would have told my dear old Nymmy, but as I have not, I have only you' (2 K 680–8; 2 H 727–30; DKM 224, 240, 285; 39 MEW 318–19).

It is not apparent from the reliable evidence that survives exactly what injustices Eleanor thought Freddy had suffered and at whose hands. None of the Marx girls seemed at all occupied with paternity in their dealings with Freddy, and all three accepted him as Lenchen's son. How long they had known of his existence, and his maternity (as it were) are not known. Possibly they were troubled about him and inclined to thoughts of guilt because he had grown up apart from his mother, so far as is known, and had enjoyed few educational advantages. Any feelings that his mother had been disadvantaged did not occur to them or did not surface in the correspondence that survives. Children were commonly put out to nurse in the 1850s, even amongst poor families like the Marxes, whose little Franziska (28 March 1851–14 April 1852) had been boarded at about the same time as the infant Freddy. Mrs Marx related this in her memoirs written in 1865: 'We gave the poor little thing to a nurse, for we could not rear her with the [three] others in three small rooms.' Lenchen, then about six months pregnant, was obviously in much the same position, except that housemaids who became pregnant were lucky to be kept on. Then in her memoirs Mrs Marx also refers to an event in the early summer of 1851 – Freddy was born on 23 June – that caused them much distress: 'it greatly contributed to increase our worries, both personal and others'. But she said that she did not 'wish to relate [it] here in detail' and gave no specifics. Marx's letters of the following August speak of infamies and tales visited on his wife, and he mentions names, but not substance:

> My wife will go under if things continue like this much longer. The constant worries, the slightest everyday struggle wears her out; and on top of that, there are the infamies of my opponents ... who seek to avenge their impotence by casting suspicions on my civil character and by disseminating the most unspeakable infamies about me. Willich, Schapper, Ruge and countless other democratic rabble make this their business.

The context here is probably the break-up of the émigré German communists into rival groups who quarrelled bitterly about money as well as politics.

More pertinently Marx had written to Engels on 31 March 1851 about a 'mystery' – 'in which you also figure' – that had given matters a 'tragi-comic turn'. But in writing that letter he was interrupted, and in the following letter of 2 April he put off relating the matter until his visit to Manchester at the end of the month. From mid-1850 the Prussian ambassador in London, and the Prussian government itself, had been conducting a campaign to discredit Marx and Engels and other communists, and in March 1851 Ferdinand von Westphalen (1799–1876), stepbrother of Mrs Marx and a civil servant in the Ministry of the Interior, was involved in moves to secure the deportation of the chief revolutionaries from Britain. Prussian methods included the use of agents to find compromising material and collect rumours and allegations that might influence the British government to comply with the plan to push the communists further afield, and Marx and Engels were circumspect in their correspondence. But it may be that the housmaid's pregnancy was under discussion. Engels, who was supporting the Marxes on his slender resources, was in a position to pay to have the infant fostered, but there is no record of any arrangements to which he may or may not have agreed.

If any of the odd comments in letters and memoirs were really about the pregnant Lenchen, then the affair seems to have been viewed as an inconvenient embarrassment by Marx and as the source of personal distress by his wife, but there is no sense that

Marx was intimately implicated, nor that Mrs Marx saw him any differently, nor that Engels himself was going to be seriously put out, because the comments that do survive indicate that everyone involved was on much the same terms as usual. The pregnant housemaid and the problem of her offspring were real – but peripheral to the domestic difficulties with money and political difficulties with spies and communists that the Marxes and Engels had to endure (R 23–4; KM 271–3; 38 CW 324–5, 402–3, 626–7).

Freddy would be an altogether minor character in any consideration of Engels's life or Marx's, were it not for a document, first published in extracts in 1962. According to the story recounted there, Freddy is suddenly a relation of Marx and his family and – in an ambiguous way – of Engels himself. Ostensibly the tale concerns Marx and his alleged affair with the housemaid, but it is Engels who plays the central role in the supposed narrative.

This typewritten document, which has been accepted by some scholars as entirely genuine and hotly disputed by others as a forgery, possibly by Nazi agents aiming to discredit socialism, appears to be a letter dated 2–4 September 1898, written by Louise Freyberger *née* Strasser (1860–1950), three years after the Engels household broke up. As Louise Kautsky, the recently divorced wife of the prominent German socialist Karl Kautsky (1854–1938), she had been asked by Engels, within a month of Lenchen's death, to keep house for him, and she arrived post haste from Vienna. In 1894 she married Dr Ludwig Freyberger, another émigré, and he came to live in Engels's house, too – much to Eleanor's displeasure, as she disliked Louise and her influence over Engels, then in his seventies (2 K 444; 2 H 725–6).

The document spins a lurid tale of death-bed revelations by Engels to Eleanor Marx, principally the claim that Marx himself was Freddy's father. Fearing gossip imputing paternity, Engels is said to have declared 'the truth', in case he should be accused, after his death, of treating Freddy shabbily. The date of the document is some six months after Eleanor's suicide, so if there was a letter, Eleanor was conveniently out of the way, though others mentioned as in on the story to some degree – such as Sam Moore (*c.* 1830–1911), Marx's English translator, and Eleanor's sister Laura – clearly were not. The addressee of the supposed letter, the prominent German socialist and trade unionist August Bebel (1840–1913), or anyone else who had been the recipient of such tales from Louise, could have checked with them.

The Freyberger 'letter' – if such it is – has put Marx and his works in a bad light, and made Engels's deathbed into high Victorian melodrama. After such a gothic story it is extraordinarily difficult to see the situation any other way, but this now well-known version of events must nonetheless be tested stringently against the facts as we have them. In particular Engels's actions – attested and alleged – must be carefully scrutinized.

At the time of Freddy's conception in 1850 and birth in 1851 the four principals in the affair, so far as we know, were Lenchen, Marx, Mrs Marx and Engels. The birth of an illegitimate child to the maid was obviously difficult and trying for the household, because the situation precluded any truly humane solution. Mrs Marx would not have wanted to lose her long-time maid, and Lenchen no doubt wished to keep her livelihood. Continued residence for Lenchen with the Marxes, together with her illegitimate baby, would have associated the household with 'free love' and moral irresponsibility, whoever the father was in fact or by repute. This was especially problematic with respect to the legitimate children, who would have been confronted – according to the standards of the time – with an example of flagrantly immoral behaviour, and one specially relevant to young girls. These were standards held by both conventional conservatives and responsible communists, albeit for somewhat different reasons. In any event such an establishment would have been poor publicity for communism, and a considerable burden for the children to bear, both legitimate and illegitimate. Lenchen could have been set up outside the family with her baby, but this was probably – with or without genuine regrets – beyond Engels's means, and certainly against his wish to spare his own family the possibility of serious embarrass-ment, as his connection with 'immorality' might well leak out, whether or not he was presumed to be the father. The Engels family were, in any case, his employers. The obvious solution was to board the child out and leave him there, and that is in fact what happened, so far as we know.

Lenchen may not have objected very much, as it was clearly for her own good to keep her situation, for the Marx family to continue unencumbered and for the communist cause to suffer no invidious criticism. The fact that she continued in the household with evident aplomb accords with this hypothesis, and with Eleanor's evident blankness on any injustice done to Freddy's mother, whose infant had gone to another home. The grievous injustice, from Eleanor's point of view, could have been the fact that Freddy had to grow up as a foster-child – no doubt a hard upbringing – away from his mother and the civilized influence of a cultured household.

Throughout their lives all four principals lived very happily together, and Lenchen ultimately served in both the Marx and the Engels households without any suggestion of reluctance. Hers is another unheard voice, as she left no written testimony other than her will, but memoirs of the two households attest to her willing service. If there were difficulties amongst the four principals of the 1850s – about finances, maternity, paternity or whatever – they were swiftly settled and never revisited. Mrs Marx would hardly have made her remarks in her correspondence about disturbing events if she knew that Karl were the father, as she was most particular about the obligations of family life and could not have wished to spread such a tale any further. Presumably she made her comments because they were about a situation – one that was outside her immediate relationship with her husband – that affected her deeply.

If Engels were the father, or had taken the rap for Karl, this story would surely have surfaced at some point in the émigré community, since spiteful gossips abounded. Indeed Engels was quite capable of dishing up that sort of thing himself. Writing to Marx in 1846 about their communist contacts near Paris, Engels indulged himself in ribaldry: 'The best of it is that in the house . . . there are 2 women, 2 men, several children, one of them dubious, and despite all this not a thing happens there. They don't even practise pederasty' (38 CW 55).

A considerable number of highly communicative people – not all of them life-long friends of Marx or Engels by any means – knew of Freddy's existence, and it seems to have been no particular secret that Freddy's mother was a close associate of both Marx and Engels. Had there ever been a serious possibility that Freddy's paternity would pose problems for either of the two – and hence for the 'Marx party' within the communist movement – the principals could easily have passed him off as a Demuth nephew or other relation.

Indeed the adult Freddy was known and loved in the family as Lenchen's son, who had suffered a great injustice and needed to be helped. Eleanor spoke of him in those terms before Engels's death and afterwards, and for that reason she is unlikely to have been the recipient of revelations on the subject of Freddy and unlikely to have sorted the Engels papers to remove any proof of Marx's paternity. If she had learned in 1895 of something scandalous she could hardly have gone on with Freddy exactly as before, and made almost exactly the same kind of comments about injustice. The correspondence that survives concerning Freddy reflects a steady, continuing interest in him on the part of the Marx girls – and vice versa – from sometime before 1882 up to his final correspondence with Laura, shortly before her suicide in 1911. Insofar as Lenchen was a second mother to her, Freddy was a kind of half-brother, and because Lenchen was in effect a member of the Marx family, Eleanor's efforts to put him on a par with the other Marx legatees of Engels's will are understandable in those terms alone. Also the Engels estate was probably her only source of spare cash. Eleanor commented quite correctly in 1892 that Freddy was part of Engels's past, but did not mention the other three principals of the original affair, because by the time of her letter they were all dead. Later when she mentioned again the injustices done to Freddy, she did not mention Engels, because by that time he was dead, too.

Engels's reported irritation with Freddy suggests that he did not want an old embarrassment exhumed, as there was no way that Freddy's circumstances could reflect well on himself and the Marxes as communists, and there were numerous ways that it could be construed to bring discredit on the movement. With Freddy on the scene in London questions might arise about his treatment in early life or just possibly his paternity, and the difficult matter for Engels of proving himself or others innocent of all callous behaviour might arise if such an ill-natured and unedifying inquiry were opened.

Engels had already put himself up for criticism in respect of the Burns sisters, and so he was party already to conventional discretion as a first line of defence. His liaisons were never widely advertised, they were never made to look like 'free love', and they never involved children – though exactly why not, we do not know. Thus they appeared – to those who were determined to inquire – to be responsible domestic relationships that had merely foregone the formalities of marriage. As he was evidently 'doing right' by the Irish girls, not too much could be made of his living arrangements by conservatives bent on gutter politics or communists with scores to settle against Marx. The situation with respect to

Freddy might well have been more difficult to explain and less easy to justify.

The most curious thing about the Freyberger 'letter' is that it contains allegations about Marx and Engels that are quite sensational, but until the 1960s quite unknown. The 'letter' was addressed to one of the most prominent socialist leaders in Germany. Did it actually reach him, or did it go astray or was it never sent? In any case, why did Louise never raise the matter again? She was nothing if not energetic and determined, and as the intention of the 'letter' was plainly to impose a revelation on the world, it seems inconceivable that she put pen to paper once, and then let the sensational story drop for no less than the *fifty-two years* that elapsed before her death in 1950.

Thus the Freyberger 'letter' is very probably inauthentic. Even if it is authentic, Louise's account of the death-bed revelation is as suspect as some of the other 'facts' in the document. And even if the tale of Engels's death-bed is truly told, the validity of his claim that Marx was Freddy's father is open to doubt. Of the two, Engels himself is a better candidate than Karl, and he was indeed living in London at the relevant time, September–October 1850. The younger, unmarried and handsomer man was the one with a taste for girls, working-class ones at that, and Lenchen was his exact contemporary. Writing to Marx from Paris in 1847 Engels let rip about *grisettes* – 'easy' working-class girls called after their cheap grey attire: 'it is absolutely essential that you get out of boring Brussels for once and come to Paris, and I for my part have a great desire to go carousing with you. . . . If I had an income of 5000 francs I would do nothing but work and amuse myself with women until I went to pieces. If there were no Frenchwomen, life wouldn't be worth living. But so long as there are *grisettes*, well and good!' (38 CW 115).

By contrast Karl was notably struck on Jenny his long-suffering wife; and from all accounts he was uxorious in the home – even if he did complain a bit in letters – and desperately anxious for a son. He mourned his two dead ones – Edgar or 'Musch' (1847–55) and Guido or 'Föxchen' (1849–50) – with particular bitterness. The younger boy had only recently died in November 1850, and on the occasion of his third daughter Franziska's birth he commented, 'My wife, alas, has been delivered of a girl, and not a boy. And what is worse, she's very poorly.' When his last surviving child, Eleanor, was born in January 1855, he wrote to Engels, 'my wife was delivered of a *bona fide* TRAVELLER – unfortunately of THE "SEX" *par excellence*. If it had been a male child, well and good'.

Lenchen and Mrs Marx were very close – Lenchen was a link for Jenny with the von Westphalens and happier days – and Frau Marx was virtually all that Helene Demuth had in the world. The two no doubt spent more time together than Jenny spent with Karl, who devoted long hours to his work in the British Museum. It seems difficult to imagine Lenchen deceiving her mistress, and if violence were perpetrated on the maid by Karl, it seems difficult to imagine Jenny allowing the household to continue as if nothing had happened.

Marx's wife Jenny complained on occasion about August Willich (1810–78), one of the expatriate '48ers, saying that he was lurking around the household with seduction on his mind. Someone like that seems a better candidate for Freddy's father than either Marx or Engels. At registration Freddy was named Henry, possibly after Karl Heinrich Marx, and Frederick, possibly after Friedrich Engels, who had no alternative Christian name but sometimes anglicized his own. The two were very possibly charged by the unhappy mother and her distraught mistress with doing the best they could for the infant – at a distance (38 CW 326; 39 CW 509; 1 K 21; KM 246–7).

The story of 'Marx's illegitimate son' has been the most obvious reading of the Freyberger 'letter'. But the document should be particularly scrutinized in the present context for its allegations about Engels, namely his behaviour on his deathbed and before. In the supposed letter Freyberger says: '[Engels] said that he did not wish his name to be besmirched. . . . He had stood in for Marx in order to save him from a serious domestic quarrel. . . . I have seen the letter which Marx wrote to General [Engels's nickname] in Manchester at the time. . . . I believe that he had this letter but, like so much of their correspondence, has destroyed it' (R 134–8).

If Engels were genuinely worried at any stage that Freddy's paternity would be laid at his door – and there is no evidence that he was – he would hardly have wanted to destroy the one piece of evidence that would have cleared him, as the Freyberger 'letter' suggests. If, as seems more likely, he cared more for Marx's name within the communist cause than for his own respectability, then – if there were a letter incriminating Marx – he might well have burnt it, but many years before Louise Freyberger arrived in his household in 1890. However, there is little likelihood that on his deathbed Engels would suddenly demonstrate an overpowering concern for his own moral reputation in the shallowest sense, and then seek to salvage it from an entirely hypothetical attack, by imputing Freddy's paternity to Marx. Indeed Engels took special care to provide for the Marx children, and if Freddy were one as well, Engels could easily have written another codicil and included him amongst the legatees. He would thus have protected himself from charges of 'shabby treatment' with substantial help rather than with unsubstantiated allegations.

Overall Engels was far more concerned for the good name of the communist movement, and for Marx's good name first and foremost within it, than he was for his own. By the time he died he had devoted fifty years to this cause, and he is unlikely to have wanted to blacken Marx's name for any reason whatsoever. The personal and the political were far too closely intertwined in his life to come apart so catastrophically, indeed they were virtually one and the same. The Freyberger 'letter' is instructive because it illustrates precisely the kind of thing that he was *least* likely to say. Political action played a large part in his personal relationships – what they were and how they were conducted – and indeed the idea of political action completely filled his personal life.

6

Continental Communist

From an early age Engels was a political animal, determined to make his mark. For him politics was not a remunerative career – his financial needs were almost entirely met, one way or another, through his family – yet communist politics was his life's work. In that work he faced two major disjunctions.

One disjunction concerned the relationship between writing – such as journalism and pamphleteering – and other forms of political action. Forms of political action apart from writing in Engels's day included speech-making, discussion-circles, public demonstrations, workers' education, the formation and dissolution of groups or parties, the establishment of co-ordinating bodies and the holding of meetings and congresses. For Engels, as for many political activists, all these – political writing and other forms of political activity – were a means to an end. But the difficulty of deciding which means to choose, or how to pursue them in combination, was always a serious one.

Obviously there comes a trade-off as time spent on one form of activity cancels the possibility of pursuing another, and in Engels's own life political writing took precedence. To a large extent this was a reflection of necessity, in that his communist politics had to be pursued clandestinely and in exile for virtually all his life, and authorial publication – despite censorship and police harassment – was generally a safer and apparently more productive option for him than organizational activity as such. On the other hand there were many socialists and communists, indeed constitutional liberals and radical democrats, who played a far larger role in the development of political parties and revolutionary organizations than did Engels and others who have since become 'standard authors'. In many cases organizational activists are now rather less studied and understood than more widely published writers – such as Engels – who concerned themselves with general questions in a way that is still intellectually accessible.

To some extent Engels struck the balance between organizational activism and political writing as he did because of personal choice. In a sense this was a continuation of his earliest opportunities to involve himself in the political world through journalistic activity and to reach a literate audience through publication. In that way his activities as a revolutionary communist were somewhat circumscribed during his lifetime, however famous they have become in retrospect. Furthermore it is perhaps arguable that in his career, writing came to stand for political action as such. This may then have choked off other forms of activity that could have been as productive politically, or more so.

The other disjunction was the tricky political position in which Engels found himself as a communist. The movement for democratic rights to participate in government was only just underway in Europe, and only just beginning to achieve constitutional concessions from which citizen participation in government could be institutionalized. In so far as this movement for representative and responsible government was opposed to established monarchical systems and the remains of a feudal social order, socialists and communists supported it wholeheartedly. And in so far as it expanded the numbers of people involving themselves in political life, organizing to promote their ends and communicating their ideas to an increasingly articulate public, socialists and communists sought an alliance with the democratic movement. In those ways socialists and communists expected to build on the principles of constitutional legality and middle-class politics, accepting them as an improvement on feudal tradition and arbitrary rule. But their position as allies to the democratic movement was somewhat undermined when their socialist and communist principles intruded. In pursuing their defining aims, they criticized democratic principles as insufficient to remedy the 'social question' of endemic poverty and the peculiar ills of industrial society.

Keeping clear of middle-class constitutionalism would perforce condemn the political writing and other activities of socialists and communists to a sectarian ghetto and would make it difficult to attract committed supporters and keep them. But forging an alliance with the democratic movement whilst maintaining a distinctively socialist and communist identity would inevitably expose them to charges of impracticality in trying to go too far too fast. More seriously it might lead to their expulsion on charges of anti-democratic subversion and socially catastrophic nihilism. In such a position socialists and communists found it easy to make enemies and difficult to keep friends, so throughout most of his life Engels fought his battle for communism in conjunction with a very small group indeed.

Middle-class democrats were committed in principle to freedoms of speech and organization, so socialists and communists could expect some toleration for their critical views and constant agitation. But socialism and communism often jeopardized democratic politics for two reasons. Firstly, because they appeared too radical for the middle-classes on the issue of redistributing property, and secondly, because they attracted official repression for their intended subversion of the existing order. Toleration within organizations for would-be allies who sought fundamental alterations from within and attracted destruction from without was consequently limited. But socialists and communists had to align themselves with the democratic movement because it offered them their best access to political influence and practical success.

Engels put his name to a letter to communists in Germany advising them as a matter of tactics to 'proceed jesuitically, put aside teutonic probity, true-heartedness and decency, and sign and push forward the bourgeois petitions for freedom of the press, a constitution, and so on. When this has been achieved a new era will dawn for c[ommunist] propaganda. . . . In a party one must support everything which helps towards progress, and have no truck with any tedious moral scruples' (6 CW 56). But as a matter of fact he recognized 'that even these radical bourgeois here [in Germany] see us as their future main enemies and have no intention of putting into our hands weapons which we would very shortly turn against themselves' (38 CW 172). In politics Engels aimed to be a communist Machiavel, fighting the battle of democracy, but he found his opponents no less cunning. For that reason his political career involved him in considerable frustration.

The guiding questions for this chapter and the next are:

From the age of 24 what political action – apart from writing – did Engels undertake?
What from that point were his achievements in politics?
What important intellectual developments occurred from 1845 onwards and how are they related to the outlook developed in Engels's early years?

I   CLASS POLITICS

Between the autumn of 1841, when he moved to Berlin to do military service, and the spring of 1845, when he took up residence in Brussels to begin a political association with Marx, Engels published some forty-six articles and pamphlets, as well as a large book and his brief contributions to *The Holy Family* – a compendium of chapters written and signed by Marx and Engels individually. Of the two Engels was by far the more prolific and successful publicist, as during the same period Marx published some thirty-nine articles of his own and a very few collaborative pieces, as well as the greater part of *The Holy Family*. But much of Marx's efforts, as in his student days, had gone into works that remained almost wholly unpublished until the twentieth century – a *Critique of Hegel's 'Philosophy of Right'* and the *Economic and Philosophical Manuscripts*.

In November 1844 Engels was at home in Barmen, and in a letter to his new associate Marx he expressed a certain frustration with the politics of the intellectual polemic. He complained about their present confinement to pamphleteering against other intellectuals, merely chastizing them in print for their preoccupation with concepts and for an insufficient engagement with the contemporary politics of social class. During the week or so that autumn when the two had been together in Paris, they had agreed to write a pamphlet in German of some ten printer's sheets – about eighty printed pages – dealing with themes from philosophy, history and idealism. Engels had quickly finished his contribution, about a dozen pages as printed. The work would not be objectionable to the censors, so Marx said in a letter to a German publishing house – which refused the work. He eventually found a publisher in Frankfurt am Main, and the 'Critique of Critical Criticism – Against Bruno Bauer and Company' was launched. Engels's targets were Carl Reichardt, Julius Faucher (1820–78) and Ernst Jungnitz (d. 1848) – all very minor followers of Bauer's tendency – while Marx took over most of the attack by discoursing at length on Edgar Bauer, Pierre-Joseph Proudhon (1809–65), Bruno Bauer and others in the school, such as Stirner.

In a storm of activity Marx greatly expanded the book and attracted criticism from Engels on two counts. One was that Engels appeared as co-author (indeed as first of the two), even though he had contributed but one-and-a-half sheets against Marx's total of over twenty. The pamphlet had become a book, *The Holy Family*, and Engels complained that the new irreligious title would cause him difficulty at home. But the way that Marx had devoted himself at such length to theoretical issues, and to intellectual opponents of little popular standing, upset Engels even more.

In Engels's view Germany was backward precisely because socialism and communism had been taken up most publicly by philosophers, rather than by practical people. On such metaphysicians he himself, Marx and (for a time) Hess had declared war. Thus philosophers such as Bruno Bauer were denigrated by Engels as poor socialists because they occupied themselves with mere speculation, and the theorist Stirner was particularly condemned as an enemy of communism because he advocated an egoism far removed from the 'community system'.

By contrast Engels was 'up to his eyebrows' in the English newspapers and books required for his study of the contemporary condition of the working class in industrial England, and he described his empirical work as 'blows' aimed at the German bourgeoisie. Further projects for his pen were readable studies of English economic developments – to show Germans the truth about industrialism – and a pamphlet against Friedrich List (1789–1846), the leading German political economist. In Engels's eyes List was a typical defender of the class system imposed by industrial development, and he required refutation in a popular form. But a full-blown critical work on political economy as a whole, which Marx had commenced in rough extracts and manuscript draft during 1844, was in Engels's view to be the definitive theoretical refutation of the economic arguments supporting or at least excusing industrial capitalism. In January 1845 he urged Marx to complete this mammoth intellectual task by April, and offered his colleague some writerly advice: 'do as I do, set yourself a date by which you will *definitely have finished*'. Engels's pleas to Marx to get the job over and done with and the results quickly into print were a continuing theme in their correspondence for the next twenty years.

Engels himself was more interested in reviewing the progress of the communist communities of England and America as positive, practical examples, and in praising French and German theorists of socialism in so far as he deemed their ideas realistic. He aimed to get the best works of socialist and communist literature to the

German public in translation, and he sought Marx's collaboration on the project, which was to include translations from François Fourier (1772–1837), Owen and the followers of the Comte de Saint-Simon (1760–1825), who had planned a highly rationalist reform of society. In considering whether to present the French and English thinkers in historical sequence Engels suggested to Marx that theoretical interest in the development of ideas should give way to practical effectiveness. The book should start off with items arranged according to their appeal to the German audience, emphasizing the communist principles the two wished to promote in contemporary political life. 'If we were to seek to give a collection of sources on the history of socialism', he wrote, 'a considerable time would, I fear, elapse before we finished it and, moreover, the thing would become boring'. Of the planned joint project only a translation by Engels – a manuscript fragment by Fourier on trade – was published, and Marx did little on the book, if anything.

Engels's politics was far removed from the philanthropy, *noblesse oblige* and religious effusions that his pantheon of 'foreign', i.e. non-German, socialists and communists variously exemplified. While he praised the achievements in practice of experimental communitarians who had established new societies in miniature, the thought of joining or emulating such groups never seems to have occurred to him. Rather he was concerned to draw lessons from their trials and errors that would impress his German audience. This was the native middle class in Elberfeld and later the émigré working class in Brussels and Paris – even New York. His idea of a practical movement in politics was very broad and in the Hegelian mode: 'the whole of English and French history during the last eighty years, English industry and the French revolution'.

When a copy of *The Holy Family* finally arrived in Barmen in March 1845 Engels praised it briefly in a letter to his co-author – and then complained that it was too long, incomprehensible to the public at large and of no obvious general interest. 'Otherwise', he noted somewhat faintly, 'the book is splendidly written', but its size was wholly at odds with the supreme contempt in which they held the writers whose work they had wanted to ridicule. In an earlier letter to Marx he had already announced that he found the 'theoretical twaddle' of philosophers and intellectuals 'daily more tedious' and that he was irritated 'by every word . . . that has to be read or written against [idealist] theology and abstraction no less than against crude materialism'.

In his own writings Engels was turning instead to 'real, live things, to historical developments and consequences'. Such an approach, he said to Marx, is 'the best we can hope for so long as we're confined exclusively to wielding a pen and cannot realise our thoughts directly with our hands, or, if need be, with our fists'. In fact he longed to get the 'wild, hot-blooded dyers and bleachers' of the Wuppertal on the move, making their protest against industrial society through communism, rather than through the individual violence – beating, stabbing and robbing the local bourgeoisie at night – that had become a commonplace occurrence. Thus the 24-year-old Engels clearly longed to move from mere writing to other forms of action in politics. And even in respect of political writing he had suspicions concerning the practical effect for German communists of his co-author's published efforts and large-scale plans (4 CW 240–2, 644; 38 CW 5, 7, 10–13, 17–18, 25, 27–8).

Though somewhat sceptical of Marx's emphasis on theoretical questions – but highly impressed by his thoroughness in arguing political issues through to basic premises – Engels joined Marx in early April 1845 in an informal political association. This was not an inevitable event, as Engels had previously been much closer to Hess. Indeed Engels had been working with Hess in Elberfeld, and the two planned for a time to edit a journal together. But Engels had his suspicions that Hess was tending towards philosophical and moral idealism. Even if Marx was not wholly practical in a political sense, he was at least empirical in his interests and razor-sharp in his writings, unlike Hess, who was given to dreamy, ill-defined speculations. Best of all Marx was utterly disinclined to preach any pseudo-Christian, quasi-religious or even moralistic socialism based on love for one's fellows and true faith in a doctrine – approaches to social reconstruction which Engels's thoroughgoing atheism had led him to reject. Engels admired Marx's insistence that the conflicting material interests of class politics formed the basis of the communist critique of existing society. Indeed class analysis was a preoccupation dating back to the 'Letters from Wuppertal'. In Marx's view the resolution of social conflict in favour of the labouring class would become the basis in practice of a new society – communism. For Engels, who ad experienced the real world of industry and commerce, here were exciting and realistic premises for political action.

In the early days of their association Engels took Marx on his first rip to England. During the weeks from 12 July to 21 August 1845 hey surveyed the resources available in Manchester and London for Marx's projected critique of political economy. Engels had lready embarked on that line of theoretical research for his outline critique in the *Deutsch-französische Jahrbücher*, and had good advice to give. Also, the two made contact with the London branch of the League of the Just, a group of loosely organized émigrés working to liberalize German political life, albeit from abroad. However, Marx's first exposure to the full force of industrialization and to the open practice of class politics in England did not deflect him from his concern with theorists – some dead, some living. Back in Brussels he began a lengthy critical satire *Die deutsche Ideologie* (*The German Ideology*) with Engels's help, but it did not find a willing publisher either as a series of articles or as a book. The vast work was an attack on Feuerbach, Bruno Bauer and Stirner for their 'pure' philosophy of humanity, and then on Karl Grün (1817–1887) (Proudhon's translator) and others in the developing school of 'true' socialism.

Marx obviously considered the conceptual speculations of these philosophers and journalists to be a real danger. Undisciplined philosophizing, as he saw it, was ultimately unconvincing and liable to lead to some truly strange conclusions about politics. Moreover the 'true socialists' were disinclined to support the constitutional reforms and civil rights for which middle-class liberals – and Marx and Engels – were working, though with different long-term goals in mind. Indeed Marx feared that the 'German ideologists', such as Bauer, and 'true socialists', such as Grün, were sowers of confusion about class relations and material interests in society – the very basis of his new outlook. In his manuscript notes he described this outlook somewhat obscurely as a new materialism, but it was in reality a class-based analysis of history and politics.

Feuerbach – the most prestigious and sophisticated of the philosophers under attack – became a highly intellectual point of departure for the exposition of communist premises. Indeed by education and interests Marx and Engels were all too readily identified by some Young Hegelians as disciples of Feuerbach, who had declared himself for an all-out inversion of idealism. But

Marx and Engels considered his materialism insufficiently social in outlook and class-conscious in content, and did not care to be known as his disciples, nor indeed anyone else's.

Almost by definition 'the German ideology' and 'true socialism' were not perceived as such an egregious threat by anyone else, and only a small fraction of the massive manuscript work appeared in print. A four-page reply to Bruno Bauer's criticism of *The Holy Family* was published by Engels, albeit anonymously, in the Rhineland press, and part of that text drew on a minute portion of *The German Ideology*. A jointly written 'circular' criticizing the 'true socialist' Hermann Kriege (1820–50), who was publishing a German newspaper for émigrés in New York, had perhaps been destined for inclusion in the larger work. The material that Engels made into historical articles on the socialist verse of Beck and the prose writings of Grün, and Marx's review of Grün's major work, were both drawn from manuscript material for the projected satire. Engels also drafted an up-date on 'true socialism' in early 1847, but did not get the article published.

Of the vast work – *The German Ideology* was estimated at some fifty printer's sheets – Engels considered the opening philosophical section on Feuerbach to be the most urgent, but could not find a taker. Engels's conception of urgency was tied to personalities in politics and to remuneration in real life, rather than to the intellectual niceties of definitive arguments. He wrote to Marx that each month that the manuscripts lay idle they lost '5–10 francs per sheet in EXCHANGEABLE VALUE', and that after a few months 'Bauer and Stirner will not fetch more than 10 francs per sheet'. Eventually, he concluded, the value to the publisher of such a topical work would sink to 'the stage where the high fee demanded as a writer's *point d'honneur* has to be completely set aside' – in reality a serious issue, as they were both short of money (38 CW 79, 112–13; see MEIR 67–71).

Before leaving Germany for Paris in the autumn of 1843, Marx had indeed achieved some political notoriety for his editorial policies on the *Rheinische Zeitung* and struggles with the censor. But away from his paper he was tending to concentrate very heavily on theoretical issues and on attacks directed at fellow theorists. These culminated in print in his *Misère de la philosophie* (*Poverty of Philosophy*) of 1847, a critique of Proudhon, whose ideas on 'co-operative' production and 'just' exchange were becoming an influence on German socialism. Though published in Brussels and

Paris, where Marx was in touch with German émigré politics, the book was in fact written in French, so that, as he commented, 'Proudhon himself will be able to reply'. Engels described Marx's plan as splendid – but noted that German-speaking communists were left tantalized. And he continued to complain to Marx that it was extremely urgent that 'your book [on economics] . . . should appear as soon as possible', since the 'fellows are all worried by the thought that such splendid ideas remain so long concealed from the people' (6 CW 73; 38 CW 109, 112).

Significantly the anonymous *Manifest der kommunistischen Partei (Communist Manifesto)*, finished by Marx in January 1848, but previously drafted during 1847 in two versions by Engels, is in style and content far more like Engels's journalism, full-length book and essays than like Marx's penetrating but convoluted critiques. The slim pamphlet is a political masterpiece, and it was reprinted and widely circulated within a few months. Engels could never have written Marx's 1843 manuscript critique of Hegel's philosophy of law, now considered a major contribution to the philosophical theory of the state, nor his Paris manuscripts of 1844 criticizing political economy, now regarded as an important text in modern 'continental' philosophy. But then however much he admired the quality of Marx's thought, Engels would not have wanted to write those works, because few people were seriously interested in the highly specialized ideas under attack, and hardly anyone could understand the points that Marx was making. Marx did not have the steady focus on intended audience, quick publication and immediate effect that was so characteristic of Engels and his writing, and Engels's developing political talents as a communist agitator were somewhat mismatched with Marx's current penchant for overblown satires.

Towards the middle of the 1840s the middle-class movement for constitutional rule took off in Germany. By late 1844 the political importance of Young Hegelian intellectuals was tending to fade, and Engels was inclined to disparage even his own earlier efforts during his Berlin days to undermine their views. His researches into the condition of the working class and the history of industrialization, which he worked on in Manchester, were also not continued much after 1845, apart from a brief postscript of 1846 to *The Condition of the Working Class in England*. In that way certain targets for attack and objects of study were shifted aside somewhat, whilst his long-standing interest in exposing the evils of class rule by the bourgeoisie took precedence in the three years to 1848. The main task of any investigation of social questions, he proclaimed, is 'the *criticism of existing society*' (4 CW 614).

Between late 1844 and early 1848 – whilst he was in Barmen, Brussels and then Paris – Engels continued with his own topical journalism, always from the communist perspective, and with his overt advertisements for the communist cause. Though he attacked the 'true socialists' in print, albeit briefly, and replied at length to the criticisms of communism published by Karl Heinzen (1809–80), a German liberal democrat turned radical republican, his main focus was on current political events and issues. His articles were written for the press in Germany, Belgium, France and England, and the political complexion of the papers that took his work ranged from socialist and communist to respectably reformist. Using German, English and finally French, Engels covered familiar ground in chronicling industrial unrest in Germany, elsewhere on the continent and in England; protesting the harassment of communist writers and sympathetic presses in various continental countries; considering the balance of political forces and relative levels of economic development in Britain, France and Germany; addressing the Irish question, the Chartist campaign and the agitation against the corn laws; and pondering the implications of the development of European constitutionalism for the future of the working-class movement.

Engels had been dedicated for some years to the 'eloquence of facts' in studying industrial society and to the exposure of hypocrisy in middle-class defences of private property. He carefully distinguished empirical studies of the working classes, which were of course politically useful, from the more serious and potentially more explosive business of exposing 'respectable society, the contradiction between its theory and its practice, the dullness of its entire mode of life'. He argued that existing society was thoroughly reprehensible and that 'by criticism of the bourgeoisie alone – namely of the bourgeoisie in its inner relationships, apart from its attitude to the proletariat – one can arrive at the necessity of a social reconstruction'. About German social criticism to date he was typically scathing: 'True, there has been talk here and there about free love, about the position of woman and her emancipation; but what has been the result? A few confused phrases, a few blue-stockings, a little hysteria and a good deal of moaning about the German family – not even one bastard came out of it!' (4 CW 643–4).

Whilst in Barmen Engels claimed that the vigour of his own communist analysis – combined with the threat of spontaneous mob violence – could move the middle classes of the Wuppertal to reject the benefits (for them) of private property and to see the virtues (for all) of communal ownership. But he expected even more enthusiasm from the working classes and even less resistance. He acknowledged that there were a number of republicans and indeed communists amongst the youth of the middle class, but their numbers would inevitably be small. Thus communists could not count on them but would instead look to the 'glorious array of working Democrats and Communists'. In Germany, he commented, 'Democracy and Communism are, as far as the working classes are concerned, quite synonymous'.

Engels took the line that *'Democracy nowadays is communism'*, and 'all European democrats . . . are more or less Communists at heart'. This was because, in his view, 'the transition from the absolute monarchy to the modern representative state in no way abolishes the poverty of the great mass of the people', but rather brings to power a new class, the bourgeoisie. By means of its capital this class presses heavily on the 'masses', and hence it is 'the opponent *par excellence* of the Communists, or socialists respectively, as representatives of the mass of the people'. In Engels's view the working class was no beneficiary of the current system and so would hardly want to defend its ideals and institutions (4 CW 647; 6 CW 5, 75–6).

By the spring of 1845 Engels had himself had practical experience in class politics, and he put this quite pointedly to Marx, saying: 'standing up in front of real, live people and holding forth to them directly and straightforwardly, so that they see and hear you is something quite different from engaging in this devilishly abstract quillpushing with an abstract audience in one's "mind's eye"' (38 CW 23).

Engels and his communist associates in the Rhineland, such as Hess, had been holding public meetings arranged on the spur of the moment and without police permission. Organisations to assist the working classes, and thereby circumvent strikes and violence, were being set up throughout Germany in late 1844, as the Silesian weavers' uprising had taken place that summer. Engels reported

that 'our own people' had gained access to the local rules committees in Cologne and Elberfeld and that in alliance with Christian
rationalists they had defeated pietist conservatives, though he did
not say on what issues. The society for the education and relief of
workers in Elberfeld was twice addressed by Engels himself, and
he sent Marx a report: 'Here in Elberfeld wondrous things are
afoot. Yesterday we held our third communist meeting in the
town's largest hall and leading inn. The first meeting was forty
strong, the second 130 and the third at least 200. All Elberfeld and
Barmen, from the financial aristocracy to *épicerie* was represented,
only the proletariat being excluded.'

Proletarian participation was presumably unthinkable, as middle-class participants would surely have stormed out, and the
police would have considered it a disorderly gathering by definition. But for the middle classes – in a respectably organized
gathering – Engels reported that communism was a tremendous
draw. He considered them to be potentially favourable to the
communist cause, as they had been frightened into intellectual
curiosity and political action by outbreaks of working-class violence against employers and landowners. Even if the police were
successful in banning further meetings as seditious, he expected
that communist publications would henceforth be voraciously
sought and widely read.

Engels was not yet, however, in direct contact with a working-
class audience. 'What the proletariat does we know not and indeed
could hardly know', he wrote to Marx from Barmen. Though he
was anxious to show them the communist way towards 'the free
development and exercise of their human nature and inborn
capacities', he dismissed this for the moment as impossible,
presumably because of swift police repression – and an even
swifter and perhaps more terrible reaction at home. Instead his
audience was drawn from the politically liberal and socially
philanthropic middle classes.

Engels's speeches of February 1845 were themselves published
in August in a radical Rhineland magazine, and his verdict on the
episode was a model of political calculation. He commented that
middle-class schemes to dupe the working classes with savings
banks, premiums and prizes for the best workers were mere
hypocrisy and sham philanthropy, rightly exposed to ridicule by
communists who had found a rare opportunity – 'in a country of
patriarchal police government' – to gain a public hearing. But in

the local societies to relieve working-class distress the twin dangers inherent in the communists' position began to surface. Their rationalist allies deserted them, because the middle classes feared a red revolution, and the Prussian government wound up the groups altogether, because it feared democratic activity (4 CW 237–40, 250; 38 CW 10, 22–4, 30, 569).

After Engels moved to Brussels in early 1845 the framework for his political activity shifted somewhat. In Belgium he could contact working-class communists and socialists directly, if not always openly, and he could pursue the organizational means to spread communist information throughout the émigré community in Belgium and France. Expatriate German labourers were working in what he considered to be more advanced conditions in industry than those employed in Germany, and so in his view they ought to be more receptive to communist and socialist ideas. Socialist and communist ideas were in any case more sophisticated in France and Belgium than in Germany, so the new class politics would be that much more potent. Émigré socialists and communists, such as Engels, aimed to influence workers in Germany, albeit indirectly for the time being. When the political situation in Germany became favourable, a network of socialists and communists – both middle-class and working-class in origin – could return, and the development of German socialism and communism would then advance in step with the most progressive wings of the movement.

Engels worked with Marx in founding a Communist Correspondence Committee in Brussels in early 1846, and similar committees were founded in London, Paris, Cologne and a number of other towns. Writing to Proudhon – already an object of considerable criticism but still a potential ally – Marx explained that the aim was to put German socialists in touch with their French and English counterparts, to inform the world about the development of socialism in Germany, and to keep Germans up to date with the progress of socialism in France and England. Marx envisaged a constant interchange of letters on 'scientific questions', with an eye on popular writings and socialist propaganda:

> In this way differences of opinion can be brought to light and an exchange of ideas and impartial criticism can take place. It will be a step made by the social movement in its *literary* manifestation to rid itself of the barriers of *nationality*. And when the moment for action comes, it will clearly be much to everyone's advantage

to be acquainted with the state of affairs abroad as well as at home (38 CW 39).

The Committee aimed to contact groups such as the League of the Just. The membership of the League comprised conspiratorial revolutionaries and visionary communists, and its adherents were located in England (where Engels had first made contact) and on the continent. In turn, the League was closely associated with the German Workers' Educational Society in London, founded in 1840 by Schapper and Moll, in order to introduce communism into popular programmes of after-hours study. The League was also a force in the International Society of Fraternal Democrats in London, founded in 1845 by Harney of *The Northern Star*, which aimed to bring left-wing émigrés into contact with Chartism and middle-class democrats. The Brussels Committee aimed to contact both kinds of group – workers' educational societies and pressure groups for democratic reform. Amongst the committee's communications were strongly worded warnings, written by Marx and Engels, about the 'true socialists' and their deleterious influence.

As Marx was still banned from France, Engels travelled to Paris during 1846 and 1847, taking up the Committee's cause: 'I went to see Étienne Cabet [author of *Voyage en Icarie*, Paris, 1842]. The old boy [Cabet was then about 58] was extremely cordial, I listened to all his stuff, told him about God and the devil, etc. I shall go there more often' (38 CW 53). More interestingly Engels reported back to the Brussels committee about his meetings with German workers – cabinet-makers living in the Faubourg St Antoine in Paris. This was a group of twelve to twenty, gathering once a week for discussion. An émigré communist – Ewerbeck – gave them lectures on German history, and then 'an extremely muddled political economy', drawn from Engels's own article on the subject in the *Deutsch-französische Jahrbücher*:

> Meanwhile I appeared. In order to establish contact with them, I twice discussed conditions in Germany since the French revolution, my point of departure being the economic relations. . . . It is a good way of attracting new people for it's entirely public; a fortnight ago the police arrived and wanted to impose a veto but allowed themselves to be placated and did nothing further. . . . I hope to be able to achieve something with the fellows, for they

all have a strong desire for instruction in economics (38 CW 61–2).

Engels's great success with these groups came later in 1846 when he obtained majority support for his definition of communist aims. In that way he was working to expunge the influence of the 'true socialist' Grün where it mattered – on the ground: 'The main thing is that the various differences I have had to thrash out with the lads hitherto are now settled: Grün's chief follower and disciple, Papa Eisermann [a German joiner], has been chucked out, the rest, so far as their influence over the great majority is concerned, have been completely routed, and I have carried through a unanimous resolution against them.'

At these gatherings Engels urged the German workers in Paris to reject Proudhonian 'reforms' of production and exchange, which he described as petty-bourgeois panaceas, and Grünian 'true socialism', which he thought insufficiently cognizant of class antagonism. Communism, which he defined very simply in three points, was the recommended alternative. Communists aimed: '1. to ensure that the interests of the proletariat prevail, as opposed to those of the bourgeoisie; 2. to do so by abolishing private property and replacing same with community of goods; 3. to recognise no means of attaining these aims other than democratic revolution by force' (38 CW 81–2).

By early 1847 Engels believed that the Paris police, suspicious of his political activities, were watching him with a view to deportation. He ceased his communist agitation for a time, and by the summer he was back in Brussels where a Democratic Association – similar to the London Fraternal Democrats – was being formed. Writing to Marx, who was temporarily in Holland (seeking money from relatives), Engels affirmed that 'nothing democratic must be allowed to take place in little Brussels without our participating', and presented the affair as a plot. Middle-class democrats, so he thought, were working against the interests of communists and of the newly-formed Brussels German Workers' Society, which was similar to the Educational Society in London. Engels – though professing embarrassment about his youthful appearance – took on the vice-presidency of the Democratic Association, and he and Marx co-operated in publicizing plans – Marx in Brussels and Engels in Paris – for an international democratic congress. The two

communists were thus balancing their efforts between working-
class and middle-class venues within organizations that were
increasingly international – and internationalist – in character. In a
letter to Marx, Engels drew out what seemed politically important
to him in this Brussels episode:

> The affair [of the Democratic Association] has made a capital
> impression on the [German Workers'] Society; for the first time
> they have had a role to play, have dominated a meeting despite
> all the plotting, and have put in his place a fellow who was
> trying to set himself up against them. . . . They have experienced
> what it means to be associated. . . . The fellows are beginning to
> feel their own importance (38 CW 122–3, 128, 130).

Through the Brussels Correspondence Committee Marx and
Engels were achieving recognition as international communists,
and the League of the Just in London approached them proposing
membership. They countered with a proposal for reorganization so
that the loose conspiratorial group would become an organized
political party representing communism as they conceived it. In
Engels's phrase their communism was summed up in the 'necessity for revolution by force', very much in the tradition of the French
revolutions of 1789 and 1830. In his view this form of mass
democratic politics involved constant contact between radical
intellectuals and 'the people', *ad hoc* forms of organization changing to meet threats and to consolidate gains, and fierce resistance
to counter-revolutionary 'reaction' and backsliding 'liberal' compromises. At the same time his conception of mass politics excluded plots, conspiracies and ill-prepared insurrections. In a
political party – as he conceived it – communism would acquire an
organization of dedicated members with as much public presence
as possible. Such communists would not be mere 'sympathizers'
whose commitments to existing parties of reform would dampen
their efforts, nor would they be hare-brained schemers whose
antics would lead to mass repression.

An international congress to found the Communist League was
agreed, and Engels – as a representative of the German workers in
Paris – attended its meetings in London in June 1847. Marx lacked
funds to make the journey. Engels arrived with a draft 'confession
of faith' or revolutionary catechism, a type of work that was useful
in converting workers to the communist cause. Discussions of the

'confession' and draft rules took place after the first congress amongst members of the League and other communists working within the various local workers' societies and correspondence committees. Engels rewrote his draft as a declaration of the 'principles of communism' in October, retaining the simple question-and-answer format. In November, having returned to Paris, he was elected once again to be a delegate from there to the second congress, as Marx was for Brussels, where his Correspondence Committee had organized a new section of the still-gestating Communist League. About the mechanics of his own election Engels was honest but un-self-aware, turning up contradictions but not seeking resolutions. Two questions in particular – the place of intrigue in democratic organizations, and the role of the middle-classes in a workers' party – did not detain him in his thought and action: 'After an extremely muddled session I was elected with a 2/3 [majority]. This time I had engaged in no intrigues whatsoever, there had been little opportunity for any. The opposition was merely a fiction; a working man was proposed for appearances' sake, but those who proposed him voted for me' (38 CW 143).

The second international congress of communists was held later that month in London. Engels wrote cheerfully to Marx about their plans to attend the sessions together, and said, 'This congress must be a decisive one, AS THIS TIME WE SHALL HAVE IT ALL OUR OWN WAY'. And he took Marx into his confidence about the policy document that he was still drafting for the Party, albeit behind the backs of its general membership in Paris:

> *Strictly between ourselves*, I've played an infernal trick on Mosi [Hess]. He had actually put through a delightfully amended confession of faith. Last Friday at the district [committee of the Communist League] I dealt with this. . . . I got them to entrust me with the task of drafting a new one which . . . will be sent to London *behind the backs of the [communist] communities*. Naturally not a soul must know about this, otherwise we shall all be unseated and there'll be the deuce of a row (38 CW 138–9, 146).

Later he wrote more specifically to Marx about his revisions: 'I think we would do best to abandon the catachetical form and call the thing Communist *Manifesto*. Since a certain amount of history has to be narrated in it, the form hitherto adopted is quite unsuitable.' Engels informed Marx that he had begun with the

question 'What is communism?' and had then gone straight on to
discuss the proletariat – its history, how it differs from earlier
workers, its antithetical relationship with the bourgeoisie, the
development of economic crises and finally, the communists' party
policy, 'in so far as it should be made public'. He described his
present version as 'wretchedly worded' but said, 'I think I can get it
through in such a form that at least there is nothing in it which
conflicts with our views' (38 CW 149).

As it happened Engels could make certain of this, because at the
second congress, where he acted as secretary, he and Marx were
charged with preparing a final version, and the two worked
together when they were back in Brussels in December. Engels
returned to Paris later in the month, and Marx – after repeated
entreaties and threats from communist leaders – sent the final
manuscript to the printers in January 1848 (for a textual comparison of the *Manifesto* and Engels's drafts, see MEIR 78–94). Because
the title substituted 'Party' for 'League', it represented something
of a coup for communists such as Marx and Engels, who had
steered clear of 'the Just'. The *Manifesto* of the Communist Party was
published in London in February 1848 at a printshop owned by a
German émigré, and the German Workers' Educational Society
covered the costs.

By January 1848 Engels was in some despair about his agitation
in Paris amongst the émigré workers on which he had spent the
best part of a year, saying 'things are going wretchedly with the
League' and complaining 'never have I encountered such sluggish-
ness and petty jealousy ... nothing can be done'. He described
some of these German workers as 'ageing boors' and others as
'aspiring petty bourgeois'. 'A class which lives, Irish-fashion, by
depressing the wages of the French', so he wrote to Marx, 'is
utterly useless'. Engels looked forward to the arrival of the rules
and manifesto from the London congress 'to liven things up
somewhat', but resolved that this was his one last attempt. 'If that
doesn't succeed', he concluded, 'I shall give up this kind of
propaganda' (38 CW 154).

The outbreak of revolution on the Continent in the early weeks
of 1848 did not so much overtake the *Manifesto* as sweep it up. Its
co-authors returned quite unexpectedly to Germany. Copies of the
document were shipped over from London, and Marx and Engels
moved back into communist politics in the Rhineland.

II RHINELAND REVOLUTIONARY

Engels was finally expelled from France for being a communist agitator in late January 1848, and he returned to Brussels to join Marx in their local and international work with the newly-founded Communist Party. But after the revolutionary events of late February in Paris, when King Louis Philippe was overthrown, Marx was ejected from Belgium as a subversive influence by panicky authorities. He was then invited back to Paris by a member of the new government of revolutionary French republicans. Their régime was merely provisional till the planned adoption – by popularly elected representatives – of a new, democratic constitution.

Up to 1848 Engels had enjoyed some success in working with and through middle-class constitutional groups and liberal newspapers. It was important to his strategy of supporting radical reform to have good relationships with editors and journalists such as Harney in Britain, Lucien Jottrand (1804–77) in Belgium, the Frenchman Ferdinand Flocon (1800–66, editor of *La Réforme*) and the Rhinelander Hermann Püttman (1811–94, editor of the *Deutsches Bürgerbuch*). But during 1848–9 Engels experienced the opposite aspect of his conditional alliance with middle-class reformists – their fear of attracting monarchical repression. The 'revolutions' of 1848–9 were really the promotion of constitutionalism through mass action and ultimately violence, though in fact popular insurrections were ill-suited to maintaining provisional governments and new republics. This was because monarchists and other authoritarians could command large-scale forces away from the large towns, which had been the scenes of successful armed insurgency.

Communists and all manner of radicals might have been useful allies for the constitutionalists in defying the old authorities, had the constitutionalists wished to begin a new order in society and to crush the defenders of the old régime without mercy. No doubt cognisant of the French revolutionary experience, in which a defence of constitutionalism had degenerated into terror, Engels's middle-class contemporaries – when they were constitutionalists at all – did not want an all-out struggle with monarchism in Germany or with self-styled defenders of public order such as Louis Bonaparte in France. Hence they did not require communists and socialists as allies. Rather they sought concessions from former authorities and military leaders, not mastery of the situation. Indeed they sometimes considered the 'left' more dangerous than the 'right'. In that way middle-class constitutionalists aimed to defend themselves from the potential threat of socialism and communism, and to achieve a constitutional régime. Their strategy was to compromise with monarchists and dictators, who promised to defend the principle of private property.

The proclamation of the Second Republic in Paris on 25 February 1848 was the signal for communists to put their own political strategy into operation, and for Marx and Engels – as co-authors of the *Manifesto* – to take over the League and make it into a Party. They expected to push middle-class constitutionalists into defeating authoritarians and monarchists, and then to press these revolutionary liberals on the 'social question'. The London inner circle transferred itself successively to Brussels and Paris, following Marx. Engels left Belgium on 20 March to join his colleagues in revolutionary France.

Riots had already erupted in Vienna and Berlin, forcing out unpopular ministers – though not monarchism as such – and demonstrations in favour of constitutional rights and social reforms had broken out in the Rhineland. Engels's first comments on the events there were excited, but prescient:

> It's a bad business in Cologne.... They [the demonstrators] wanted to go into the attack, but instead of supplying themselves with weapons, which were easily obtainable, they went to the town hall unarmed and let themselves be surrounded... The thing was initiated without rhyme or reason ... they could very well have gone into the attack and in 2 hours all would have been over. But everything was organised with appalling stupidity.

'Otherwise', he continued, 'the news from Germany is splendid', but the outcome of revolutionary events was far from certain. Engels's method of class-analysis by no means precluded the study of individual actions in politics. Moreover he assigned to them a considerable degree of indeterminacy. Hence he noted that success was dependent on the actions of King Friedrich Wilhelm IV: if only he would dig his heels in and stick to his feudal ways! 'But the devil only knows what this capricious and crazy individual will do' (38 CW 159–60).

Engels's correspondence and works written during the revolutionary events of 1848–9 reflected very precisely his view that a
successful revolution would resemble in crucial ways the events
that took place in France from 1789 to 1793. But his model was, of
course, the French revolution as portrayed within the traditions of
romantic rebellion and Young Hegelian historiography, in which
he had schooled himself: 'the whole European social movement
today is only the ... *dénoument* of the drama which began in Paris
in 1789, and now has the whole of Europe for its stage'. In
particular he extolled the most radical of the successive revolutionary governments as the harbinger of contemporary class struggle:
'there were men ... whose iron energy ensured that from May 31,
1792 [the Jacobin uprising] to July 26, 1794 [the coup of 9–10
Thermidor] ... not a single bourgeois dared show his face' (6 CW
5).

In the *Deutsche-Brüsseler Zeitung* for 27 February he wrote of the
current revolutionary events in a vividly apocalyptic style: 'News
has just arrived that the people have won and proclaimed the
Republic. We confess that we had not dared hope for this brilliant
success by the Paris proletariat. . . . Our age, the age of democracy,
is breaking. The flames of the Tuileries and the Palais Royal are the
dawn of the proletariat. Everywhere the rule of the bourgeoisie will
now come crashing down, or be dashed to pieces' (6 CW 558).

Mass armed action, particularly of the 'people' or the 'workers'
in urban areas, was exactly what he aimed to foment and assist.
Writing to his brother-in-law from Paris in March, Engels identified
the major political forces in France by social class. But he defined
class ostensively rather than analytically: 'the big bourgeoisie,
speculators on the Bourse, bankers, manufacturers and big merchants, the old conservatives and liberals'. Next were 'the petty
bourgeoisie, the middle class, the bulk of the National Guard
[citizen militia] ... the "reasonable radicals"'. And finally there
were 'the people, the Parisian workers, who are now holding Paris
by force of arms'.

Almost as an afterthought Engels mentioned the peasantry as
supporters of the 'petty bourgeoisie', whom he despised for their
vacillations between left and right. As his eye was on a victorious
revolution he dismissed the Legitimists, who wished to revive the
Bourbon monarchy, and the Bonapartists, who wished to revive
the Napoleonic empire, as isolated sectarians. Had he had his eye
on counter-revolution as such, rather than on mere 'set-backs', he

might have taken the Bonapartists – who were the eventual victors – more seriously from the beginning. Instead his expectation was that middle-class vacillation, and consequent ruling-class 'uppishness', would lead to further armed action by the outraged masses. In May he commented in those terms on the situation in Berlin, where 'the rule of officials and aristocrats grows daily more insolent, irritates the people, the people revolt and ... [liberal] spinelessness and cowardice lead us straight towards fresh revolutions' (38 CW 167–8, 176).

Conversely Engels rejected any revolutionary conspiracy or small-scale insurgency, particularly when it was 'inserted' into a locality from abroad. The formation of a volunteer legion of German émigrés in France, and the plan to march them into Germany to establish republican rule through military action – province by province – was scorned by him as a doomed crusade. While he viewed the group as unsound on the 'social question' and hardly even socialist, he was in addition never friendly to the political strategy they espoused. Instead he worked in Paris to dispatch communists – largely unarmed and relatively unorganized – into Germany to work with whatever constitutional and radical forces they could find. Armed action by popular forces, aroused through demonstrations and the written word, was the method by which he expected the revolution to progress. While local communists and the more distant authorities of the Party had a role to play in exhorting revolution and drafting demands, this never extended to enforcing or even recommending a particular leadership structure in the field.

Engels aimed to make his contribution to the revolution in the first instance by continuing his work as a journalist. In early April he joined Marx in Cologne on his revived newspaper the *Neue Rheinische Zeitung*. Marx was editor-in-chief, and his associates included his friend Wilhelm Wolff (1809–64) and Engels's friend Weerth, along with three other communists – Ernst Dronke (1822–91), Heinrich Bürgers (1820–78) and Ferdinand Wolf (sometimes 'Wolff' but in my text always 'Wolf', 1812–95) – later joined by the poet Freiligrath. Advice, exhortation and criticism flowed in some 300 issues over twelve months, beginning on 1 June.

While serving as a writer and deputy-editor of Marx's paper Engels also made himself active once again as a Wuppertal communist, returning to Barmen. Writing to his editor on 25 April Engels commented, 'the mood of the bourgeoisie is really ugly', and he noted that 'the workers are beginning to bestir themselves a little, still in a very crude way, but as a mass'. Direct discussion of the 'social question' was not on, he reckoned, as repression would be swift. The workers' own political activity – in which they formed themselves into 'coalitions', i.e. factions and sects – could only be 'a hindrance' to the class unity that communists were seeking to promote. Without that unity they would lose their main chance, which was to threaten and cajole the middle classes into action against the old régime.

In particular Engels commented that if even one copy of the seventeen demands published by the Communist Party reached the Wuppertal, 'all would be lost' (38 CW 173). This was a flysheet based on the concluding paragraphs of section II of the much longer *Manifesto*, and it was published in German in Paris in March, reprinted in the press in Germany and widely circulated. The document was signed by Marx, Schapper, Heinrich Bauer, Engels, Moll and Wolff. The Communists called for a unified German republic, a parliamentary government, and universal (i.e. manhood) suffrage at 21. They advocated arming of the people, which was to be co-ordinated with a militarization of labour. Other demands included free legal services, an end to all feudal obligations, complete separation of church and state, and free education. Their economic programme comprised the nationalization of productive resources such as mines and transport, as well as large agricultural estates. Other aspects of the market economy would be managed centrally: state mortgages and tenancies for peasants, state control of banking and currency, one salary grading for civil servants, a guaranteed livelihood through national workshops, and provision for the incapacitated. The communists also proposed a curtailment of the right of inheritance, the introduction of graduated taxes, and the abolition of duties on consumption. Overall through these measures they aimed to bind the interests of the conservative bourgeoisie to the revolutionary government through legal action. And they wanted to appeal beyond 'the German proletariat' to the 'petty bourgeoisie and the small peasants', so that through their representatives in democratic politics these groups would support a programme of constitutional and political reforms 'with all possible energy' (7 CW 3–7).

Back in Cologne Engels was involved, along with Marx, in the activities of the local Democratic Society (where they made speeches) and the Workers' Association (of which Marx was briefly president). The high point of these activities was the organization of the Cologne Committee of Public Safety. This took place after a mass meeting of 13 September, and the editors of the *Neue Rheinische Zeitung* – who had been subject to police inquiry since July – were elected members. A mass meeting at Worringen on the Rhine was held on 17 September to stimulate resistance in the Rhineland to the actions of the Prussian government, which was opposed to the liberalizing measures passed by the German National Assembly, sitting as a constituent assembly for all of Germany at Frankfurt. The communist Schapper was president of the Worringen public meeting and Engels secretary.

Prussian reaction began to strike in earnest on 26 September when the authorities declared a state of siege in Cologne. The militia was disbanded, and the *Neue Rheinische Zeitung*, amongst other democratic publications, was suspended. The arrest of agitators such as Engels was ordered, and the warrants were publicized. Moving swiftly from Barmen to Belgium and then to France, Engels escaped, but did not seem to grasp that the siege was over within a week and the newspaper back in print within a fortnight. Instead of returning immediately to Cologne he set out in early October to walk to Switzerland by way of the Loire and Burgundy. He arrived at Neuchâtel in early November, then moved on and stayed over two months in Berne. Possibly he feared a row with unfriendly shareholders of Marx's paper, and possibly he feared further reprisals from the authorities in Cologne.

Or possibly there was simply an element of holiday-making in the episode, during which Engels enjoyed himself thoroughly. Taking a walking tour in the middle of the 1848 revolutions might seem an odd activity for a communist, but it was quite consistent with Engels's character and personality, since he was capable of pursuing activities together which to others might seem discordant or even contradictory. He was never keen to be a martyr or to disgrace his family utterly, and he was always determined on a wide range of cultural pursuits, including oenology. Also he was then still 27, so a little fun and a measure of frivolity are perhaps understandable.

'One does not readily part from France', Engels observed in his manuscript notes on the trip. These are very much in the style of his early travel writing, with somewhat up-dated allusions:

La belle France! The French certainly have a beautiful country and they are right to be proud of it. . . . And what wine! What a diversity, from Bordeaux to Burgundy . . . from Petit Mâcon or Chablis to Chambertin . . . and from that to sparkling champagne! . . . With a few bottles one can experience every intermediate state from a [Philippe] Musard [1793–1859] quadrille to the *Marseillaise*, from the exultation of the cancan to the tempestuous fever heat of revolution.

Compared with France, England was a poor place because of its 'coal-smoke and cattle-raising . . . and no wine', and Germany was damned by Engels as a land of 'beer, schnapps and rye bread, of rivers and revolutions that have dried up' (7 CW 511–12, 514). Politics, of course, came to the fore in his writing, as the political connection between the peasantry and the emerging Bonapartist counter-revolution was becoming evident, much to his rage as a communist:

When, in February of this year, a revolution took place in which the proletariat appeared for the first time with demands of its own, the peasants showed not the faintest comprehension. . . . Every peasant I spoke to was just as enthusiastic about Louis Napoleon as he was full of hatred for Paris. These two passions and the most unthinking, bovine amazement at the whole European upheaval are the sum total of the French peasant's politics.

Most fluently and most extraordinarily of all, Engels praised the 'red republic of the burgundian wine-harvest'. The language is completely that of the young Bremen *bon viveur*:

If only one could have had one's pockets full of money in that red republic! The 1848 harvest was so infinitely rich . . . better than '46, perhaps even better than '34! . . . It will therefore readily be believed that I spent more time lying in the grass with the vintners and their girls, eating grapes, drinking wine, chatting and laughing, than marching [on]. . . . The more so since one can eat one's fill of grapes sixty times over each day and has thus the best of excuses at each vineyard to establish contact with these constantly laughing and obliging people of both sexes (7 CW 521–2, 526–9).

Once in Switzerland Engels aimed to write political journalism from his haven, and he took these characteristic instructions from Marx on 29 November, attentive as ever to personalities: 'Write in detail about *Proudhon* and, since your geography is good, about the dirty business in Hungary.... Don't forget me in the piece on Proudhon, since our articles are reprinted by a great many French newspapers' (38 CW 181).

Since his Manchester days Engels had been praising and publicizing Marx's prospective and published works, and he once again obliged his associate. Writing of Proudhon's *Qu'est-ce que la propriété?* (*What is Property?*, Paris, 1841) and his *Philosophie de la misère* (*Philosophy of Poverty*, Paris, 1846), he summed up the Frenchman's achievements in social criticism as 'zero' and praised Marx's counterblast as 'witty', 'thorough' and 'a thousand times more French than Proudhon's pretentious monstrosity'. Engels called Proudhon's performance as an elected deputy in the constituent assembly 'the St. Vitus's dance of the enraged bourgeois' and described his speech-making to the Paris workers as incomprehensible mystification (8 CW 129–32). Proudhon's Hegelian analysis of economics and his profession of working-class socialism made him a formidable rival to the communism promoted by Marx and Engels, and unhappily for them he was well placed in France, where revolutionary insurgency and militant constitutionalism were the most sophisticated in Europe. Marx and Engels had abandoned any hope of making him an ally, finding him personally and intellectually repellent, and so had embarked on a strategy of destroying his influence as best they could. Even writing in French, as Marx did, their attempts met with little success, and the events of 1848–9 in France proceeded without significant intervention from the Communist Party, whose inner-circle was entirely German.

Up to his flight in October Engels had published over fifty articles in the *Neue Rheinische Zeitung*, reporting first-hand on politics in Cologne and the Wupper Valley. He also covered the rest of Germany, France, Belgium, Austria, Denmark, Poland and Italy, using the press and other sources, amplifying the news with comment. His fiercest rhetoric concerned the unsuccessful June rising of 1848, when Parisians mounted violent protests against the republican government. Its proposals to curtail the national workshops and to restrict newly-won civil liberties caused an urban outburst. Once again Engels invoked the events of the French revolution and saw contemporary events as their continuation: 'The people as well as the bourgeoisie sense that the revolution which they are experiencing will be more significant than that of 1789 or 1793'. *'The June revolution is the revolution of despair'*, he continued, and 'the workers know that they are involved in a *fight to the death'*. Similarly 'the bourgeoisie declared the workers to be ... *enemies of society* who must be destroyed'. His conclusion was an epitaph – the first of many – on what he saw as a brave attempt at proletarian revolution: 'The courage with which the workers have fought is truly marvellous. For three full days, 30,000 to 40,000 workers were able to hold their own against ... generals who did not shrink from using methods employed in Algeria! They have been crushed and in large part massacred' (7 CW 130, 139, 143).

From Switzerland Engels contributed over thirty-five articles in the *Neue Rheinische Zeitung*, mostly on Swiss politics. The Communist Party was committed to an indivisible republic in Germany, as federal arrangements seemed to them a ruse by which reaction could flourish in odd corners of the nation. Moreover they considered that federalism would be a drag on Germany's further economic development, since the country's administrative system would remain somewhat fragmented. Engels used the current crisis in Swiss politics to point up the disadvantages of federalism, taking explicit instructions from Marx (38 CW 181). Engels's petition for permission to reside in Berne, which survives in draft, was Machiavellian on this point, as he argued that: 'Berne affords me the opportunity to study in the work of the Swiss Federal Assembly the practical effect of a Constitution from which Germany in any case can learn much, particularly at a time when the German people may be in a position to give itself a Constitution similar to this in one or another respect' (8 CW 497–8).

As part of the same overall outlook Engels also delivered himself of strongly-worded opinions on the political struggles within the Austrian Empire. His opening articles on the Magyar struggle connected contemporary politics with his own vivid view of the French revolutionary tradition: 'For the first time in the revolutionary movement of 1848, for the first time since 1793 ... we meet with a truly revolutionary figure, a man who in the name of his people dares to accept the challenge of a desperate struggle, who for his nation is [Georges Jacques] Danton [1759–94] and [Lazare Nicolas] Carnot [1753–1823] in one person – *Lajos Kossuth* [1802–1894]'.

Good revolutionary organisation, in Engels's terms, was local and popular. Its leadership emerged in the heat of the moment and depended for its authority on mass support:

> Mass uprising, national manufacture of arms, issue of bank-notes, short shrift for anyone hindering the revolutionary move-ment, revolution in permanence – in short, all the main features of the glorious year 1793 are found again in the Hungary which Kossuth has armed, organised and inspired with enthusiasm. This [was a] revolutionary organisation, which on pain of utter ruin had to be completed, so to speak, in 24 hours.

Engels supported Hungarian independence as a liberal move-ment, but he condemned independence for the small Slavic peoples as potentially or actually reactionary. Pan-Slavism, a move-ment to unify the Slavic peoples, was either a fantasy, because the various peoples were at different stages of development, or it was a cover for the Russian knout – his phrase for tsarist despotism. His hostility to reaction, especially tsarism, was based on his abhor-rence of absolute rule. Russia had been untouched by the events of 1848, save for renewed action by the tsarist régime against liberals and westernisers. Suspicion of Russian diplomatic machinations against constitutionalism in western Europe was undoubtedly justified in historical fact, and Engels had seen this force at work. Five years earlier the tsar and his agents had put pressure on the Prussian monarchy to close the *Rheinische Zeitung* and root out the dangerous doctrines – constitutionalism and rule of law repre-sentative and responsible government – that it was propounding.

Politics in war-torn Austria-Hungary raised the issue of nationalism in a particularly acute form, as it cross-cut revolution-ary alliances and plans for the reorganization of the Empire. Generally in his writings on the nationalities – in uproar through-out the 1848 events – Engels reflected the popular anthropolgy of the mid-nineteenth century. This gave credence, even scientific status, to a concept of race which linked physiognomy and other physical characteristics to national characteristics and then to gradations of civilized development. To that view he applied his Young Hegelian outlook on history, according to which freedom was being realized through the development of liberal conscious-ness and constitutional self-government amongst progress peoples:

Among all the large and small nations of Austria, only three standard-bearers of progress took an active part in history, and still retain their vitality – the *Germans*, the *Poles* and the *Magyars*. Hence they are now revolutionary.

All the other large and small nationalities and peoples are destined to perish before long in the revolutionary world storm. For that reason they are now counter-revolutionary.

Engels's judgements on whole peoples reflected the real struggles and hard choices of the time, when democratic rights were difficult to achieve and easy to lose. In those circumstances he felt obliged to identify potential enemies to the cause of constitutionalism – though he may not have been correct in his allegations – because actual enemies were causing numerous deaths amongst the democrats whom he was supporting. His pronouncements may have had some value as advice or exhortation at the time, but even so their sweeping finality seems at odds with the very liberalism – given its stress on individual educability and citizen participation in politics – that he was concerned to defend:

There is no country in Europe which does not have in some corner or other one or several ruined fragments of peoples.... These relics of a nation mercilessly trampled under foot in the course of history, as Hegel says, these *residual fragments of peoples* always become fanatical standard-bearers of counter-revolution and remain so until their complete extirpation or loss of their national character, just as their whole existence in general is itself a protest against a great historical revolution (8 CW 227–8, 230, 234).

More strikingly Engels argued that even the democrats amongst the pan-Slav movement were mere moralists obsessed with concepts such as justice, humanity, freedom, equality and fraternity. These made them blind to the true facts of world-historical development, which was economic in origin. In support of this argument he cited the recent Mexican War of 1846–8 in which the 'energetic Yankees' seized 'splendid California' from the 'lazy Mexicans'. This war was a blow only to the theories of justice and humanity which supposedly united the two republics. Engels was all for the American interest, which could 'create large cities, open up communications by steamship, construct a railway from New

York to San Francisco' and hence 'really open the Pacific Ocean to civilisation' – echoes of his early linkage of the Young Hegelian view of history with the development of modern industry and communications. The '"independence" of a few Spanish Californians and Texans' might suffer, he admitted, and 'in some places "justice" and other moral principles may be violated'. 'But', he concluded, 'what does that matter compared to such facts of world-historic significance?' (8 CW 365–6).

Whilst writing for Marx's paper Engels participated in the activities of local Swiss Workers' Associations and was appointed a delegate from Lausanne – as 'an old fighter for the proletariat' – to the first Congress of workers in Berne. There he was elected to the central commission and again acted as secretary (8 CW 505). But in all he said he was bored with living abroad and wrote to Marx in late December: 'If there are sufficient grounds for believing that I shall not be detained for questioning, I shall come at once. After that they may, so far as I'm concerned, place me before 10,000 juries, but when you're arrested for questioning you're not allowed to smoke, and I won't let myself in for that' (38 CW 183).

In late January 1849 Engels evidently had sufficient assurances of safety and so returned to the Rhineland to rejoin the *Neue Rheinische Zeitung*. After that he published about 150 articles, and during his time on the paper he doubtless had a hand in many times that number. Most of his work was concerned with further reporting on the Hungarian campaigns, in which liberal constitutionalism, ethnic separatism and imperial traditionalism were intermingled. He attempted to decipher this patchwork war, to which he attached European importance. As we have seen, the revolutionary Hungarians and progressive Slavs were his heroes, fighting against Austrian imperialism and reactionary pan-Slavism. But the purely military aspects of the war occupied his attention greatly, and he considered the Hungarian commanders – whose forces were vastly inferior to those of the Austrians and their Russian allies – to be the most gifted commanders of his time.

Indeed the Hungarians were attempting to pursue the kind of policy Engels had in mind for Germany – national unification under a liberal constitution, combined with assimilation of small 'backward' nationalities. In that way they would be absorbed into the realm of modern commercial civilization. But his analysis also showed considerable sensitivity to the international dimensions of class politics, when he argued that the balance of local struggles might be decisively affected by pressure of diplomacy or by intervention from abroad: '*Austria* wages a war of oppression against the Magyars, *Russia* attacks them from behind, and *Prussia* stands at the border, warrant in hand, to arrest the refugees and hand them over to their executioners'. He argued that if Hungary were made independent, Poland restored to nationhood, Austria won over to liberal constitutionalism and Italy unified under a republic, then 'Prussia would disintegrate and Russia would be forced back to the borders of Asia' (8 CW 438; 9 CW 461–2).

Legal action against Marx's paper continued into early 1849, and a trial began on 7 February at which Engels, along with Marx and their publisher Hermann Korff, were accused of insulting the public prosecutor and subjecting the police to calumny. The charges were based on articles reporting the role these agencies had played in arresting various Rhineland democrats the summer before.

Marx and Engels then published the speeches they had made in their own defence. In his, Engels argued that it was for the jury to interpret an old law in the light of new political and social conditions. These included a new freedom for the press to place the actions of officials before the public. If the jury believed that the press must falsify events to fit the whims of ministers and policemen, or else remain silent altogether, then – so he announced rhetorically – they should pronounce him guilty (8 CW 318–19, 322). The two were acquitted.

On 8 May 1849 there was a democratic uprising in Elberfeld, and Engels entered the revolution in armed service. The German National or 'Frankfurt' Assembly had produced a constitution for the unification of the German states and principalities under an emperor. In late April this imperial constitution was rejected by the king of Prussia, and other German rulers, who wished to maintain and pursue their dynastic interests in defiance of the proposed liberalization. Armed revolts in support of constitutional rule broke out in many German towns and cities – notably Dresden, where Bakunin, Born and Wagner took part. Several towns in the Rhineland were similarly disturbed. Engels wrote up a report on the Elberfeld rising for the *Neue Rheinische Zeitung*, using the Düsseldorf press as his source, and he left immediately on 10 May.

The Prussian army was dispatched to put down the disorders in the Rhineland, and Engels joined his local committee of public safety in organizing measures to resist the troops. After a busy week in Elberfeld he reported on his activities to his readership in Cologne, commenting that the *Neue Rheinische Zeitung* was now personally represented at the barricades, and that he had arrived there with two cases of captured cartridges. Evidently he put his experience as a bombardier and artillery officer at the disposal of the local committee, since he supervised the town's defensive installations and barricades. To do so he had had to deny any political interest as a communist in the current struggle and to promise to concern himself exclusively with military matters in defending the imperial constitution. Local liberals did not see the communists as trustworthy allies in *their* revolution, and steps were taken to forestall the influence of radical ideas and to forewarn the public.

By 14 May the local committee was calling for Engels's expulsion from the Wuppertal, as they feared that he would proclaim a 'red republic'. He had to leave, after calming down – so he said – the militant workers and volunteer soldiers who were outraged at losing him (9 CW 447–9). After that rebuff, Engels – according to his own account – led an armed raid on a Prussian arsenal to secure more weapons for the democratic resistance. Officially the episode was described as an armed band of 30–40 men led by Engels and another Rhineland communist Johann Jansen (1825–49), 'both on horseback and armed with sabres and pistols':

> The detachment immediately formed up in front of the arsenal and placed sentries at the doors. Then *Engels* went up to sergeant *Starke* with his pistol drawn, asked him whether any weapons were still available and, on receiving the answer that the weapons had already been taken by force ... ordered him to go into the arsenal with him. Personal resistance ... would have been useless. ... The two army men therefore had to yield to force and allow the arsenal to be entered. There *Engels* chose several items of armament and uniform and had them brought out into the yard ... haversacks, helmets, trousers, cartridge pouches, pistols, sabres, drums, footwear, and one rifle (10 CW 168, 603–4).

For that act of rebellion further warrants were issued for Engels's arrest in June, but by that time he – and Marx – had departed for Frankfurt, the centre of constitutional unrest.

The *Neue Rheinische Zeitung* lasted until 19 May 1849, when an

increasingly conservative Prussian government – alarmed at further constitutional demonstrations – forced it to cease publication.
This was accomplished indirectly by threatening Marx and other
non-Prussian editors with deportation. Marx had renounced his
citizenship in December 1845, so that the Prussians would have no
pretext for securing the co-operation of foreign governments in
their attempts to silence him as an émigré radical, and this decision
was now turned against him at home.

On arrival in south-west Germany Engels and Marx did what
they could to encourage an open and successful insurrection
against the Prussian monarchy in favour of constitutional rule. For
that they suffered harassment and arrest. At Kaiserslautern they
found democrats and communists, principally Willich, amongst
several hundred armed volunteers, mostly workers and students.
But Marx left immediately for Paris, 'with the sole aim of collecting
additional material for my work on the history of political economy', as he explained in the French press in late July. Possibly
this reason was given for public consumption, disguising his real
intention, which was to make contact with insurgents in France.
He contacted political groups working against the increasingly
conservative régime, then at war with the Roman republic on
behalf of the Pope. Indeed he expected riots and upheavals in
France, and there were demonstrations and armed action against
the government in Paris and Lyons. But he did not write about
those events with any great enthusiasm after they failed, and
repression again took hold. Of course Marx had no military
experience or very practical interest in it, and he had a growing
family to look after – the reverse of Engels's situation. Earlier in the
month Marx had been ordered by the French Ministry of the
Interior to leave the capital and reside in the remote and swampy
Morbihan in Brittany. In mid-August his appeal was refused, and
so he departed for England where, stateless, he could secure
residence (9 CW 477–9, 480–1, 525–7; 38 CW 199).

Engels, by contrast, chose to stay on in Germany and join the
remnants of armed resistance to Prussian troops in Baden and the
Bavarian Palatinate. Writing in a local paper on 2 June he summed
up the revolutionary events of 1848–9 on which he had been a
studious commentator and sometime eye-witness. Middle-class
timorousness and perfidy had wrecked even moderate constitutionalism and laid Germany, indeed all Europe, open to a monarchical and absolutist counter-revolution. Democratic forces would

now have to fight against overwhelming odds: 'In short, in the great struggle for freedom which is spreading through the whole of Europe, the Palatinate and Baden will stand on the side of freedom against slavery, of revolution against counter-revolution, of the people against the sovereigns, of revolutionary France, Hungary and Germany against absolutist Russia, Austria, Prussia and Bavaria' (9 CW 476).

Engels joined Willich's corps of democratic insurgents, consisting of about 800 men, which was part of an irregular army of some thousands. Pursued by Prussian forces, the constitutional rebels retreated steadily, skirmishing with the regulars. They experienced a final defeat at Rastatt near the French border, where Engels's friend Moll fell under fire. By 12 July the last remnants of the workers' army had moved south and crossed into Switzerland, Engels amongst them.

Writing two weeks later to Jenny Marx, Engels said that he had at first dissociated himself from the so-called revolution in Baden. But when the Prussians had arrived, so he informed her, the urge to take part in the war became irresistible. Engels's strongest motivation for joining in the affair seems to have been his desire to give the Prussian king one in the eye. Engels had joined Willich as his adjutant and now boasted that he himself – as one of the 'democratic gentry' – had preserved the honour of the *Neue Rheinische Zeitung*. 'The whistle of bullets is really quite a trivial matter', he informed Mrs Marx. He longed to get in contact with Karl, as 'our column, which fought well, bores me'. In battle, it seems, he found Willich brave and adroit, but otherwise considered him a 'tedious ideologist and a true socialist'. 'There isn't anything to do here', he complained (38 CW 203–4).

Marx was keen – for a variety of reasons – that Engels should write up his experiences: 'Had you not taken part in the actual fighting, we couldn't have put forward our views about that frolic. . . . I am positive that the thing will sell and bring you money.' And he related to Engels his latest editorial scheme – 'a politico-economic (monthly) periodical . . . which would have to be largely written by us two'. In August he invited Engels to come along to London in order to pursue the project. As usual the scheme combined the communist mission they shared in politics with the immediate necessity to support life and limb in a world where the capitalist economy prevailed. 'In London', Marx wrote, 'we shall get down to business' (38 CW 207, 213).

The communists were now dispersed – Ferdinand Wolf in London with Marx, Dronke in Paris, Wilhelm Wolff in Zürich. Marx advised Engels to come for his own safety as 'the Prussians would shoot you twice over: 1) because of Baden, 2) because of Elberfeld' (38 CW 212, 213). Engels travelled from Switzerland to Genoa, because crossing France would not have been safe for a known radical. He then proceeded by ship on a five-week voyage, and arrived in London about 12 November 1849. His intention was to help Marx run a German-language periodical, once again in exile. Engels was then very nearly 29.

Underlying Engels's role in what became permanent emigration was a continuing political strategy of somewhat tenuous value. As we have seen, this involved the development of a network of workers and intellectuals who would disperse themselves when mass political insurgence took place. Without pre-arranged direction they were to inspire a far-reaching reconstruction of society and then safeguard those measures against reaction. Indeed during the revolutionary events of 1848–9 Marx and Engels had considered the Communist League to be formally dissolved, and they had worked with a broad – and barely organized – democratic front. This long-planned strategy was abandoned only in the spring of 1849 when they gave up on the treacherous middle classes and urged downtrodden German workers to protect their own interests – as best they could.

In effect the political strategy pursued by Engels and Marx required the complete collapse of traditional monarchism, either through internal revolution or through external war. And it also seemed to require a curious double-think on the part of the middle classes – they were to accept the communists as allies in the struggle for constitutionalism, whilst knowing of their declared intention to better the workers at bourgeois expense. The peasantry, who were not schooled by industry in the modern class struggle, simply confounded the communists altogether, except in so far as these victims of rural backwardness might be lured almost unthinkingly into action on the side of progress.

On Engels's understanding of history the further development of industrialization would eventually enable the French revolutionary script to be played out. In his view progress in social development would have to include the collective control of productive resources as well as the democratic control of government. But insurgent revolutionary forces, according to his strategy, would have to institutionalize and defend those measures against all their enemies with only spontaneous leadership and hastily assembled forces. Neither Marx nor Engels was ever keen to involve himself closely and wholeheartedly with armed revolutionary 'cells', as that strategy smacked of wild-eyed conspiracies. Engels's one military adventure was very much a romantic's last stand. Nor did they ever seek to participate personally in middle-class representative institutions, as that strategy smacked of reformism and compromise with the class of oppressors. Engels could perhaps have attempted to gain elected office – as did Wilhelm Wolff – during the brief flowering of German parliamentary politics in 1848–9, but he did not, and he showed little inclination to take that road later on in life, when similar opportunities might have been developed.

After the events of 1848–9 Engels achieved immense influence as an 'ideas man' in German socialism, with the curious twist that the most important ideas, so he believed, were really those of Marx. But how and whether this influence was connected with worthwhile efforts in the pursuit of class politics was in practice beyond his control, a situation which he very largely accepted. Writing was backed up with more writing, and in content his thought ascended to higher and higher levels of theorizing. This made it more general in its intended coverage and effect, but more and more remote from the hard decisions and risky actions of local and national politics. The theoretical works he undertook in England during the next forty-five years were the ones which he thought had most intellectual merit. Through those writings he became famous, even revered as a founder of Marxism.

7

Emigration

In emigration and then in employment Engels could no longer maintain the close contact with local and national political action that he had established during his days – before the revolution and during the events themselves – as a political journalist and communist agitator. His situation after the uprisings of 1848–9 did not offer him the temptation of compromise; rather it compromised him at the outset. He had to stay on the right side of Her Majesty's Government in order to remain in England, as a return to politics amongst German émigrés on the continent was now too risky, and only the United States or some even remoter haven offered any other possibilities. There is some slight suggestion that Engels and Marx may have considered leaving England early on for the New World, and then rejected the idea as their fear of persecution died down. Writing to Wilhelm Wolff on 1 May 1851 Engels commented that he hoped that 'Lupus' would come to England to stay, as 'you would have more opportunities here than in America and it's not so easy, once you're there, to come back again'. 'It's frightful in America', he concluded, 'The devil take the public there. Sooner a galley-slave in Turkey than a journalist in America' (38 CW 341).

Indeed Engels had to appear respectable in Manchester in order to keep his job, so his chances of continuing as an agitator for the communist cause were heavily circumscribed by office hours and largely proscribed by his social position. Writing to Marx on 17 March 1851 – after about four months in Manchester – Engels complained, 'I am dreadfully irritated by the stupidity of the arrangements here, which make regular and uninterrupted swotting virtually impossible' (38 CW 316). As his contact with day-to-day communist and even reformist politics necessarily declined in emigration, so his writing ascended to broader areas of concern, higher levels of abstraction and sometimes rather remote preoccupations. Moreover as Marx's masterwork on political economy began to appear in print, so Engels took on the job of promoting it to an audience, first in Germany and then beyond, which would have to cope with its formidable difficulties of style and content.

On his arrival in England Engels was not to know, on the eve of his twenty-ninth birthday, that his emigration would become permanent. Throughout the remaining years of his life – he lived until he was 74 – he expected the class struggle in Europe to break out now and again into open civil wars, and the international communist movement – of which he had been a founder – to play its role in providing political activists. In his first years in England this expectation was especially strong. But it is evident that in middle age he became absorbed in his domestic relationships, which had settled into stability, and were distinctly non-German in character. Moreover his role in supporting the Marxes – out of friendship for the family and out of devotion to Marx's critique of political economy – was most easily pursued in England on two counts: Engels could make money in the business in Manchester, and Marx could work on his researches in London.

Engels was in any case somewhat anglicized, having travelled, lived and worked extensively in England. Residing there kept him away from his family's prying eyes, and his name at a goodly remove from local papers and gossip. In 1860 he obtained permission to travel to Prussia for his father's funeral, and in 1861 on the accession of King Wilhelm (1797–1888) an amnesty was granted for deserters. Technically Engels was in this category, since he had not responded to the call-up of the autumn of 1850, when a threat from Austria had prompted mobilization. He seems to have secured the necessary consular testimonials for renaturalization, a convenience which Marx was ultimately refused.

Engels was thus no longer troubled with nationality problems in Prussia, but even so was quite understandably in no firm mind to return permanently to live and work in Germany. Direct engagement as a communist in local and national politics would once again entail difficulties with the law and the government. Writing to Bebel just after Marx's death in 1883, Engels declined to move back to Germany, Switzerland or anywhere else on the continent, saying that he simply would not go to live in a country from which he could be expelled. Hence he was only safe in America, which at best he would merely visit (he did so as a tourist for six weeks in 1888), and in England, where he would remain. In countries other than England – which had no radical labour movement in which to participate – he would have to occupy himself with 'practical agitation', so he said, and would therefore lose an enormous amount of time. In work of that kind he felt he was interchangeable with others, but in 'theoretical work' – for which there was peace and quiet in England – he could not yet see who would replace 'me and M[arx]'. At 63, he concluded, he would be crazy to exchange his peaceful asylum in London for anywhere else. Political meetings and journalistic battles, so he wrote, would necessarily spoil the clarity of his vision (41 CW 314–15, 617, 621; 36 MEW 21).

I   AN INDEPENDENT WRITER

During his first months in England Engels attempted to replicate his activities of the preceding years – communist journalism and political agitation – by living in London in association with Marx and assisting him on his third venture as a full-time editor. This was the revived *Neue Rheinische Zeitung*, now subtitled 'Political-Economic Review', rather than the more *engagé* 'Organ of Democracy', the sub-title of its immediate predecessor of 1848–9. The journal was printed in Hamburg, published in London and aimed at the diaspora of '48ers now scattered all over Europe, onwards to New York and even beyond to the American mid-west. As a bi-monthly the periodical was somewhat removed from the immediate whirl of local, national and international reporting, and it was no longer genuinely in and of the Rhineland. Instead it was more historical and theoretical in content, focusing on the recent uprisings in France and Germany and on their predecessors in revolts as far back as the sixteenth century, offering critical evaluations of the past and encouragement for the future. In that way it looked back to the theoretical emphasis of the *Deutsch-französische Jahrbücher* and the assiduous internationalism of the Brussels Correspondence Committee and the Central Committee of the League of Communists as it was just before 1848. Writing to a Swiss bookseller about distributing the journal there, Engels described their efforts as follows:

Besides the general introduction (by Marx), the first issue will contain a first article by me on the campaign for an imperial constitution, an article by little [Wilhelm] Wolff on the last days of the Frankfurt and Stuttgart parliaments, a survey of [current] events by Marx and myself and, if feasible, the first of a series of

lectures on economics which Marx is giving at the Workers'
Society here. Also miscellanea, perhaps something more by red
[Ferdinand] Wolf. The latter, Marx, Weerth and I, are now here
and Lupus [Wilhelm Wolff] will, if at all possible, be joining us
shortly (38 CW 222).

Not all of these items appeared in the first number or even in
others, but the letter captures rather well the kind of enterprise
that the new London-based *Neue Rheinische Zeitung* was supposed
to be, and something of the determination shown by its editors and
associates to maintain a political presence in Germany. The paper
went through six numbers before folding after a year, and it was a
failure financially and politically. Engels coped with this disaster
by making the decision in November 1850 to return to the family
firm for his living – in order to help with Marx's – and to leave
communist quarters in London for a necessarily bourgeois lifestyle
in Manchester.

The Communist League in London was then splitting between
Marx's faction and another involving Willich and Schapper, and
the German Workers' Educational Society was subject to similar
strains. From 1851 there were also arrests and persecutions of
democrats in Germany, and harassment of those in emigration. By
late 1852 the League was finished. International efforts on the part
of the '48ers of all shades of opinion – not just communist – to
unify themselves into organizations to promote democracy fell
apart in similar ways, as in the absence of popular agitation there
was little external necessity to make them achieve agreement in
political terms. For liberal constitutionalists, radical reformers and
communist revolutionaries alike the period was one of retrench-
ment and introspection. Engels pursued his interest in communism by using the lively journalism and intellectual intensity that
were so characteristic of his formative years. He did this against the
odds, and thus maintained an important continuity in his thought
and interests. Without that persistence it seems unlikely that his
immensely influential works of the 1870s and 1880s would ever
have emerged.

In the 1840s Engels's 'criticism of existing society' had moved on
from an investigation of proletarian living and working conditions
to a strategy of exposing reactionaries and their sometime allies
amongst the middle classes. Also included in 'existing society', of
course, were democrats and communist rebels, whose activities

and strategies were open to analysis and evaluation as well. In the 1850s his articles reflected his own experiences in the German uprising, his international perspective on the history and current development of European class-politics, and his specialized interest in military campaigns and modern warfare. To some extent his choice of topic was constrained by what he could sell to editors and publishers, and he was very largely successful in finding outlets for the sort of work he wished to do. This was quite in contrast to Marx, who could not support himself and his family from his own specialism, the critique of political economy, and so was forced into occasional journalism, which he deeply resented. Indeed in the early 1850s it was Engels who wrote articles for the American press for Marx, and also translated Marx's articles, as Marx himself took some years to acquire the fluency in English that he needed to make anything at all on his own account in journalism.

On arrival in London Engels wrote and published 'Letters' from Germany and France, as they were somewhat misleadingly entitled by his editor Harney, now running a Chartist monthly called *The Democratic Review*. Engels's bitter conspectus of events in January – July 1850 outlined the terms of political analysis that he and Marx followed in the next few years. In both countries reactionaries were fighting successfully against the institution of constitutional rights. In Prussia the king had rejected the 'imperial' constitution drafted by a popular assembly at Frankfurt, and had imposed his own constitution in Prussia. Then he insisted on several re-drafts to make the franchise and representation more favourable to the aristocracy and landowners, and also limited the power of the elected chambers compared with his own. 'His Majesty [Friedrich Wilhelm IV] forces upon the good Prussians a new Constitution. . . . His parliament amends it by striking out everything like a remnant of popular rights', Engels wrote. Similar events were taking place in France, under the direction of Louis Bonaparte, president of the new republic: 'The electoral "Reform" Law has passed, and the people of Paris have not moved. Universal Suffrage has been destroyed, without the slightest attempt at disturbance or demonstration, and the working people of France are again what they were under [King] Louis Philippe: political Pariahs, without recognised rights, without votes, without muskets.'

Engels continued that he did not expect anything serious by way of rebellion there until events took their logical conclusion and the republic was wound up by its president or by one of the royalist factions. The coup d'état of December 1851 by Louis Bonaparte bore out his analysis of right-wing political strategy, but after this dramatic event the French people failed to rise 'from their torpor' – much to Engels's distress. Engels's view of French politics was highly coloured by his enthusiasm for the revolutionary events symbolized in a litany of inspirational dates, 1789–1793–1830–1848, and he seemed to reason that a people with that tradition behind them would rise swiftly against the authoritarian reaction, which he encapsulated in a sequence of counter-revolutionary dates, 1794–1815. His political enthusiasm for France was further fuelled by his despair and disgust with German politics, which was hardly even constitutional in the first place and only feebly revolutionary by comparison with its more advanced neighbour. His distaste for what he considered to be the even more authoritarian and reactionary régimes to the east in Austria-Hungary and Russia filled out his overview of European political development (10 CW 13, 22, 34, 40).

Those feelings about France and Germany, which dated from Engels's earliest experiences in politics, emerged in his article *Die deutsche Reichsverfassungskampagne* ('The Campaign for the German Imperial Constitution'), published for the German émigré community in the London *Neue Rheinische Zeitung* for March–April 1850. This was a detailed account of the rebellion in south-west Germany, much of it based on his testimony as an eye-witness, and it was subsequently excerpted in the Rhineland press. His outlook placed class struggle within a Young Hegelian view of human progress as the development of European politics and civilization: 'Ever since the defeat of [the Paris uprising in] June 1848 the question for the civilised part of the European continent has stood thus: either the rule of the revolutionary proletariat or the rule of the classes who ruled before [the French revolution of] February [1848].'

About the campaign for the imperial constitution in Germany Engels was scathing, arguing that it had foundered 'because of its own half-heartedness and wretched internal state'. Those who supported the constitution did not really want to fight, since they were of 'the petty bourgeoisie' and partook of 'the German ideology', and those revolutionary democrats who wanted to fight did not really support the constitution, since it was still monarchical and thus insufficiently radical. The best he could say for the campaign was that it had contributed to the sharpening of class antagonisms in Germany, and the worst was that it had been a failure from the very start, politically and militarily. 'Its only prospect of succeeding lay outside of Germany, in the victory of the [protesting] republicans in Paris on June 13 [1848], and June 13 came to nothing', he concluded (10 CW 237–8).

For readers of *The Democratic Review* Engels also provided an English-language synopsis in April–June 1850 of his and Marx's works on recent Continental events: 'Two Years of a Revolution: 1848 and 1849'. In it he presented Marx as both a revisionist historian whose class-analysis of politics provided a superior explanation for the fall of Louis Philippe, and a communist seer predicting that the current reaction portended a universal war. Thus the 'next French revolution will be forced to extend itself beyond the limits of the national territory ... which alone will allow free development to the social revolution of the nineteenth century' (10 CW 369). But Engels's major work of this period – the London summer of 1850 – was an independent work of history, 'Der deutsche Bauernkrieg' ('The Peasant War in Germany'), published in the last, double number of Marx's *Neue Rheinische Zeitung* for November.

The point of writing a lengthy study of late fifteenth- and early sixteenth-century peasant revolts was clearly to raise revolutionary consciousness in contemporary Germany. Engels's argument was that, unbeknown to his contemporaries, Germany had a significant revolutionary history, moreover one that predated the *annus mirabilis* of 1789 in France. The piece was highly characteristic of Engels's eclectic communism – Hegelian dialectical method, Young Hegelian activism, progressive German nationalism, revolutionary liberalism and committed proletarian socialism – and it was wholly in line with his usual method of work. He had one major source – Wilhelm Zimmermann's *Allgemeine Geschichte des grossen Bauernkrieges* (*General History of the Great Peasant Revolt*) (3 vols, Stuttgart, 1841–3) – and an over-riding political purpose in taking on the subject. His project was to persuade his audience of democrats at home in Germany and abroad in the émigré community that they still had a mission in German politics, that mass political action could be expected to develop in the towns and countryside, and that in the modern industrial world an international perspective on politics was a necessity.

'It is high time to remind the German people' of the 'clumsy yet powerful and tenacious figures of the Great Peasant War', Engels wrote, and he argued that the conflict of three hundred years past was not impossibly distant from the present struggle. Indeed in both cases the opponents who had to be fought were still 'essentially the same', the revolution was betrayed by 'traitorous classes and groups', and it was unfortunate that in the recent uprising there had not been more of 'the robust vandalism of the Peasant War'.

Engels's exposition opened with an analysis of medieval industry and the corresponding class structure of society, comparing and contrasting this with France in 1789 and Germany in 1848. His view of history and his approach to contemporary political analysis were clearly one and the same: underneath an ideological 'screen' of apparently 'religious' or 'political' difference there lay the reality of class interest and class struggle, which it was his political purpose to clarify and sharpen. Indeed he had been making speeches and appearances during his time in London with much the same intent. He proposed a toast to the Paris insurgents at a banquet in honour of the second anniversary of the February revolution of 1848. He also made a speech to the fraternal democrats when they met to commemorate Maximilien Robespierre (1758–94) in April, taking the opportunity to remind the English of their revolutionary tradition and their radicals, such as the mid-seventeenth-century Levellers. And in another speech in September he reportedly remarked that there would shortly be another continental revolution. But on that occasion, he opined, the people of England would no longer provide shelter for reactionaries, as they had for the likes of ex-King Louis Philippe of France, Prince Metternich (1773–1859) of Austria and Prince Wilhelm of Prussia. Instead future 'enemies of the people' could go to 'their friend Nicholas of Russia who would perhaps give them a small kingdom in Siberia'. According to the press report this remark raised 'loud laughter'. In December he journeyed up from Manchester to treat his audience of English democrats to what *The Northern Star* described as 'a long and elaborate statement of the cause of the failures abroad, and the consequent reaction, showing that it equally arose from the ignorance of the people and the treachery of their leaders'.

When available in London Engels was a popular speaker, invited because of his journalistic background and personal involvement in democratic politics. His works of political analysis and history were part of his scheme to inform and inflame. For that reason it is easy to criticize his articles and pamphlets as scantily researched and overwhelmingly partisan, and it is not surprising that his work is of peripheral interest to historians today. Indeed it was not Engels's purpose to win favour with historians at all. Rather his approach can still be judged in political terms, as class interest and class struggle have by no means faded from view. His works, using inadequate and even very dated material, are still persuasive and inspirational in promoting constitutional and other democratic rights as well as in sharpening awareness of economic inequality and disparities in power.

On Marx's behalf Engels wrote a series of English-language articles – later known as 'Revolution and Counter-Revolution in Germany' – for the *New-York Daily Tribune*. They were published between August 1851 and September 1852, and continued his critical journalism. Engels acceded to Marx's request for copy to send to the paper, but inquired what attitude he should adopt, as he knew 'nothing about the POLITICS of the *New-York Tribune* beyond the fact that they are American Whigs [predecessors to the Republicans]'. Engels, ever attentive to his audience, but now increasingly concerned with scholarly accuracy, reported difficulties: 'Herewith an article of a sort. Various circumstances have conspired to spoil the thing.' 'All I could do was scrape the bottom of the barrel, and rely on memory. . . . [My] almost total ignorance of the paper and its readership [precluded] any proper plan' (10 CW 399, 411–12, 419, 434, 607, 611, 624, 637; 38 CW 419, 434).

After the demise of the London *Neue Rheinische Zeitung* Marx evidently had ambitions centred on Cologne for a further periodical (which never materialized), and he wrote to Engels in Manchester saying, 'You must seriously consider what you are going to write about'. For subject matter England would not do, nor was there much to say about France – as the late review had covered recent events in detail. 'Could you not perhaps, in conjunction with [Giuseppe] Mazzini's [1805–72] latest things, tackle the rotten Italians along with their revolution?' Marx inquired. Marx was upset at the publication of democratic manifestos calling for immediate military action against 'the kings and aristocrats of Europe' in order to catch 'the popular tide' – which he sardonically amended to 'popular stagnation'. This was yet more 'Schapper and Willich' to him, i.e. ill-prepared, foolhardy interventionism, doomed to failure. Connecting the recent call-to-arms with Mazzini's very similar enthusiasms, he urged Engels to involve himself in a military analysis that would demolish these pretensions. Engels duly obliged, making reference to his own previous work as military correspondent for the Cologne *Neue Rheinische Zeitung*, when he had reported on the Hungarian campaigns of 1849 and other manifestations of nationalist politics in the Austrian Empire (38 CW 246–50, 254).

Engels subsequently began research in his spare time in Manchester into the military history of the French revolutionary wars. The occasion for this exercise was the preparation of a long study (unpublished in his lifetime) on the conditions and prospects for a fictitious war a year hence, and his purpose was of course to douse the current mood of émigré adventurism with cold water. This forthcoming 'war', in Engels's view, would be waged by a resurrected 'Holy Alliance' of Prussia, Austria and Russia against a new French revolution, hurling itself once again into Europe to fight reaction. Engels's prognosis was not encouraging for proletarian forces in this hypothetical struggle, as he argued that 'the chances of superiority . . . are at least as much in favour of the Coalition [of reactionary powers] as in favour of the revolution'. Victory for the proletariat in a new form of warfare would come only with 'the complete abolition of all class distinctions and the complete concentration of all the means of production, in Germany and France' *and* with 'the co-operation of Britain' – the European triarchy once again. Marx's inquiries and interest in such military affairs thus set the stage for an extensive programme of 'autodidacticism' in Manchester, by which Engels came to specialize in the military aspects of revolutionary class struggles, both historical and contemporary (10 CW 550, 553; 38 CW 370).

This line of study represented a certain deflection from the finer details of contemporary class politics, and a consequent distancing of Engels from more immediate concerns that might then have engaged a large popular audience much more directly. Indeed Marx and his associate Engels were perceived amongst the émigrés as compromisers and turncoats because of their pronounced caution with respect to any immediate continuation of the armed revolutionary struggle for democracy. Engels's plans for a series of articles on events in France over the period 1830–48 for Harney's Chartist journal did not materialize, as Marx's desire to distance himself from the Willich and Schapper faction of the Communist League, and indeed from émigré factionalism as such, came between Engels and his friendship with the influential English editor. Writing to Engels in February 1851 Marx announced:

> I am greatly pleased by the public, authentic isolation in which we two, you and I, now find ourselves. It is wholly in accord with our attitude and our principles. The system of mutual concessions, half-measures tolerated for decency's sake, and the obligation to bear one's share of public ridicule in the party along with all these jackasses, all this is now over (38 CW 286).

In reply Engels agreed:

> One comes to realise more and more that emigration is an institution which inevitably turns a man into a fool, an ass and a base rascal unless he withdraws wholly therefrom, and unless he is content to be an independent writer who doesn't give a tinker's curse for the so-called revolutionary party. It is a real SCHOOL OF SCANDAL AND MEANNESS in which the hindmost donkey becomes the foremost saviour of his country (38 CW 287).

Writing once again to Marx, Engels confirmed that they needed neither popularity with any public nor support from any party, and that their position was 'completely independent of such ludicrous trifles'. At some point 'these gentry' would want them, and then they could dictate their own terms. But until that time they would at least have some peace and quiet.

> How can people like us . . . fit into a 'party'? And what have we, who spit on popularity, who don't know what to make of ourselves if we show signs of growing popular, to do with a 'party', i.e. a herd of jackasses who swear by us because they think we're of the same kidney as they? Truly, it is no loss if we are no longer held to be the 'right and adequate expression' of the ignorant curs with whom we have been thrown together over the past few years.

Engels's view was that they two were really more revolutionary than the other radicals, but more inclined to take things coolly after their experiences in Germany, and were now merely in need of outlets for their ideas, either quarterlies or 'fat books', the latter being more feasible. 'What price all the tittle-tattle the entire émigré crowd can muster against you, when you answer it with your political economy?', Engels wrote to Marx. That remark displays a highly rationalistic optimism with respect to the political effect of a specialized treatise on economics, and it is somewhat at odds with their view of their former comrades – now as influential as anyone in the world of democratic politics – as jackasses. Marx even said that he preferred contemporary authoritarian governments to 'all this 1848 democracy', which should be given time to moulder away.

Writing to Dronke in Switzerland Engels expressed his satisfaction at having left the Communist League and the German Workers' Educational Society behind. Thus he was 'rid of the entire loud-mouthed, muddle-headed impotent émigré rabble' in London, and at long last he was able to work again undisturbed in Manchester. He explained that he was making good use of his time swotting, and 'if anything should blow up again, the advantage we shall have over them will this time be of quite a different order, and in fields, furthermore, of which they have small inkling'. His 'Personal Column' at the close of the letter gives an insight into the life of émigré communists, looking back over their experiences of the 1840s and merely enduring the 1850s. Engels inquired about Dronke as husband and father, and about his friendly relations with Moses Hess – but 'with an eye to Mrs. Moses'. In Engels's mind she was still on the make. He reported that in Hamburg his friend Weerth was, like himself, 'writing business letters pending the next set-to', having brought 'nothing back from his travels in Spain, not even the clap'. 'Red [Ferdinand] Wolf has gone through various phases ... and *Père* Marx goes daily to the library and is adding amazingly to his knowledge – but also his family.' 'Finally as to myself', Engels concluded, 'I drink rum and water, swot and spend my time 'twixt [cotton] TWIST and tedium'.

Engels bolstered this strategy of isolation and specialist publication with a view of revolution as a time when the rules of social development assume a 'much more physical character' and 'the material force of necessity makes itself more strongly felt'. As a representative of a party, 'one is dragged into this whirlpool of irresistible natural necessity', he wrote. That immersion was no advantage compared with one's political independence – 'although one does, of course, end up by being dragged into it'. Engels's first few months in Manchester were crucial to the following forty years, as early in 1851 he adopted a strategy of associating himself only indirectly with political parties, both German and English, and thus becoming an 'influence' rather than a leader as such. In compensation he substituted – in a process of very gradual development – an increasingly intense dedication to defending the theories that Marx was developing with ever greater specificity and sophistication (38 CW 288, 289–90, 377, 382–3).

In the spring of 1851 Marx entertained (but only briefly) the idea of a two-volume study of the events of 1848–9. As Engels was already devoting himself to military science, so Marx noted, could he not embark on a fresh study of the Hungarian campaigns? Engels replied that he would be happy enough, if he had the materials available, because 'there's no easier way to make an ass of oneself than by trying to argue about military history without having all the facts at one's finger-tips'. It was all right working with scanty sources for a newspaper when all journals were equally ill-informed, but in writing after the event he needed sufficient material to enable the reading public to say of every crucial occasion, 'here such and such ought to have been done, and here what was done was right'. Writing to his compatriot Joseph Wiedemeyer (1818–66), then still in Frankfurt, Engels asked for advice and sources, such as German military manuals, other books and detailed maps, saying that he intended to devote himself systematically to the military aspect of the next movement in the democratic struggle, for which historical study was essential. Without 'laborious research', he commented, 'one achieves nothing worthwhile', and it was evidently his intention to build on what he had already learned when he was with the army in Berlin and with the irregulars in Baden: 'What I now actually need, you will better understand if I remind you that – disregarding, of course, my promotion in Baden – I never rose higher than a Royal Prussian bombardier in the *Landwehr* [army reserve].'

Engels explained that he was concerned to brush up on elementary knowledge of military science – tactics, fortifications, engineering, weapons. After that he wanted 'something really sound on artillery, since I have forgotten a great deal and there is much I simply don't know'. Characteristically he said that he was most interested in finding out about what is 'practical and really exists', and he commented that he had found inaccuracies in the standard work on battle plans for the French revolutionary wars of 1792–1814 (38 CW 325, 328, 370–2).

Thus Engels came to cover the diplomatic and military background to the Russo-Turkish War alongside its current development during 1853, setting his journalism – about a dozen or so articles – within his familiar, long-established political context:

> Russia is decidely a conquering nation, and was so for a century, until the great movement of 1789 called into potent activity an antagonist of formidable nature. We mean the European Revolution, the explosive force of democratic ideas and man's native thirst for freedom. Since that epoch there have been in reality but two powers on the continent of Europe – Russia and Absolutism, the Revolution and Democracy (12 CW 17).

As the conflict widened in 1854 and 1855 to include Britain and France – who were fighting in alliance with Turkey against Russia – Engels continued with over fifty articles for the *New-York Daily Tribune*. Occasionally his material was translated back into German by Marx for publication in the *Neue Oder-Zeitung* of Breslau, a middle-class, moderate paper and virtually the only outlet available to the 'Marx party' in Germany, as the radical press had collapsed. Marx, needing money and having to sacrifice his unpaid work on political economy, wrote many, many times more articles during the 1850s than his Manchester colleague, who had far less time available.

In March 1854 Engels sought to escape from his hated employment and so applied to become a full-time journalist on military affairs with the *Daily News* of London. He was rejected by the paper, and he presumed that this was on political grounds, despite his carefully-worded disclaimer. Indeed this disclaimer was sincere in so far as he sought in journalism to find outlets, reach a public and undertake specialist research:

> As to politics, I should mix them up as little as possible with military criticism. There is but one good line of policy in war: to go at it with the greatest rapidity and energy, to beat your opponent, and force him to submit to your terms. . . . I should stick to the principle, that military science, like mathematics or geography, has no particular political opinion (39 CW 425).

Engels's interests moved on after 1856 to the Anglo-Persian War, the 'opium' wars in China and the Indian Mutiny of 1857 in another dozen or so articles, giving due weight to great-power strategy, the importance of international trade routes and, on occasion, the sufferings and struggles of the peoples of the east. As ever, his approach to these events was highly coloured by his Young Hegelian view of civilization as the progressive development of western culture and technology:

> The English have just concluded an Asiatic war [the Anglo-Persian war of 1856–7], and are entering upon another [the second opium war of 1856–60 with China]. . . . In Persia, the European system of military organisation has been engrafted upon Asiatic barbarity; in China, the rotting semi-civilisation of the oldest State in the world meets the Europeans with its own resources. Persia has been signally defeated, while distracted, half-dissolved China has hit upon a system of resistance . . . the mass of the people take an active, nay, a fanatical part in the struggle against the foreigners (15 CW 278–81).

The judgement on imperialism passed by Engels involved a rejection of chauvinism, a good deal of sympathy for the innocent victims, and an appreciation of the power of popular, even guerrilla struggles against conventional armies. Overall he presented an analysis of contemporary wars as episodes in a global conflict initiated by the aggressive commercial powers in the west. Writing in 1858 after the reconquest of India by Britain, he took the long view:

> The great rebellion [of 1857], stirred up by the mutiny of the Bengal army, is indeed, it appears, dying out. . . . The cruelty of the retribution dealt out by the British troops, goaded on by exaggerated and false reports of the atrocities attributed to the natives . . . have not created any particular fondness for the victors. . . . The two great Asiatic powers, England and Russia . . . must come into direct collision. . . . Thence westward [from Pekin] a line will ere long be drawn across the breadth of the Asiatic continent, on which this collision of rival interests will constantly take place (15 CW 610).

From 1857 Engels turned his specialization in military matters to financial advantage by agreeing to help Marx with a series of articles for *The New American Cyclopaedia*, an offshoot of the

New-York Daily Tribune. This was the progressive American paper that had been giving Marx the only steady employment – albeit as a freelancer – that he ever had. Using standard sources Engels wrote long articles on 'Infantry' and 'Fortification', but worked mostly on snippets for the As, Bs and Cs, e.g. 'Adjutant', 'Bombardier' and 'Catapult' (18 CW 545–6).

Then in 1859 Engels produced his first substantial work for some years, the pamphlet *Po und Rhein* (*Po and Rhine*), which was strongly supported by Marx. Great power conflict, internal German politics and the stirrings of democratic revolutionaries presented an irresistible opportunity for Engels to intervene – as a journalist – in Germany. In doing so he took pleasure in attacking once again some familiar targets: reactionary militarism in Germany, by appealing to military science; Bonapartism in France, by appealing to the integrity of the German nation; and fissiparous nationalism all over Europe, by dismissing small ethnic groups as politically non-viable. Marx advised a plan of anonymous publication, so that Engels's argument would be taken seriously and not immediately dismissed as the work of socialists. This was followed later by an acknowledgement of Engels's authorship in the press, as 'it is all to the good', he wrote, 'if you yourself take the stage'.

Briefly Engels argued that Germany's defence did not require the maintenance of Austrian hegemony in northern Italy, and that the military men who argued thus were exposing Germany to danger. Their claim that Germany required a secure frontier beyond the Alps would also justify French incursions into the Rhineland, whilst making them militarily difficult to resist if German troops were bogged down on the Po supporting Austrian reactionaries against nationalist rebels. Engels was certain that the French emperor would have to undertake aggressive wars – against Austria and Germany – in order to keep his military clientele satisfied with spoils and his democratic critics occupied with national ambitions. Writing to Ferdinand Lassalle (1825–64) Engels made explicit the theory of external war and internal collapse that underlay his general strategy for the kind of democratic revolution that would vastly increase the power of communists: 'It would be difficult to imagine a better basis for a thorough-going German revolution than that provided by a Franco-Russian alliance.... In such a crisis all existing powers must necessarily be ruined and all the parties crumble one after another ... in such a struggle the moment must necessarily come when only the most ruthless and resolute party is in a position to save the nation.'

But, Engels stipulated, 'we [Germans] must not cede an inch of Prussian Poland . . .'. His overall theory of European politics now seems oddly nationalistic for a democratic socialist, but in the context of his own intellectual development – looking back to his days as a revolutionary liberal and Young Hegelian nationalist – these views were unexceptionable. He wrote that the map of Europe was not yet definitively established, so any changes 'must increasingly tend by and large to give the big and viable nations their *real* natural frontiers'. These frontiers, however, were to be determined by 'language and fellow-feeling', with military considerations taking second place. Yet in his view there were still 'remnants of peoples . . . that are no longer capable of national existence'. Such peoples would have to remain incorporated within larger nations and thus merge completely, or else 'be conserved as merely ethnographic relics with no political significance'. With respect to Germany he argued strongly for unity amongst the various states and principalities, rather than incursions into 'all the Italian rubbish'. And in the context of great power adjustments, he wrote, 'Germany should not be asked, as has been the custom, to make all the sacrifices alone'. His later position on the tricky Polish question was consistent with these views. He supported an independent Poland, but as a barrier to Russian reaction, and his proposed boundaries gave only subordinate attention to language and nationalist aspirations, as the Poles did not in his opinion make up a 'big and viable nation' (16 CW 254–5; 40 CW 393, 446; 16 MEW 153–63).

Engels's pamphlet was widely noticed in the German press, and he took the opportunity to advertise himself to the *Allgemeine Militär-Zeitung* of Darmstadt as a potential contributor, commenting that he had good sources on military matters in England, which was – save for Russia – 'our only natural and necessary ally against Bonapartism'. He also mentioned his service as a one-year volunteer in the artillery and his participation 'on the side of the insurgents' in the campaign in Baden (18 CW 407). Overlapping this work were his further contributions on military affairs for *The Volunteer Journal for Lancashire and Cheshire*, a periodical directed at the newly-organized volunteer forces, then arming to protect England from a widely-perceived Bonapartist threat of invasion. The organization of those bodies had a certain appeal for Engels, as they were voluntary in recruitment, democratic in electing officers, and something of a contrast to the regular forces, whose highly traditional forms of selection and organization had been roundly blamed – though Engels was hardly the only one making this charge – for the disasters of the late Crimean campaign. For his local brigades, which were largely middle-class, he reported on various reviews and inspections, but more interestingly he advised them on French armaments and tactics. He also discoursed extensively on the history and contemporary construction of the rifle, an admittedly 'dry' subject, yet suggesting that 'no intelligent soldier ought to be ignorant of the principles on which his arms are constructed'. The non-commissioned officers of most continental armies, he wrote, would be expected to know these matters, and the majority of volunteers, '"the intelligence of the country", ought to be as well up in the knowledge of their fire-arms as they!' (18 CW 459).

In the early 1860s there was a revival of democratic politics in the guise of popular nationalism in Italy and Germany. The prospects for insurrection in the course of the Austro-French War in Italy seemed good, as indeed proved the case with the campaigns of Giuseppe Garibaldi (1807–82). Marx was briefly back in the editorial chair with a renewed version of *Das Volk*, a London-based weekly that originated from the German Workers' Educational Society, with which he had re-established contact. The inner circle of the paper included Marx, Engels, Freiligrath and Wolff, the familiar names known to Engels as 'our party'. The venture lasted four months, during which time he reviewed events in the Italian campaigns (16 CW 624).

Capitalizing on the success of *Po and Rhine*, Engels produced an anonymous sequel *Savoyen, Nizza und der Rhein* (*Savoy, Nice and the Rhine*), published in Berlin in 1860. Far from finding Russia moving into alliance with Germany against Bonapartism, Engels now argued that the French emperor was uniquely suited to Russian machinations, as he had to make war and appear the conqueror in order to survive. In this necessity he was bound to demand the German left bank of the Rhine, using arguments and methods the same as those he was employing in order to annex the Savoy and Nice. On the one hand Engels appealed to a unified German nationalism to resist a Franco-Russian alliance, and on the other to a new ally in the form of the Russian serfs. 'The contest that has now broken out in Russia between the ruling and the oppressed classes of the rural population is already undermining the entire system of Russian foreign policy', he wrote. Industrial and agricultural development there would eventually reach a point where the existing social conditions could no longer be endured. Revolution was a necessity in Russia, but also an impossibility without violent change, and with that change Russian foreign policy, as currently pursued by reactionaries, would collapse as well (16 CW 602–3, 609–10). Whatever his fascination with military strategy and high diplomacy, the class-perspective inevitably surfaced in Engels's thinking – when his editors were willing – and it played a crucial role in his historical vision.

When the American Civil War began in 1861 Marx lost his living from the *New-York Daily Tribune*, as interest in European news had declined. He then begn to contribute to the liberal Vienna paper *Die Presse*, edited by his former contact with the Breslau *Neue Oder-Zeitung*. On the usual arrangements Engels contributed articles and materials, reviewing the new war in very excited terms:

> The American Civil War presents a spectacle without parallel in the annals of military history. The vast extent of the disputed territory; the far-flung front of the lines of operation; the numerical strength of the hostile armies, the creation of which hardly drew any support from a prior organisational basis; the fabulous cost of these armies; the manner of commanding them . . . are all new in the eyes of the European onlooker (19 CW 186).

Predictably Engels had no truck with the 'adventurous idlers' of the Confederacy and their 'truly Bonapartist spirit'. But for the Union he offered critical support, remarking that it was absurd to send raw volunteers into battle at Bull Run on 21 July 1861. He looked back to the first great democratic army, that of the French revolution, which had made similar mistakes between 1792 and 1795 – before going on to win victories against the reactionary allied powers (19 CW 186–7).

Engels also covered the short Austro-Prussian War of 1866 for the *Manchester Guardian*, writing 'impartially' and from the 'military point of view', treating the brief campaign as an important test for the victorious Prussians in building up a modern army. Then from July 1870 to February 1871 he covered the Franco-Prussian War in fifty-nine articles for the London *Pall Mall Gazette*. One of their correspondents had approached Marx, who intended to do 'something political', and had suggested to Engels that he do 'something military'. Engels was well up on the relative strengths of the French and Prussian forces and energetic enough in retirement to comment on events day-by-day from reports. Because the paper was conservative there is little class-analysis in his work, and it was then that he became known amongst the Marx family as 'the General' (33 MEW 6).

As the possibilities for democratic and even working-class politics in Germany began to improve, so Engels's attention was inevitably drawn back to familiar ground. Lassalle, ex-'48er and founder in 1863 of the General Association of German Workers, was emerging as the major spokesman for working-class socialism in Germany. Writing to Marx in 1863 Engels commented:

> Lassalle's goings-on and the rumpus they have created in Germany are really becoming obnoxious. It's high time you finished your book [on political economy]; if only to provide us with propagandists of a different kind. In other respects, it's quite a good thing that an audience for anti-bourgeois stuff should be recaptured in this way, though it's disastrous that friend Izzy [their anti-semitic nickname for Lassalle] should thereby carve out a position for himself (41 CW 473).

As émigrés Marx and Engels were not well placed to defend the interests of their party of communists, though their supporters in Germany, Wilhelm Liebknecht (1826–1900) and Bebel, then founded a Union of German Workers' Associations. This somewhat amorphous organization arose from the German Workers' Educational Associations and was intended to undermine the influence of the Lassalleans, who very soon lost their leader. Engels had met the '48er Liebknecht briefly in Switzerland in 1849 and had then associated with him in London. In 1862 Liebknecht returned to Germany and active, on-the-spot politics. To counter an apparent Lassallean political success, Engels fired off a pamphlet *Die preussische Militärfrage und die deutsche Arbeiterpartei* (*The Prussian Military Question and the German Workers' Party*) in 1865, which was the first substantial work to appear under his own name for twenty years. In it he argued that the Prussian government had merely offered political concessions to the workers – such as extensions of the suffrage – when the ruling interests wanted to frighten the 'bourgeois opposition'. Once working-class agitation became dangerous to the established order it would be stifled, and political rights revoked.

More interestingly Engels then argued that 'the more workers who are trained in the use of weapons the better'. In that way he found a working-class interest in the imposition of conscription, which he described as the 'natural corollary of universal suffrage'. Arming the workers would be especially useful if the bourgeoisie were 'untrue to itself' and gave in to the reactionary elements in society. The proletariat should then either drive the middle classes ahead politically, or capitulate to them in the short term and hope to re-group. Engels's notion of driving on the bourgeoisie was not related by him to the revolutionary force of firearms but to the civil struggles of English workers, who had been pressing for concessions since the Reform Bill of 1832, as French workers had been doing since the July revolution of 1830. If there were short-term capitulation by the proletariat, on the other hand, it would be like the failure of the European workers' movement between 1848 and 1850. This was an alternative that he totally deplored, but he did not detail how – even if there were external war and internal collapse – armed revolutionaries could have saved the day for progressive politics (20 CW 67, 77–8).

Keeping in touch with the now fast-moving events of German politics was an increasing problem for Engels, as his aim was to assure Marx's influence – though not in fact organizational leadership – in the only political arena in which they wished to be intimately involved at the national and local level. They were tied to Germany by language, heritage and all their important contacts, but frustratingly removed from real exposure to their intended audience. Indeed Engels was more than a little compromised, and he wrote these revealing lines to Marx in 1865:

> But one can see that Izzy [Lassalle] has given the movement a Tory-Chartist character. . . . This nauseating toadying to the reaction comes through everywhere. . . . You wait and see, the louts will be saying, what's that Engels after, what has he been doing all the time, how can he speak in our name and tell us what to do, the fellow's up there in Manchester exploiting the workers, etc. (42 CW 88).

Subsequently in 1868 Engels argued in Liebknecht's paper, the

Demokratisches Wochenblatt, that his political predictions had come true, as the Lassallean political organization had been dissolved through government action. The mistake that the Lassalleans had made, according to Engels, was to confuse universal suffrage with a genuine liberalization – right to free expression, right of association, right of assembly – which the Prussian government would not grant. Naïvely the Lassalleans had expected that genuine power would follow merely from exercising the vote in general elections. As usual he contrasted German political development unfavourably with that of France, saying:

> One has only to go to France to realise what tame elections it [universal suffrage] can give rise to, if one has only a large and ignorant rural population, a well-organised bureaucracy, a well-regimented press, associations sufficiently kept down by the police and no political meetings at all. . . . And yet the French proletariat has the advantage over the German of . . . longer experience of struggle and organization (21 CW 20–1).

In 1869 Engels published a short tribute to Marx which poignantly captured the situation of 'our party' – Marx, Engels and Liebknecht – as he saw it. Lassalle was really another Proudhon: 'It has become the habit in Germany to regard Ferdinand Lassalle as the founder of the German workers' movement. And yet nothing could be less correct. . . . If the workers acclaimed his teachings, was this because those teachings were new to them, or because they had long been more or less familiar to the thinkers amongst them?' Engels's message was that the movement of the 'forties' had already been forgotten, along with its political and socialist literature. But it was now necessary, so he stated, to recall that a well-organized socialist party had once existed, and that its individual members had continued quietly (i.e. from abroad) to prepare the ground of which Lassalle had later taken possession. Lassalle was indeed highly talented and well-educated, but he was 'neither the initial founder of the German workers' movement nor was he an original thinker'. He had vulgarized the writings of his forerunner and intellectual superior – Karl Marx.

Engels urged his readers to recall that there had also existed a man – the very same Karl Marx – who, as well as organizing the nascent party of socialism, had also devoted his life's work to the scientific study of the social question. In fact he had already published some of the most significant results of his researches as his 'contribution' to the 'critique of political economy' in 1859. Moreover from 1864 his great achievement had been to found and subsequently direct a descendant of the Brussels Correspondence Committee, the London-based International Working Men's Association – though Engels did not mention that Prussian law forbade local associations there to affiliate openly with such a 'foreign organisation'.

Engels's tribute was written to help with the publicity for the first volume of Marx's *Das Kapital* (*Capital*), published only two years previously, and to help the 'Marx party' at the forthcoming foundation congress of German social-democrats at Eisenach. But overall his article on Marx presents an unmistakable impression of pathos, because it reveals the plight of émigré politicians. They were losing political ground back home, perhaps forever. As a partner in a capitalist firm Engels could not even associate himself openly with Marx's International, and as an émigré he was necessarily removed from the events surrounding the formation of the world's first mass party of socialists – at least 10 000 strong – in his native Germany.

Lassalle was the object of sustained, vicious criticism by Marx and Engels for his intellectual shallowness, political compromises and personal foibles – he had an aristocratic mistress and was killed in a duel. On those matters they had their point, even if the language was intemperate and repellent. But in assessing the achievements of the 'Marx party', Lassalle is a useful contrast, because he stayed in Germany, played a role in electoral politics, generated a considerable following, and thus avoided the remoteness, obscurity and ambiguity into which the London communists had variously but necessarily faded (21 CW 24, 59–60, 64).

On 'retirement' in 1869 Engels freed himself at last from commercial demands on his energies. He liberated Marx from financial pressures to produce reams of journalism, which had also been a drain on his own time. And he moved on from his 'militariana' into much more substantial and influential areas of intellectual endeavour. In those works Marx's name was very much to the fore.

Publicizing Marx was nothing new to Engels, but he was now in a position somewhat different from that of the preceding two decades. Marx had actually published the first volume of *Capital* in 1867, and there was open, though restricted working-class politics in Germany. Hence Engels was able to take up his role as publicist for Marx on a much larger scale. This was particularly true with respect to the International, where he took on the role of corresponding secretary and representative for various branches outside Germany and Britain, much as in the Brussels days when he represented Marx's views in Paris. In developing Marx's ideas, and Marx's political persona, Engels came to figure prominently – albeit through journalism, correspondence and intermediaries – in German politics and to write the most intellectually ambitious works of his career.

II   MATERIALISM AND SCIENCE

An opportunity for Engels to assist in presenting Marx's substantial work on political economy to the public first arose when, in mid-1859, Marx finally produced an instalment on his critique. This was the slim volume *Zur Kritik der politischen Ökonomie* (*A Contribution to the Critique of Political Economy*), published in Berlin, which Engels immediately reviewed in August for the short-lived London paper *Das Volk*, edited by Marx. Engels took as his major text for exposition not the substantive propositions concerning 'the commodity' and 'money or simple circulation' that Marx had expounded in the main chapters of the book but rather the brief preface (already published in *Das Volk*) in which the 'guiding thread' of his studies had been summarized into a single tantalizing paragraph. In itself this marks a major point of interpretation, because in presenting Marx to the public Engels generally concentrated on delineating Marx's method and setting an intellectual context for his work, rather than on reproducing his economic theory in detail and deducing its consequences for political action.

Engels denominated Marx's outlook 'the materialist conception of history' and in that way located it firmly in the context of the debates of the mid-1840s. Those debates, in which they had both been involved, had concerned Young Hegelian idealism, in which politics and history were conceptualized as progressive stages in the development of ideas. But at the time Marx and Engels also dealt with Feuerbachian materialism, in which anthropology was supposed to take the place of Hegelian concepts, thus 'inverting' Young Hegelian thought. Marx and Engels were attempting to supplant Young Hegelian politics and post-Feuerbachian philoso-

phy with their own 'new materialism' and proletarian communism, and to that end they proposed to undertake a highly politicized history of the development of civilization – up to its current
culmination in industrial, class-divided society.

The continuation of those debates was identified by Engels in
1859 as the contemporary task of the 'proletarian party' in Germany – i.e. the 'Marx party' of communists. In Engels's words,
they had been 'propelled on to the political stage by the [1848]
February Revolution [in Paris]' and had thus been 'prevented from
pursuing purely scientific aims'. The 'development of the materialist conception in respect of even a single historical example'
required, so he said, 'years of quiet research' in mastering an
abundance of material.

Ten years of exile away from Germany had considerably altered
Engels's political perceptions, or at least the way that he chose to
interest the public in his politics. The communist movement was
now less associated in the first instance with the mass movement
for constitutional democracy than with the 'Marx party' and the
scientific results established – however slowly over the years – by
its leading light. In fact Engels claimed that the withdrawal from
democratic politics undertaken by 'our party' during the 1850s – 'a
time when it became increasingly impossible to exert any influence
on Germany from abroad' – was its salvation, as the elaboration of
this new scientific outlook prevented the demoralization that
overtook the other ex-'48ers. In that way he pushed Marx's critique
of political economy up a notch in abstraction, presenting it as an
'elaboration' of an 'outlook' and finding its highest significance in a
more general intellectual context than was readily apparent from
Marx's text itself. Thus the very task of committed communists
came to include, in Engels's vision, profound and highly abstract
studies in the philosophy of science.

The criticisms that Engels had actually made of Marx in the 1840s
– that he should direct his work to contemporary issues and
personalities, that he should produce it quickly as journalism and
that he should face real audiences and sway the crowds – virtually
disappeared in the English exile to which Engels's sense of political
vocation had then become adapted. In his career Engels touched
extremes of political participation that Marx did not attempt –
sustained popular agitation and even armed conflict. And he
touched an extreme of intellectual endeavour that did not occupy
Marx directly – the reconciliation of philosophy and science on a

Hegelian model. In undertaking this work Engels the reviewer, journalist and popular writer promoted Marx in terms that were somewhat removed from Marx's own, and made him a vehicle for views that were not expressed explicitly in his writings. Engels expounded those ideas under his own name, but made Marx ultimately responsible: 'Marx was and is the only one who could undertake the work of extracting from the Hegelian logic the kernel containing Hegel's real discoveries in this field, and of establishing the dialectical method, divested of its idealist wrappings, in the simple form in which it becomes the only correct mode of the development of thought.'

Engels had been prepared for some time to take on the task of working out the method which underlay Marx's critique of political economy, and that project, he wrote, would itself produce results as significant as Marx's basic materialist outlook. That materialist outlook had been encapsulated by Marx in a sweeping generalisation – 'the mode of production of material life conditions the general process of social, political and intellectual life' – but however wide-ranging, it was not an outlook that addressed itself explicitly to the higher questions in which Engels was interested (see MST *passim*). In particular he was concerned to put communist conclusions on to what he believed was a proper scientific footing. For him the key areas of study that linked Marx's social science, which was based on the development of productive activities in society down through history, with modern physical science, which was based on matter-in-motion materialism and demonstrable causal explanations, were human physiology, comparative anatomy and molecular chemistry.

The study of physiology, and the organic and inorganic chemical processes which figure in the organs of living creatures, had occupied Engels off and on from the time of *The German Ideology*. This was because Feuerbach's materialist inversion of idealist philosophy had made 'man', and indeed the physical processes of biology, a focus of philosophical debate. In the context of the time those philosophical issues were also political. A materialist philosophy, if convincing, would have profound implications for the Christian, theistic and pseudo-theistic political theories that interested parties were urging on the limited but widening circle of active participants in politics.

In the 1840s Engels had used the sciences of physiology and chemistry in order to criticize the views of Young Hegelian philosophers, whom he had caught wandering into uninformed speculations about human nature and communist society. But he had not used those sciences as reasons for adopting a simplistic Feuerbachian materialism as a philosophical view. Whilst he was a thorough-going atheist and scathing critic of other-worldly idealism, his own perception of politics was highly historical and progressively rationalist in the Young Hegelian manner. He was not then a philosophical reductionist keen to explain all phenomena in exclusively material terms, or even to see all behaviour in terms of biological imperatives. Instead his communist or 'new materialist' focus on productive activity gave science an important role as a key to the development of technology. For Marx and Engels – the 'new materialists' – science as technology was crucial in showing how human beings had developed their capacities through productive activities. Those activities had transcended mere biology and were now becoming increasingly rational. On this 'new materialist' view humans as a species had characteristically progressed through 'modes of production' ranging from primitive tribalism to industrial capitalism. In future a form of industrial communism was expected to resolve the 'social question' with which Engels had been acquainted since early youth and had lately been preoccupied.

Thus Engels's Young Hegelian communism assigned a special role to technology and industry in the development of human history up to the present, and on his view modern science – in all its manifestations – would henceforth become increasingly important in creating the conditions under which communism would become a political reality. His 'autodidacticism' in tracing this process and contributing to it was extremely wide, because his conception of science as *Wissenschaft* covered any disciplined field of study, whether chemistry, mathematics, logic or other areas of philosophy. Indeed his assumption that philosophy and science could be reconciled was what made his search for a method common to both a sensible undertaking, and that unificatory approach was derived directly from the 'natural philosophy' of classical times in which all those studies had originally been located. Therefore he was critical of conceptions of science and philosophy that divided one from the other, and he was synthetic in offering his own solution. That solution consisted in reconciling Hegelian dialectics from philosophy with positive knowledge from science.

The young Engels of the early 1840s had of course been keen to reconcile Hegelian dialectic with contemporary science, but the science in question had then been political economy – a *social* science in which matter-in-motion did not figure. In the mid-1840s he turned what he knew of physiology and chemistry against 'ideologists' and 'true socialists' in arguments, such as those in *The German Ideology*, that did not require a matter-in-motion material-ism either, but merely a reference (often a gross one) to the realities of physical life for human beings. Arguments of that character were supposed to explicate an 'outlook' on history that identified and promoted class struggle as crucial to any truthful conception of human social development.

In the 1850s, however, Engels's interest in physiology and chemistry came to figure in a somewhat different context, as he began to work on a philosophical problem in epistemology. That happened when he addressed the relationship between philoso-phy and science directly, and suggested a specific reconciliation: materialist outlook and dialectical method. Thus he turned his interest in the physical sciences philosophically on to Hegel him-self, rather than politically on to his rivals. In that way he used the positive results established over the previous twenty years or so in science as proof that the Hegelian dialectical method – when properly explicated – was in fact compatible with the materialism on which science itself was based. Crucially this was a matter-in-motion materialism, working on the assumption that particles and energy were fundamental to all phenomena and therefore the terms from which causal explanations must ultimately be con-structed. On that basis science, especially chemistry and physics, had advanced very rapidly, accumulating what he described as a great 'stock of data'.

Thus Engels developed an abstract, philosophical interest in reconciling Hegelian dialectical method and modern physical science, indeed he claimed to be improving on both as a conse-quence. In that way he skipped over precisely the area into which Marx had put his own greatest efforts. Marx's special project was a substantive work of social science, founded on a logical analysis of political economy and committed to the overthrow of contempor-ary class-divided society. By contrast in his review of Marx's first published instalment Engels wrote: 'Here there was, therefore, a question to be solved which was not connected with political economy as such. How was science to be dealt with?' According to

Engels this was a question that only Marx could resolve – though the great man had not in fact attempted it himself.

In Engels's view all Marx's 'literary productions' were founded on a fundamental materialism of the matter-in-motion type – though he cited no explicit textual evidence. He merely announced that 'action in each particular case [that came under historical investigation] was initiated by direct material causes'. Hence 'political action and its results', he concluded, 'originated in material causes'. But in all Engels's work this implied connection between physical science – which was said to be based on a matter-in-motion materialism – and social sciences or humane studies – which in fact do not explore human behaviour directly in those terms – was merely asserted and never satisfactorily explicated and defended (see MEIR 96–158).

In his review of 1859 Engels moved on to treat, albeit very briefly, Marx's critique of political economy itself, giving the reader the implicit assumption that Marx's work was as well established – indeed established on the same basis and in the same way – as the latest discoveries in the natural sciences. But in presenting Marx's results or 'outlook' Engels also likened his work substantively to Hegel's, saying that the great philosopher's epoch-making conception of history was the direct theoretical precondition of the new materialist outlook. Indeed Engels, whilst critical as a Young Hegelian of Hegel's pantheistic idealism, nevertheless retained from the beginning a very positive evaluation of Hegel. Specifically Engels endorsed Hegel's comprehensive 'outlook', because it brought all reality under philosophical review, and Hegel's unique 'method', because it demonstrated development through contradiction. Thus he made Marx and his 'new materialism' the successor to Hegel's monumental achievements (16 CW 465–77). Amongst the books and manuscripts in Hegel's attempted incorporation of all knowledge within philosophy was of course his *Vorlesungen über die Naturphilosophie* (*Philosophy of Nature*), published in Berlin in 1842. That book was again attracting Engels's attention just before he wrote his review in the summer of 1859.

Writing to Marx on 14 July 1858 Engels asked for the loan of Hegel's *Philosophy of Nature*, as he was doing 'a little physiology . . . combined with comparative anatomy'. 'Here one comes upon highly speculative things', he continued, 'all of which, however, have only recently been discovered'. Engels was curious to find out whether 'the old man' Hegel had not had 'some inkling' of these latest developments. But in any case, Engels was already convinced that the Hegelian dialectical method and philosophical appropriation of science were valid, and indeed discoveries over the intervening thirty years had demonstrated this to his satisfaction. In particular he cited the advances made in organic chemistry, and the revolution wrought by the microscope in physiology. The discovery of the cell in plants and later in animals by two German scientists – Theodor Schwann (1810–82) and Mathias Schleiden (1804–81) – especially excited him. The cell, he wrote, 'is Hegelian "being in itself", and its development follows the Hegelian process step by step right up to the final emergence of the "idea" – i.e. each completed organism', whatever the form. Indeed the identification of corresponding structures between higher and lower animals – from 'man' down to 'insects, crustaceans, tapeworms, etc.' – confirmed for Engels all of 'Hegel's stuff about the qualitative leap in the quantitative sequence'. Underlying those discoveries in cell-biology was the recent demonstration by 'an Englishman' (James Joule, 1818–89) that physical forces change from one form into another in specific quantitative proportions, 'so that e.g. a certain quantity of one, e.g. electricity, corresponds to a certain quantity of each of the others, e.g. magnetism, light, heat, chemical affinity ... and motion'. That law, in Engels's view, was 'splendid material proof of how the reflex categories [delineated by Hegel] dissolve one into the other' (40 CW 326–7).

Unsurprisingly Engels was also keen on *The Origin of Species* by Charles Darwin (1809–82), when it was published in 1859, and he subsequently claimed that it provided further confirmation for his views on the way that science and philosophy were to be reconciled. Writing to Marx on 13 December he commented on Darwin's book, remarking on the inferior, non-dialectical method, but suggesting that the theory of evolution was consistent with the grand reconciliation of philosophy and science on which he was working. In that reconciliation he had already located studies as diverse as Marx's political economy, contemporary cell biology and recently discovered laws of physics: 'Darwin, by the way, whom I'm reading just now, is absolutely splendid. . . . Never before has so grandiose an attempt been made to demonstrate historical evolution in Nature, and certainly never to such good effect. One does, of course, have to put up with the crude English method' (40 CW 551). By the 1860s Engels was friends with the German chemist Carl Schorlemmer (1834–92) of Owen's College in Manchester.

Schorlemmer was later the first professor of Organic Chemistry in Britain, and through their acquaintance Engels found it easy to keep abreast of discoveries in the physical sciences.

When Marx asked Engels to review his *Contribution to the Critique of Political Economy* he suggested something 'brief on the method and what is new in the content'. And then more explicitly he admonished Engels not to forget two important points: '1. that it [his *Critique*] extirpates Proudhonism root and branch, and 2. that the *specifically* social, by no means *absolute* character of bourgeois production is analysed straight away'. Marx undoubtedly saw Engels's piece before publication and subsequently pronounced himself pleased with the publicity: '*Your articles* on my affair have been reprinted in the German papers from New York to California (with the tiny little *Volk* we hooked the whole of the German-American press). . . .' But as Engels did not actually mention Proudhon in the review, and as he treated Marx's analysis of the commodity only at the end – and specifically as an instance of 'the German dialectical method' – the claim by McLellan that Marx had himself dictated the main points of the (anonymous) notice seems overdrawn (40 CW 471, 473, 502; KM 310; see MEIR, 96–117).

Engels's major preoccupation over his remaining thirty-five years of intellectual activity was the further development of his grand framework for knowledge, his defence of the dialectical method for establishing it, and his argument that Marx's work was best explicated within that philosophical context. That context arose from the Young Hegelian perspective that he had adopted very early in his intellectual career. In the mid-1840s he was involved full-time in politics, and in the 1850s and 1860s he was in full-time employment. Only after his 'retirement' in the 1870s did he find time and occasions in which to tackle such highly abstract issues at length.

By 1873 Engels's commitments to the International – taken on when he moved from Manchester to London – had been much reduced, because the General Council had been relocated to New York after The Hague Congress of the previous year. An outbreak of what he called 'shallow materialist popularisation' in the philosophy of science had occurred during the 1860s, and this was given 'new impetus by the coming into fashion of Darwinism'. The writers that he had in mind were Karl Vogt (1817–95), Ludwig Büchner (1824–99), and Jakob Moleschott (1822–93), promoters of 'scientific systems' that allegedly validated their schemes for social reform. Engels's comments were written on the first pages of notebooks that later became his *Dialektik der Natur* (*Dialectics of Nature*), commenced in 1873 and continued into the 1880s, though the manuscripts were not published in his lifetime. Instead some of his results and views appeared in published works of more immediate political import, such as *Herrn Eugen Dühring's Umwälzung der Wissenschaft* (known as Anti-Dühring), first issued in 1877–8 as articles for the socialist press.

Engels was entirely clear about his reasons for engaging in the vast researches required to overturn the systems currently in vogue. He said that he could very well have left the writers alone and abandoned them 'to their not-unpraiseworthy if narrow occupation of teaching atheism, etc., to the German philistine' – but for two considerations. These were '1. abuse directed [by them] against philosophy ... which in spite of everything is the glory of Germany, and 2. the presumption of applying the theories about nature [e.g. Darwinism] to society and of reforming socialism'. In a few brief phrases he set down the essence of his own dialectical outlook:

> Two philosophical tendencies, the metaphysical with fixed categories, the dialectical (Aristotle and especially Hegel) with fluid categories ... all logic develops only from these progressing contradictions ... the dialectics of the mind is only the reflection of the forms of motion of the real world, both of nature and of history. ... Philosophy takes its revenge posthumously on natural science for the latter having deserted it ... [e.g.] Hegel – whose encylcopaedic comprehensive treatment and rational grouping of the natural sciences is a greater achievement than all the materialistic nonsense put together (25 CW 482–6).

Engels planned to demonstrate in his researches that natural science contained dilemmas which could only be resolved dialectically, as had already happened, so he argued, in the famous mathematical disputes between Sir Isaac Newton (1642–1727) and Gottfried Leibniz (1646–1716) over the calculus. Eventually, if slowly, scientists would realize that the dialectical method yielded scientific knowledge. The main laws of this method were 'transformation of quantity into quality – mutual penetration of polar opposites and transformation into each other when carried to extremes – development through contradiction or negation of the negation – spiral form of development'. To demonstrate this universal interconnection of all phenomena he proposed to show that the sciences are reflections of a dialectical reality. His work would therefore include critical coverage of mathematics, celestial mechanics, physics, chemistry, biology including Darwin, Darwinian politics and theory of society, and human development through labour (25 CW 313–14).

Whereas in the 1840s Engels had used class struggle – as a well-developed idea in theory and as a documented empirical reality – to discredit the economists and philosophers with whom he had political disagreements, in the 1850s and onwards this no longer satisfied him intellectually. Whilst he consistently claimed that his communist politics was founded on the contradictions of class-conflict and was dedicated to their resolution in a classless society, the wide-ranging and abstract character of his later dialectical studies inevitably distanced him somewhat from the more immediately political preoccupations characteristic of his earlier years. He spent considerable energy acquiring the specialised knowledge necessary to outline and support the high abstractions of his materialist dialectic. Knowledge of that dialectic was required, in his view, so that he could explicate Marx's work and authenticate its scientific character.

It is clear that the level of abstraction at which Engels pitched his publicity for communism – and hence his view of his readership – had changed considerably since his popular drafts for the *Communist Manifesto*, his impassioned first book *The Condition of the Working Class in England* and his spirited article 'Outlines of a Critique of Political Economy'. Whilst the later works overlap these early writings to some extent, the imposition of the more elaborate and perhaps forbidding intellectual context made the class struggle seem, at one level anyway, a problem for specialist theoreticians. His fame and reputation were ultimately built up on the late writings in which he developed his dialectical philosophy of science.

There is no denying that the late 'scientific' works of Engels have been more widely read than his early ones, and that his materialist dialectic has been influential in communist – and anti-communist – politics. But the nature of this influence must be carefully considered. Did his preoccupation with the reconciliation of philosophy and science – in terms of a matter-in-motion materialism and a Hegelian dialectic – really help the 'Marx party', subsequent

Marxists, or indeed socialists of any kind to get to grips with the harsh realities of class politics? It has been argued that he was responsible in part for purveying a determinism that discouraged political initiative amongst socialists, and that he encouraged by example a kind of rarefied theorizing that distracted them from mass politics. On the other hand he made proletarian socialism more respectable intellectually in Germany and elsewhere than had previously been the case, and in that way he created additional interest in class politics and in Marx's conceptualization of capitalism (L 244–58; AM 235–60).

In terms of Engels's own career as an ardent communist another awkward question arises. Was he perhaps moving into such abstract issues as a way of compensating for the very real frustrations and successive disappointments experienced by the 'Marx party'? This was a party of London émigrés, working in Germany through agents – sometimes rather wayward ones – such as Liebknecht and Bebel. The 'party' was in any case allied in a highly problematic way with the middle-class movement for constitutional rights and political power. Speaking in French at the London Congress of the International in September 1871 Engels commented that 'the politics which are needed are working class politics . . . the workers' party must be constituted not as the tail of some bourgeois party, but as an independent party with its own objective'. 'Political freedoms', he continued, 'the right of assembly and association, and the freedom of the press' – 'these are our weapons'. But the power to use those weapons was in fact in the hands of the middle classes themselves (22 CW 417).

Moreover the 'Marx party' was constantly squeezed within the socialist movement itself. On the right there were power-seekers, notably the Lassalleans, who were prepared to compromise with an existing régime in order to obtain political and economic concessions, as the 'Marxists' were not. On the left there were anarchists, most notably the Bakuninists, who claimed to reject any state whatsoever in principle and indeed all structures of power within the socialist movement. Writing in an Italian almanac for 1874, 'Federico Engels' ridiculed any anarchistic expectations that a social revolution could abolish all authority. A revolution is certainly the most authoritarian thing there is, he announced, and it would use highly authoritarian means – rifles, bayonets and cannon – so that one part of the population could impose its will on another (23 CW 425).

Other than large-scale revolution based on a flowering of constitutional rights and working-class participation in politics, it is
difficult to see what would constitute a success for the 'workers'
party', as envisaged by Engels. When the somewhat inchoate
events of contemporary democratic revolt proved disappointing,
the anguish must have been intense. In so far as his view of
revolutionary theory as a science provided political leaders with
recruits for the cause, Engels's work promoted class politics
directly – even if he personally functioned only indirectly as a kind
of adviser to the socialist movement. Whilst he maintained a lively
and stimulating correspondence with a broad range of socialists
throughout the world, including representatives of socialism in
France, Austria, Hungary, Spain, Italy, numerous other countries
and most particularly with the Germans, he was not an officer in a
national party or other such organization in which decisions were
taken and binding commitments to action enforced. His advice
was sought, considered and amended in contexts where he himself
did not function directly, and his views had the prestige that they
did because he had made himself well known as a theorist. Indeed
his advice made little sense without the theory and would not have
been much considered at the time nor today had he not made his
reputation as the principal exponent of Marx's unique brand of
communism. He made only one important personal appearance at
an international socialist congress, albeit as a late-arriving non-
participant. This was the meeting of the Second International held
in Zürich in 1893, at which – as a grand old man indeed – he was
called upon to close the sessions as an honorary president.

Engels's best political opportunity to promote his scheme for
reconciling philosophy and science, and to publicize Marx's place
within it, came when he agreed with Liebknecht in 1875 that it
would be a good idea to attack Eugen von Dühring (1833–1921), a
blind lecturer at the University of Berlin and would-be social
reformer. Politically this was a continuation of his attacks on what
he considered to be 'petty-bourgeois socialism', as he had recently
written a series of articles 'Zur Wohnungsfrage' ('The Housing
Question') for Liebknecht's *Volksstaat*, the official paper of the
German Social-Democratic Party. In that work, later reprinted, he
ridiculed Proudhonian schemes for private ownership and other
nostrums intended to ameliorate class conflict, quoting *inter alia*
from Marx's *Capital* (just going into a second edition) and his own
Condition of the Working Class in England (last printed in 1848).

Dühring had just published a number of popular works, presenting similar schemes for the reconciliation of wealth and poverty. He had situated those plans within a grand philosophy of science, which Engels criticized in design as well as in detail. In dismissing Dühring he published a series of long articles in *Vorwärts*, the paper of the Socialist Workers' Party of Germany, newly formed at Gotha when Lassalleans – from the General Association of German Workers – and 'Eisenachers' – from Bebel's and Liebknecht's Social-Democratic Workers' Party – were at last united in 1875. Engels's articles were collected in 1878 into a weighty volume, which became his second and final full-length book. The formal title – 'Herr Eugen Dühring's Revolution in Science' – was an ironically inverted parody of Dühring's attribution of a 'revolution' in political economy to the American writer Henry Charles Carey (1793–1879), whom Marx despised for his notion that class-relations in capitalist society could be 'harmonized'. Engels composed his attack on a scale similar to Dühring's own works, and in it he outlined a philosophical system that was somewhat similar in scope and level of abstraction, covering philosophy, political economy and socialism.

No doubt this made Engels's *Anti-Dühring* a credible critique, and it put his name before a substantial public. But it also involved meeting Dühring the philosophical socialist on his own ground, a tactic about which Engels had expressed a good deal of reluctance in the 1840s when he warned Marx of the dangers. Whilst noting that problem in his preface, Engels advised his readers that he had taken the opportunity to set forth 'in a positive form my views on controversial issues which are today of quite general scientific or practical interest'. And whilst disclaiming any ambition to create a rival system, he none the less hoped that the reader would not fail to observe 'the connection inherent in the various views which I have advanced' (25 CW 6).

Engels continued this project in further works, including *The Origin of the Family, Private Property and the State*, which had been intended for publication in *Die Neue Zeit*. This was the socialist 'theoretical' monthly edited by Kautsky, who was a strong admirer of Engels and the first important Marxist to be born after 1848. However, Engels did not think that he could trim his views to fit the anti-socialist law, introduced in 1878 by Imperial Chancellor Prince Otto von Bismarck (1815–98), and so the work was published in Switzerland. Ostensibly the short book used recent anthropological studies (and relevant notebooks inherited from Marx) to trace in more detail than had been possible in the 1840s the development of technology in pre-historical times, the history of marital practice and domestic labour, and changes in other social structures consequent upon both those factors. Darwinian evolutionary explanation featured in Engels's account of the prehistoric origins of the modern monogamous family, and he attempted somewhat unsuccessfully to reconcile this 'materialist' line of explanation concerning the family and private property with his 'new materialist' account, relating technological change to the state.

On the one hand Engels's *Origin* reflected a 'scientific' approach to society that was far more widely advertised and accepted than Marx's – namely social Darwinism – and on the other it addressed issues of increasing political importance – namely the 'woman question'. As the *Origin* dealt explicitly with the position of women in historical development up to the present and with the role they might expect to play in a communist society of the future, it was one of Engels's most popular, often reprinted and widely translated works. In particular, he addressed questions concerning civil, economic and familial rights that aligned him with the movement for the emancipation of women. For him their struggle was part of the progressive development of constitutional rights and democratic government in the west. That view of progress, of course, formed the overarching framework of his entire politics. On the other hand the *Origin* was not the work of a wholly self-critical feminist. His analysis failed to probe deeply into the position of women, because he presumed a different nature (especially in sexual matters) for them, as well as different domestic responsibilities, compared with the behaviour and roles that he assigned, sometimes implicitly, to men. In that way the work bears a highly ambiguous relation to the methods and aspirations of modern socialist feminism (see EF 480–9).

The 'new materialist' outlook on the prehistorical and historical development of class society also acquired a 'scientific' basis in evolutionary biology – supplied by Engels. In a manuscript work of 1876 on the part played by labour in the transition from ape to man he presented a Darwinian – and occasionally Lamarckian – analysis of primate evolution. He argued that the progressive development of the physiological organs and intellectual capacities needed for human productive activities were crucial features in human development. Significantly that work was published in *Die Neue Zeit* just posthumously in 1895–6, and so reinforced the rapprochement between 'scientific socialism', as Engels conceived it, and the increasingly influential Darwinian theories of human history and politics.

Engels's much translated and reprinted eulogy for Marx reveals very clearly how he aimed to link Marx with Darwinian biology and the physics of matter-in-motion. 'Just as Darwin discovered the law of development of organic nature', he wrote, 'so Marx discovered the law of development of human history'. But in addition he had discovered a 'special law of motion' governing the capitalist mode of production – the law of surplus value. For Engels, Marx was a giant of modern science capable of the most abstract theoretical work, but also a 'revolutionist' who experienced particular joy when some new discovery had an immediate effect on industry and historical development (2 SW 167–8). Whilst Marx in fact had immense enthusiasm for highly abstract arguments in social science, and very occasionally for drawing limited analogies between those arguments and carefully selected developments in the physical sciences, it is highly doubtful that he saw himself as the greatest reconciler of philosophy and science since Hegel, as Engels claimed. Moreover it is open to considerable question whether Marx's works can be read to best effect – in their original historical context or in relation to contemporary society – by viewing them in the way that Engels recommended. Given the opportunities that he had for ringing endorsements, Marx's own response to Engels's works was decidedly restrained (see MEIR 121–58).

The summation of Engels's philosophical project was *Ludwig Feuerbach und der Ausgang der klassischen deutschen Philosophie* (*Ludwig Feuerbach and the End of Classical German Philosophy*), a long review published in 1886 in Kautsky's *Die Neue Zeit*, reprinted as a pamphlet in 1888, then swiftly translated into Russian and French. In his brief introduction to the work Engels mentioned that whilst writing it he had once again perused the manuscript *German Ideology* of 1845–7, but had found it insufficiently philosophical and therefore of no current use. The long section on Feuerbach seemed to him to consist of merely economic material that now appeared very primitive compared with Marx's later achievements in *Capital* – whereas in the 1840s Engels had considered Marx's material on Feuerbach to be 'philosophical' and worthy of quick publication.

After Marx's death in 1883 Engels began to speak proprietorially for them both. Hence in this work of the mid-1880s he planned to give a fresh account of their relationship to Hegelian philosophy – 'how we proceeded, as well as of how we separated, from it' – and an overdue acknowledgement of their debt to the post-Hegelian materialist philosopher Feuerbach. Engels produced a classic Young Hegelian reading of Hegel, finding in the great philosopher's most famous proposition – all that is real is rational, and all that is rational is real – a revolutionary message, once the Hegelian dialectic of change through contradiction had been correctly applied. The true significance and revolutionary character of Hegelian philosophy was that 'it dealt the death blow to the finality of productions of human thought and mind', especially in political and economic structures. To that view Engels added a 'materialist' underpinning – the dialectic was said to be thoroughly in accord with the present state of natural science. Moreover it was said to be a reflection in the brain of the immutable character of all developmental processes, whether physical, social or logical. Those truths, he concluded, represented the encyclopaedic wealth of the Hegelian system, recreated on a 'materialist' basis.

For Engels what was demonstrably true of nature must also be true of the human sciences, and within those studies he gave pride of place to Marx's work on the historical development of classes, the political development of the state and the cultural development of ideologies, such as religion. Thus in *Ludwig Feuerbach* Engels elaborated at much greater length the project of reconciling science and philosophy, which was first made explicit in his 1859 review of Marx's *Contribution*. Moreover he connected that project explicitly with his early admiration for Hegel's encyclopaedic philosophy and for the Young Hegelians' critical dialectic, thereby incorporating Marx into a framework ultimately derived from the intellectual development that he – Engels – had experienced independently. In fact *Ludwig Feuerbach* of 1886–8 is very similar in genre and structure to his very first philosophical pamphlet *Schelling and Revelation* of 1842, because in both he identified the Hegelian dialectic as the way to make progress in philosophy. In his early work he had defended the way that the Young Hegelians had applied a critical dialectic to religion – and politics. Then in his late work he defended the way that Marx had applied a 'materialist' dialectic to economics – and politics (SWOV 595–601; MEIR 118–31).

Within this grand and intellectually ambitious project Engels was of course concerned with presenting what he considered to be the essential content of Marx's economic work, and promoting it to as wide an audience as possible. He gave particular advice to Marx on that point in a letter of June 1867 when volume one of *Capital* was in proof. Engels doubted that 'your philistine' could cope with the kind of abstract thinking that Marx had employed in analysing the concept of value, which was crucial to his critical work on the concept of money. His work on money, in turn, was crucial to his overall discussion of capital. Engels recommended a larger number of short sections, each with its own heading. 'You ought to have treated this part in the manner of Hegel's *Encyclopaedia*', he wrote, 'with short paragraphs, each dialectical transition emphasised by means of a special heading'. Though the results would have looked somewhat like a school text-book, a large class of readers would have found it, so he claimed, considerably easier to understand. But with characteristic judiciousness Marx took only some of the suggestions: 'With regard to the development of the *form of value*, I have both followed and *not* followed your advice, thus striking a dialectical attitude in this matter, too.' Marx followed Engels's plan in constructing a simplified treatment of the analysis of value, but he incorporated it into an appendix for 'non-dialectical' readers (42 CW 382, 384). Then in subsequent editions it was merged into the first chapter.

Engels reviewed the first volume of *Capital* for a variety of papers, including a notice in his hometown *Elberfelder Zeitung*. From the first sentence it was crystal clear whom he meant to upset: 'A learned treatise of fifty quires proves to us that the total capital of all our bankers, merchants, manufacturers and wealthy property-holders is nothing but the accumulated and unpaid labour of the working-class!' He continued his discussion by relating Marx to the socialism that had become familiar in German politics. In his work Marx had intended, so Engels wrote, to give the socialist struggle a scientific basis. Neither Fourier nor Proudhon, nor even Lassalle had been able to provide this. Lassalle in particular was a well known practical agitator, but by contrast in Marx readers could get a systematic, scientific theory. And only science, according to Engels, could pronounce the final word in politics (20 CW 214–15).

Hence Engels also devoted considerable effort to editing further editions of *Capital*, assisting Marx whilst he was alive and then continuing on his own after 1883. His work, most notably on the fourth edition of 1890, and his advice on translations, most notably the English one by Moore and Aveling of 1887, were crucial in establishing standard texts. After Marx's death Engels published and republished further works, writing almost two dozen prefaces and introductions, producing these at an average rate of about two a year. In those short but widely read pieces he generally took the opportunity to explain the 'outlook' and 'method' implied in Marx's thought as he understood it, and then added glosses, notes and sometimes alterations to Marx's text to make his point.

Thus on occasion Engels associated Marx with a search for causal explanation, an overall assumption of determinism, and an ultimate reference to a matter-in-motion materialism that were not explicitly stated in the original writings. Of course, in Engels's view, matter-in-motion materialism and modern physical science were necessarily included in the 'dialectic' method. But as actually applied by Marx – who acknowledged his use of Hegel's dialectic but never addressed himself at length on the subject – that claim is at least questionable. Marx's work fits uneasily into the causal determination and materialist science that Engels proclaimed, so the exact role and content of the dialectic in the Marxian *oeuvre* remains an important subject for debate. This is despite Engels's attempts to resolve the issue, indeed to beg the question.

Engels devoted an enormous amount of time to editing the economic manuscripts that Marx left behind on his death. Some of those voluminous works appeared as volume two of *Capital* in 1885, with a second edition in 1893, and volume three followed in 1894. Because variorum editions are now in progress and access to the manuscripts is difficult, generalizations about his editorial work cannot be made with reasonable certainty as yet, and judgements about his role as editor will have to await detailed textual comparison. His editing of what is sometimes known as the fourth volume of *Capital* – *Theorien über den Mehrwert* (*Theories of Surplus Value*) – was largely handed over to Kautsky in 1889, on grounds of failing eyesight, though Engels was later in some distress at Kautsky's lack of progress (37 MEW 143).

Engels's *métier* was pre-eminently the popular pamphlet. Three chapters from *Anti-Dühring* on socialism appeared in 1880 in a French translation under the title *Socialisme utopique et socialisme scientifique* (*Socialism Utopian and Scientific*), just after the foundation of a French socialist party in 1879. The short book was in turn published in German in 1882, and distributed illegally in defiance of the anti-socialist law. Writing in that year to his long-time friend Friedrich Sorge, ex-'48er and socialist émigré to New York (where he had directed the International), Engels advertised his work, saying 'most people are too idle to read thick books like *Capital*, and so a little pamphlet does the job much more quickly' (35 MEW 396). By 1890 the anti-socialist law had expired, and by 1891 the 'little pamphlet' had gone through four editions in German, and tens of thousands of copies were in circulation. It was translated into English in 1892, and by that date was published, so the author claimed, in ten languages. This was the *Communist Manifesto* of its time, but arguably it was even more influential, and it went out under Engels's name alone. *Socialism Utopian and Scientific* was the work from which millions of conversions to Marxism were made, and it was Engels's greatest achievement as a publicist for Marx. Or rather it was his greatest success for the way he wished to present his deceased colleague to the socialist public. For that reason it merits careful consideration, as through it Engels decisively influenced the way that socialists perceived Marx and read his works, and hence the way that socialism and communism were subsequently developed throughout the world.

Whilst acknowledging that modern socialism was a practical movement rooted in class antagonism, Engels also set out to explicate and explain the historical development of socialism as a theory. This was a project left unfinished from the mid-1840s, when he had contemplated producing a library of the best socialist authors. Although socialism had of course been founded on contemporary material facts, it was also – so Engels maintained – necessarily connected with the development of modern philosophy and science. In particular he cited the rationalism of the Enlightenment that, in his view, formed the intellectual basis of the French revolution. In the days of post-revolutionary disappointment, that approach to social reform was succeeded by the utopian socialism of Saint-Simon, Fourier and Owen. Engels credited those well-known writers with 'stupendously grand thoughts', but indicated that their alleged absolute truths about politics necessarily led to intellectual conflicts. Those conflicts could only be resolved by a scientific socialism.

For Engels scientific socialism had its roots in German philosophy, the most impressive intellectual movement in history. Those important works of the mind had culminated in Hegel, whose philosophical system had this particularly important merit: 'for the first time the whole world, natural, historical, intellectual, is represented as a process, i.e., as in constant motion, change, transformation, development'. Hegel had produced a philosophy of dialectics, the attempt 'to trace out the internal connection that makes a continuous whole of all this movement and development'. On Engels's view dialectics 'comprehends things and their representations, ideas, in their essential connection, concatenation, motion, origin, and ending'. Proof of the validity of dialectics came not from philosophy itself, but from nature, as understood by physical scientists. Unbeknown to themselves modern scientists – working within a simplistic, or as Engels said, a 'metaphysical' materialism – were daily furnishing proof that 'in the last resort, Nature works dialectically'. 'She does not move in the eternal oneness of a perpetually recurring circle', he wrote, 'but goes through a real historical evolution'. Central within this development was 'the process of evolution of man himself'. In that connection, 'Darwin must be named before all others'.

No longer should socialists be preoccupied with inventing 'a system of society as perfect as possible', Engels wrote. Instead they should 'examine the historico-economic succession of events' – the ones from which the class-struggle had developed. The class-struggle was now documented by facts, he noted, and he associated factual criticisms of existing society with the struggles of working-class political activists. Their publications 'gave the lie to the teachings of bourgeois [political] economy', and indeed he had done that kind of work himself in the late 1830s and early 1840s.

But in Engels's view a class analysis of history, including the condition of contemporary society and the possibilities within it for future development, could not advance any further until the inner contradictions that led ultimately to revolutionary action, and the inner secret encapsulated in the concept 'surplus value', had been exposed through the 'dialectical' investigation undertaken by Marx. With those developments in theory – 'the materialistic conception of history and the revelation of the secret of capitalist production through surplus value' – socialism became a science. Both of those theoretical developments were, of course, ascribed by Engels to Marx. Casting Marx's 'materialist conception of history' as a search for 'final causes', Engels then offered readers of his pamphlet a précis of the *Communist Manifesto* (SWOV 380,

399–416). Thus the classic popular work of communist theory was now secured by Engels in a theoretical context that had reconciled 'dialectically' – so he thought – the commanding heights of modern philosophy with the powerful discoveries of physical science.

Conclusion: Politician and Theorist

Engels died of cancer of the throat on 5 August 1895, after an illness of about six months. Some thirty years earlier he had written (in the young Jenny Marx's scrapbook) that his chief characteristic was 'knowing everything by halves' and that his idea of happiness was 'Château Margaux 1848' (1 K 300). Those two remarks could well stand as his epitaph.

In accordance with Engels's instructions his body was cremated and his ashes scattered in the sea off Eastbourne, an act undertaken by Eleanor Marx, Edward Aveling and Eduard Bernstein (1850–1932), who had edited the German social-democratic paper *Der Sozialdemokrat* from Switzerland during the years of the anti-socialist law. The estate was worth nearly £30 000, and Engels left £1000 to help with election expenses for socialist candidates in Germany. After the reduced sum for 'Pumps', the remainder was divided between the surviving Marx daughters Laura and Eleanor (three-eighths each, holding one-third each for their dead sister's children), and Louise Freyberger, who had the benefit of the final quarter plus the furniture and £250 for being an executor (along with Sam Moore and Bernstein). Engels rather unwisely divided his literary effects between the German Social-Democratic Workers' Party (his library, including Marx's books, and his own letters) and Eleanor Marx (Marx's manuscripts and his letters). This arrangement did not please all his surviving associates at the time, and it led to a dispersal of manuscripts and papers that has made research and publication very difficult (2 H 727–8).

In this study of Engels's life and thought I have attempted to provide a context that will be helpful for further reading and research, and pursuing that aim has entailed paying considerable attention to his early years. Other studies do not, in my view, link Engels's youthful development with his later career at all effectively. Over the course of his life there are very real continuities in aims and opinions, and indeed those continuities must be stressed if he is to emerge as his own man, and not as a mere adjunct to Marx – which he was not. Moreover I have placed Engels's personal and family relationships at the centre of this biography, because they are not ancillary to a consideration of his political activities and views, but form the context in which his work as a politician and theorist took place, so I have produced 'nested' chronological accounts. Thus in considering who Engels actually was, what in particular he was doing, and what in fact he achieved, I have departed substantially from his own view of his career as a politician and theorist, and from the biographical tradition that has subsequently grown up around him.

The revolutionary liberalism and progressive nationalism of Engels's youth were derived from his early contact with the romantic movement and Hegelian philosophy as they were applied to the politics of the day. From that basis his views and activities developed in an intelligible way over his career. Thus his early concerns – revolutionary constitutionalism, popular participation in politics, individual rights to free expression, inequality in social class, industrial development, German nationalism, and rationalistic internationalism can all be traced in recognizable, albeit revised form throughout his later works. Allying himself politically and intellectually with Marx in the mid-1840s was thus no great revelation, as what they had in common was of more significance than anything Marx imparted to Engels as they began to work together. Indeed Engels's experience as a popular journalist and pamphleteer, his contacts with mass politics in England and his outline critique of political economy were arguably highly influential on Marx, who was more than a little prone to bury himself in convoluted arguments and to address his audience on his own terms.

The crucial turning point in Engels's life came in late 1850 when he resolved to move to Manchester. There he began to settle into full-time employment in industry and into personal relationships and domesticity. Those developments necessarily distanced him somewhat from the active involvement in German politics and in communist organizations that he had been pursuing over the previous five years. In compensation he began to carve out a role for himself that was not only intellectually more ambitious than his previous orientation but also – paradoxically – more dependent in a certain sense on Marx. Writing as a popular philosopher of science Engels erected a conceptual structure around Marx's work, thus using his ideas – or rather some version of his ideas – in a manner that Marx himself did not attempt. But in that way Engels limited himself somewhat in his investigations, as he treated

Marx's conclusions as foregone and did not tackle certain subjects – such as empirical research into working-class life and theoretical issues in political economy – on his own anymore.

Thus the output of the later Engels reflected very clearly certain intellectual ambitions of the Young Hegelian movement – an encyclopaedic outlook on all knowledge in general, a reconciliation of science and philosophy in particular, a theory of historical progress pivoting on the French revolution, and a key role in politics for intellectuals. It was their job to make discoveries in theory and to incorporate them into practice. Those Young Hegelian ambitions were allied, of course, to a view of industrial development and proletarian communism that he had acquired early in his career, again independently of Marx.

Indeed the political strategy which the two pursued together had also been acquired independently of each other. This was a radicalized liberalism linking the middle-class struggle for democratic rights with an expansion of those rights to include the working-classes. At that point democratic politics would begin to bear on the property rights enjoyed by the middle classes, because communists were committed to a settlement of the 'social question' through mass political action. Engels, in association with Marx, was thus dedicated to a strategy that was problematic in at least two ways: the middle classes rightly mistrusted the communists as would-be allies against authoritarians and so forebore to make thorough-going revolutions; and the communists were all too easily outflanked when authoritarian and middle-class régimes offered strategic concessions of power and resources to the working-classes.

Engels saw himself, rightly, as a fighter for constitutionalism and middle-class democracy in the first instance, indeed for a whole catalogue of human rights, and that aspect of his politics has been neglected. But as constitutional governments were established in the 1860s and 1870s, the struggle for democratic rights in politics was at least somewhat successful, and so it no longer looked revolutionary by definition. Using and pursuing democratic rights within a 'bourgeois' régime began to appear rather more like some kind of compromise, indeed a negation of the proletarian rule that communists aimed to achieve, and so the revolutionary rhetoric employed by Engels then sat rather oddly with his advocacy of proletarian participation in electoral politics.

Within the communist and socialist camp Engels stood –

through his empirical work as well as his political theory – for a distinctively working-class outlook, in that he viewed communism as a logical outcome of industrial development and mass politics. That aspect of his political thought has survived, since it has proved useful in stirring up revolution against élitist and reactionary governments on the one hand, and resisting utopias and nostrums amongst socialists on the other. But there are notable gaps in his political theory and corresponding lacunae in his communist politics. He advocated a revolutionary practice based on democratic rights and representative institutions, a politics of consensus-building amongst groups, societies, parties, committees, international associations, etc. Within those groups his practice was largely in accord with the conventional principles of representation in debate and obligation to obedience that are the heritage of European liberalism. But he also acknowledged very readily that pursuing a revolution entailed military action, and he accepted the necessity for some degree of authoritarianism within the revolutionary armed forces. Moreover he also suggested that authoritarianism had a role to play in defending working-class gains in political power and in settling the 'social question' in their favour. The justification of such authoritarian measures posed little problem for him, as he could argue for them on a majoritarian basis, identifying the revolutionaries with an alliance of classes – ultimately including peasant farmers – forming the majority in society.

But Engels did not explore in much detail some of the difficulties inherent in those views, either in his theory or in his practice. His studies of revolutionary failure – the French revolution of 1789 and subsequent revolutionary wars, further changes of régime in France in 1830, 1848 and 1871, and the events of 1848–9 in Germany – did not lead him to make constructive changes in his political analysis and activity. Rather he seemed to provide eulogies for working-class bravery in the midst of political disaster and then to escape, perhaps, into more abstract and – as he thought – more resolvable questions in the philosophy of science. His lack of success in the revolutionary politics of the mid-nineteenth century was not, of course, conclusive proof that national revolutions could never be made through class-alliance, that workers' interests could never be protected and pursued through mass democracy and organized armed force, that international solidarity amongst social-ists could never triumph over prejudice and chauvinism, and that some drastically different approach – whether anarchist or élitist – was in fact necessary. But it is notable that his politics was very remarkably and perhaps rather unconstructively consistent.

For that reason Engels's influence has chiefly been on the theoretical side of Marxism, and his 'dialectics' and 'materialism' are notably memorialized in official Soviet philosophy, subject of course to minor amendment in the light of subsequent scientific discoveries. His view that 'dialectics' and 'materialism' are fundamental to Marxism, and hence to any understanding of Marx's works, has been very generally accepted and on occasion hotly defended by non-Marxist commentators and anti-Marxist critics alike. However, shortly after Engels's death doubts about the complete validity of his commentary on Marx began to creep into the Marxist movement. Those doubts have led some writers to propose relatively minor adjustments to Engels's deterministic social science – which was particularly relevant to the Marxist prediction of capitalist catastrophe. But doubts about Engels have also led other theorists to reject his materialistic natural philosophy – which was relevant to the Marxist understanding of human action altogether. As further materials on Engels and Marx become available in scholarly editions, we can expect the debate to continue and sharpen, so that the exact similarities and differences between Engels and Marx can be traced in their theoretical work and practical activities. From that exercise we might expect some enlightenment in social science and on political action, if only that certain ideas and strategies might be eliminated as poorly founded in reason and inadequate in experience.

Of course to some within the Marxist and anti-Marxist camps the very idea that Engels can be examined as a theorist and politician separately from Marx, and that this exercise might disclose differences between the two, is anathema. That position is simply unscholarly and must be rejected, as it assumes a conclusion – namely that as theorists and politicians Marx and Engels were interchangeable – which must in fact be proved. On more respectable grounds there are defenders of Engels's 'dialectics' and 'materialism' today outside the world of official Soviet philosophy. The best contemporary arguments for his views stress their continuity in principle with later discoveries in the physical and natural sciences, which are based on assumptions about 'matter' that are arguably similar – or at least similar enough – to Engels's own. Any reputable social science, so the argument runs, must display such continuity with natural and physical science, as modern standards of truth in theory and validity in application – whatever the discipline – are set by the scientific materialism on which the natural and physical sciences are founded. Dualisms which attempt to provide some alternative foundation for social science have failed, and must necessarily be abandoned. Engels's principles of 'dialectics', so his defenders claim, have ample confirmation in physical and natural science, in philosophy and logic, and in social phenomena as analysed most notably by Marx, so there is little reason to believe that they are wrong or worthless. On that basis the process of tracing the correspondence between dialectical principles and phenomena of all kinds ought very well to continue, as the reconciliation of science and philosophy that Engels proposed represents a synoptic approach to knowledge that is valuable in itself.

Critics of the 'materialism' and 'dialectics' propounded by Engels have argued, in turn, that the continuity between physical and social science that undoubtedly exists is still inadequately understood, and that it is far too early to announce that social science rests on exactly the same materialism as that which physical scientists currently employ. Indeed what counts as material is under continuous review by scientists themselves and is not necessarily the same nor even very similar amongst the different physical and natural sciences. Whether the physical and social sciences – not to mention history and logic – can ever be unified on some 'materialist' basis remains an open question, and certainly the adoption of Engels's materialism – even as revised in the light of subsequent physics – can form no overall foundation for the current practice of social science. The application and use of physical science within contemporary social science is very much a possibility, but that exercise is different from any attempt to make 'scientific materialism' a necessary presumption. Indeed doing so puts social science into a straitjacket that severely limits creative inquiry and poses certain questions – about the causal basis and ultimate predictability of human actions – that are currently unanswerable. By contrast contemporary social science necessarily requires and in fact uses a mixture of assumptions, methods and explanatory frameworks. In that way there is indeed continuity between social and physical scientists, because they are in their practice committed to an open-ended approach with respect to methods and assumptions. At the very least Engels's claims for the universality of his scientific 'materialism' and 'dialectics' are premature.

Moreover, so his critics have argued, Engels's principles of 'dialectics' are themselves redundancies, rather than explanations, because they are allegedly true of all phenomena. Tracing them more or less persuasively in such changes as occur in social phenomena (or indeed in any other) does not prove that any particular 'materialism' must necessarily underlie social science, nor does 'dialectics' provide a method for research in any contemporary science worthy of the name. The result of a 'dialectical' analysis does not count as knowledge, since at best it merely translates science into a realm of esoteric concepts that reputable scientists do not themselves employ.

Unfortunately very little of the commentary on Engels concerns itself with philosophy of science as such and proceeds at a respectable standard of argument. Mostly his 'materialism' and 'dialectics' are read back into Marx, without serious attention to the ways in which the two bodies of work clearly diverge and hence to an alternative reading of Marx. That exercise – reading Engels into Marx – is then used as evidence or indeed proof for the view that Engels's 'materialism' and 'dialectics' are true as he claimed and still valid in all sciences. Or it is used as 'evidence' or 'proof' that as Marx 'agreed' with Engels's 'materialism' and 'dialectics', Marx's work may be defended or attacked with reference to the reconciliation of philosophy and science mounted by Engels. In actuality any argument concerning the truth and validity of Engels's claims about scientific materialism and dialectical method must be supported by intellectually respectable arguments (see the Guide to Further Reading below). The mere fact – if such it is – that Marx agreed with them is in itself no item of proof. Moreover Engels's reading of Marx must be tested against alternative interpretations, to see which results in a better understanding of Marx's *oeuvre* in its original context and which provides a more fruitful interpretation of his social theory today.

My study of Engels's life and thought has shown that in his early years he developed a well integrated outlook that later formed the foundation for his popularizations of Marx, and that it is a mistake to presume that the content of those popularizations flowed directly from Marx's works themselves or from some unexplained misunderstanding of them on Engels's part. Consideration of Engels's intellectual development from his earliest days onwards thus sets the scene for a more informed evaluation of the works in which he made use of Marx's ideas in theory and followed his lead in practice. That project in turn makes an evaluation of Marx's thought and practice all the more necessary and promising, as the points of similarity and contrast with Engels can then be isolated and assessed.

As a politician Engels's work was severely circumscribed by the strategy that he inherited from the politics of revolutionary constitutionalism, and as a theorist he lacked the ability and training for sustained analysis in social science. Unlike Marx, for instance, he was notably lacking in intellectual caution concerning philosophies of science and history. As a political agitator Engels had real gifts, but his use of those talents declined considerably after the debâcle of 1848–9. His greatest successes were with popular pamphlets, and in that respect he went from strength to strength. Modestly he directed attention in those works to Marx, and thus obscured his own contribution to socialist politics. In his writing there is much for the political philosopher and social scientist to criticize, but as an 'autodidact in philosophy' he has no equal in modern western thought.

Guide to Further Reading

The 'classic' biography of Engels is Gustav Mayer's *Friedrich Engels* (vol. 1, J. Springer, Berlin, 1920; vol. 1, 2nd edn, with vol. 2, Martinus Nijhoff, The Hague, 1934; repr. Kiepenheuer und Witsch, Cologne, 1971). There is an abridged English version in one volume, translated by Gilbert and Helen Highet and edited by R. H. S. Crossman (Chapman and Hall, London, 1936; repr. H. Fertig, New York, 1969). Mayer's work is inspirational, as he was a historian of the German workers' movement and biographer of Lassalle, but his strong identification with his subject, and with his subject's version of events, makes his work somewhat uncritical. Textual scholarship on Engels and Marx and their relationship has in any case advanced an enormous amount in the half-century or so since the biography was first published complete.

W. O. Henderson's two-volume biography in English, *The Life of Friedrich Engels* (Frank Cass, London, 1976) contains an enormous amount of factual detail about Engels and his associates, and it surveys the collected correspondence and memoirs at considerable length. But the author is out of his depth with the intellectual background and political theory required to make sense of Engels's writings. Engels's youthful experiences get short shrift, and his later activities and works are never put into an appropriate context in terms of his lifetime ambitions and achievements as a politician and theorist.

The 'official' biography published under the auspices of the East German Institute of Marxism-Leninism is translated into English as *Frederick Engels: A Biography* (ed. Heinrich Gemkow *et al.*, Verlag Zeit im Bild, Dresden, 1972). Whilst the work is largely uncritical of Engels's thought and virtually hagiographical on his life, it still presents a large amount of well-attested information about him and his associates.

David McLellan's *Engels* ('Fontana Modern Masters', Fontana/Collins, Glasgow, 1977) and my own *Engels* ('Past Masters', Oxford University Press, Oxford, 1981) provide very brief surveys of Engels's life and works, using modern scholarship on sources and an analytical approach to his thought. Both books reflect the reassessment of Marx and Marxism that has occurred in the west since the 1960s, and both authors provide a critical treatment of the historical and theoretical issues that arise. McLellan is particularly good in using material from memoirs, and I pay detailed attention to the way that Engels interpreted Marx.

Maximilien Rubel, Marx's first bibliographer and leading textual scholar, has indicated the necessity for a re-examination of Engels's role in interpreting Marx and has sketched the issues involved, albeit very briefly. His essay, which provoked stern objections from East German and Soviet participants at a Wuppertal conference on Engels in 1970, is reprinted as 'The "Marx Legend", or Engels, Founder of Marxism', in *Rubel on Karl Marx* (ed. Joseph O'Malley and Keith Algozin, Cambridge University Press, New York and Cambridge, 1981, pp. 15–25).

That issue – Engels's interpretation of Marx – is central to my study *Marx and Engels: The Intellectual Relationship* (Wheatsheaf, Brighton, 1983), which also develops the outlook of the early Engels before he met Marx, and the outlook of the late Engels after Marx had died. In that way an accurate context for their works of theory is developed, and similarities and differences between the two are discussed in terms of their views on science and method. Whilst their theoretical writings are of course considered in relation to contemporary politics, a sequel, *Marx and Engels: The Political Relationship*, will move beyond the canonical works of social theory to analyse the journalism and other materials relevant to their political activities.

Norman Levine has published two studies of the Marx–Engels relationship, *The Tragic Deception: Marx contra Engels* (Clio Press, Santa Barbara and Oxford, 1975), and *Dialogue within the Dialectic* (George Allen and Unwin, London, 1984). There are many points of agreement between us, but Levine's avowed purpose of 'Hegelianizing' Marx creates obscurities in his analysis. The first book presents a somewhat dramatized account of Engels's thought, treated thematically, in 'tragic' opposition to Marx's. Levine's second book contains an interesting start to an evaluation of Engels's role as editor of Marx's manuscripts, and a thoughtful attempt to relate the theoretical issues that arise in considering the Marx–Engels relationship to later developments in Marxist thought and politics.

Within the Marxist camp there have been rigorous debates about some aspects of the Marx–Engels relationship, particularly on the compatibility of a 'dialectics of nature' with a conception of science that can reliably be imputed to Marx. Donald Clark Hodges in 'Engels' Contribution to Marxism', *The Socialist Register* (1965) pp. 297–310, and Richard Gunn in 'Is Nature Dialectical?', *Marxism Today*, vol. 21, no. 2 (February 1977) pp. 45–52, have been critical of Engels's views on general grounds and critical of him as an interpreter of Marx, as has Lucio Colletti in *Marxism and Hegel* (trans. Lawrence Garner, New Left Books, London, 1973). Colletti also discusses Engels as an interpreter of Hegel.

Engels's views on a dialectic of nature, and his 'materialistic' and 'scientific' interpretation of Marx's work, have been sympathetically treated by John Hoffman and Sebastiano Timpanaro. Hoffman's defence of the application of the dialectic to nature is outlined in his *Marxism and the Theory of Praxis* (Lawrence and Wishart, London, 1975) and 'The Dialectics of Nature: "The Natural-Historical Foundation of our Outlook"', *Marxism Today*, vol. 21, no. 1 (January 1977) pp. 11–18. Timpanaro defends the 'decisive primacy' of biology and the physical sciences in his *On Materialism* (trans. Lawrence Garner, New Left Books, London, 1975).

In his articles Gareth Stedman Jones has attempted to link the intellectual development of the early Engels as a Young Hegelian with the views and concerns of his subsequent career as a 'dialectician' and 'scientific socialist', though Jones's treatment of the biographical and theoretical issues involved – especially with respect to Marx – is necessarily very brief: 'Engels and the End of Classical German Philosophy', *New Left Review*, no. 79 (1973) pp. 17–36; 'Engels and the Genesis of Marxism', *New Left Review*, no. 106 (1977) pp. 79–104; and 'Engels and the History of Marxism', in *The History of Marxism*, vol. 1 (ed. Eric J. Hobsbawm, Harvester Press, Brighton, 1982) pp. 290–326.

George Lichtheim's *Marxism: An Historical and Critical Study* (2nd edn, Routledge and Kegan Paul, London, 1964) covers the intellectual background to the careers of Marx and Engels and discusses the way that later Marxists used – and abused – their works. This is still an excellent and reliable study, despite its age, as Lichtheim had a gift for raising questions clearly, using relevant sources and suggesting pertinent answers.

By contrast Richard N. Hunt's two-volume work *The Political Ideas of Marx and Engels* (Macmillan, London, 1975 and 1984) seems to squeeze the texts cited into a predetermined thesis on various 'theories of the state' that Marx primarily – and Engels somewhat secondarily – are alleged to have held.

Engels appears conspicuously in David McLellan's *Karl Marx: His Life and Thought* (Macmillan, London, 1973), and in the two-volume *Eleanor Marx* by Yvonne Kapp (Lawrence and Wishart, London, 1972 and 1976). The classic collection of memoirs is *Reminiscences of Marx and Engels* (Progress Publishers, Moscow, n.d.). For the German reader there is *Friedrich Engels: Dokumente seines Lebens* (ed. Manfred Kliem, Röderberg-Verlag, Frankfurt a.M., 1977), which features a comprehensive collection of photographs and facsimiles, especially items connected with the Engels clan and local history in the Wuppertal. There is also the collection of memoirs and other materials *Gespräche mit Marx und Engels* in two volumes (ed. Hans Magnus Enzensberger, Insel Verlag, Frankfurt a.M., 1973).

There are three German studies of the young Engels, but none convincingly links his early experience with his later career and thought: Reinhart Seeger, *Friedrich Engels: Die religiöse Entwicklung des Spätpietisten und Frühsozialisten* (Akademischer Verlag, Halle, 1935); Karl Kupisch, *Vom Pietismus zum Kommunismus* (Lettner-Verlag, Berlin, 1953); and Horst Ullrich's two-volume study *Der junge Engels* (Deutscher Verlag der Wissenschaften, Berlin, 1961 and 1966).

Engels's book *The Condition of the Working Class in England* is discussed appreciatively and at length in Steven Marcus's *Engels, Manchester and the Working Class* (Random House, New York, 1974), but the context is that of literary criticism – with excursions into psychology – rather than that of Engels's career in politics. There is a brief critical treatment of Engels's work in Asa Briggs, *Victorian Cities* (Penguin Books, Harmondsworth, 1968) pp. 88–138.

Quite a number of studies have now been overtaken by developments in textual scholarship and historical analysis, including David Riazanov's *Karl Marx and Friedrich Engels* (trans. Joshua Kunitz, International Publishers, New York, 1927; intro. Dirk Struik, repr. Monthly Review Press, New York, 1973); Grace Carlton, *Friedrich Engels: The Shadow Prophet* (Pall Mall Press, London, 1965); Fritz Nova, *Friedrich Engels: His Contributions to Political Theory* (Vision Press, London, 1968); and Alvin Gouldner's *The Two Marxisms* (Macmillan, London, 1980).

The English edition of the *Complete Works* of Marx and Engels (Lawrence and Wishart, London, 1975 etc.) is nearly complete with respect to Engels. The introductory material and comments in the notes accord uncritically with Engels's own framework for interpreting Marx's life and thought, though occasionally certain 'errors' are ascribed to the 'junior partner'.

Despite the interpretive weaknesses, the edition is extremely useful for the historical and biographical material collected in the references, the indexing, textual scholarship and illustrations. Similar constraints affect the parent edition, *Marx-Engels Gesamtausgabe* (Dietz Verlag, Berlin, 1972 etc.), where publication has not yet caught up with the English version. Every volume of text is accompanied by an apparatus volume, in which each work in the Marx–Engels canon is introduced with an essay that presents invaluable factual detail on political context, circumstances of publication and contemporary reception.

Index

Index